The Resurrection Of
Johnny
Cash

HURT, REDEMPTION, AND
AMERICAN RECORDINGS

The Resurrection of Johnny Cash
HURT, REDEMPTION, AND *AMERICAN RECORDINGS*
GRAEME THOMSON

A Jawbone Book
First Edition 2011
Published in the UK and the USA by Jawbone Press
2a Union Court,
20–22 Union Road,
London SW4 6JP,
England
www.jawbonepress.com

ISBN 978-1-906002-36-7

DESIGN: Elizabeth Owens
EDITOR: John Morrish

Printed by Everbest Printing Co. Ltd, China

1 2 3 4 5 15 14 13 12 11

Contents

LEFT: "He had the guts to do it," says Bruce Lundvall: Cash enters Folsom Prison in January 1968 to record his landmark album. ABOVE: With fellow Highwayman Kris Kristofferson in the difficult 80s. "The band was the one place where he still seemed to be centred," says Rosanne Cash. RIGHT: With Sam Phillips at Sun Records, 1956. BELOW: The Cheese Years: with Waylon Jennings, Jessi Colter, June Carter Cash, and Ray Charles on the set of *Johnny Cash: Spring Fever*, 1978.

ABOVE LEFT: With June and Johnny Depp at the famous
Viper Room gig, December 7 1993. LEFT: Vivid Cash portraits
by Jon Langford, co-producer of the 1988 tribute album *'Til
Things Get Brighter*. THIS PAGE, TOP: Recording 'Man In
Black' with Christian metal band One Bad Pig in March
1993. ABOVE: Singing 'It Ain't Me Babe' at Bob Dylan's 30th
Anniversary Concert, October 16 1992. Rick Rubin was in
the audience. RIGHT: The One Bad Pig Silly String Incident.

LEFT: An intimate portrait from the mid 90s. "He would come to the session every day dressed as if he were going to a funeral," said engineer Sylvia Massey. "He had a sadness about him." BELOW LEFT: Recording at home in Hendersonville, 1994. RIGHT: Playing South By Southwest, March 1994. "Part of what clicked him over again was that he did a stripped-down show at SXSW," says Rodney Crowell. "That raw thing revitalised him again for a new audience."

Cash and Rick Rubin in the studio recording *Unchained*, 1996. "He was completely re-energised by this relationship," says Rosanne Cash. "It was so beautiful, it was as if two long lost brothers had found each other."

LEFT: **Hammerstein Ballroom, New York, 1999: a rare – and brief – public performance during his final years, at the tribute concert held in his honour, also featuring U2, Bruce Springsteen, Bob Dylan, Wyclef Jean, and Willie Nelson.**
BELOW LEFT: **With Rubin and Tom Petty during the** *Unchained* **sessions, 1996.** THIS PAGE: **A country King Lear: Cash at St James' Episcopal Church, Los Angeles, recording 'Danny Boy' for** *The Man Comes Around*, **2002.**

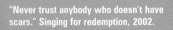
"Never trust anybody who doesn't have scars." Singing for redemption, 2002.

Prologue
The Man Turns Around

he British leg of Johnny Cash's 1993 European tour was all wrapped up in a single day. On February 3 he appeared at Butlin's Southcoast World in Bognor Regis, a resort town about 50 miles south west of London. The booking possessed all the giddy glamour one might reasonably expect when an ageing country singer without a record deal turns up at a dowdy, down-at-heel seaside holiday camp in late winter. Everything about the occasion seemed a trifle careworn and out-of-season, and that included Cash, who trotted with brisk, perfunctory efficiency through his afternoon set and evening performance to a crowd primarily comprised of elderly diehards – many decked out in the faux-Wild West regalia of rhinestone, spurs, and Stetsons – and slightly bewildered families.

Anybody looking for a symbolic summation of the hard road Cash had travelled in the previous two decades needn't have looked too far. The message could hardly have been spelt out more clearly had it adorned one of the gaudy flashing signs that advertised the Autosplash ride, mini-supermarket, and fairground stalls. Cash had gone from raising hell within the towering walls of San Quentin to grinding through the gears at the last outpost on the cabaret circuit; he had morphed from twitching, genre-busting maverick into a family entertainer at the kind of resort where the tide was always out.

This was several years before the All Tomorrow's Parties music festival began the process of reinventing Butlin's as a post-ironic destination for alternative music fans. In February 1993 there was no hint of such winking revisionism; everything was what it seemed. Southcoast World's forthcoming attractions included such past-their-prime acts as soul veteran Edwin Starr and some bastard variation of The Village People, as well as zero-credibility British comics Timmy

Mallet, Little & Large, and The Krankies. Cash was not keeping the kind of company that spoke of a career travelling in an upwardly trajectory. There was no convoy of breathless tastemakers and hip hacks rushing to catch a glimpse of his reflected glory or crown him King Patriarch of Generation X. This was a different time. Q magazine – which specialised in displaying a humorous irreverence to rock's sacred cows – sent a writer, but only to capture the sheer incongruity of it all, to mark what seemed to be a significant and symbolic point in the decline of an icon from another time.

"There was a certain air of resignation about him, and the show was pretty much going through the motions," recalls journalist Mick Houghton, who interviewed Cash at Butlin's. "The first show in the afternoon was dire, actually, although the second one had more energy about it. To me it was a bit 'how the mighty have fallen'. I felt a tinge of sadness, there was something forlorn and shabby about it all. When you see these places in daylight it all looks incredibly tacky, the rides seemed a bit rusty – and somehow I felt the same about Johnny Cash."

As an American, Cash would not necessarily have recognised the cultural significance of playing somewhere like Bognor Regis. It was just another show on the schedule, one of the hundred-plus dates he still played each year that kept his career rolling along ever since the record sales had dried up. The charmless specifics of the booking at Southcoast World – the damp, grey sea air hanging like a shroud; Cash's nagging cold; the teen disco called Hollywoods – were in the end less important in themselves than the way in which they seemed to encapsulate where he had landed towards the tail end of his career.

In the early 90s, Cash was a bruised legend whose future lay some distance behind him. He was in continual pain through a bewildering and cruel variety of illnesses, broken bones, and the aftershock of a second, punishing bout of drug addiction, and his career wasn't in much better shape than his body; he had been dropped in 1986 by Columbia, his record company of nearly 30 years. It's tempting to conclude that Cash had simply floundered in the slipstream of the colossal changes which had swept through Nashville in the 80s, when the advent and escalation of country music radio and the thirst for younger, sleeker exponents of the art form had transformed the industry.

That was part of the story, certainly, but wasn't Cash supposed to be bigger than that? Alone among country's big cats, wasn't he in possession of the kind of pan-generational, multi-platform appeal that enabled him to survive the changing seasons of the recording industry? Seemingly not. In truth Cash had been heading further off course since the mid 70s, partly under his own steam and partly pulled by riptides beyond his control.

Now, mere days away from his 61st birthday, all the signs indicated that he was ready for a future of benign and unchallenging semi-retirement; he was already the youngest member of the Country Music Hall of Fame. When he wasn't playing insalubrious venues like Southcoast World, or Roadie's Roadhouse, Mississauga, or an Amusement Park at Sandusky, Ohio, he was preparing to open the Cash Country entertainment complex in Branson, Missouri. The small town in the Ozarks had become a kind of benevolent home for creatively spent country singers like Roy Clark, Boxcar Willie, and Mel Tillis, troupers who had enjoyed their day in the spotlight but knew when it was time to settle for sentiment and nostalgia. Cash had enjoyed a fine run, better than most, but his days as a creatively vibrant artist seemed well and truly over.

Cut to a little under a year later.

On December 7 1993, Johnny Cash played a solo acoustic gig – his first ever – at the Viper Room nightclub on Sunset Boulevard. He was introduced on stage by Johnny Depp. The select audience of 150 included some of the hippest people in America, among them Sean Penn, Juliette Lewis, Henry Rollins, and assorted Red Hot Chili Peppers. They listened to Cash sing his life for over an hour in something close to awe, hurried back home, and raved about it to anyone within earshot.

He had recently performed 'The Wanderer' on U2's latest album, *Zooropa*, released in July. By the end of 1993 it had sold three million copies, at a conservative estimate at least 200 times as many units as Cash's last album, *The Mystery Of Life*. His big bass baritone had taken hold of the song and inhabited it utterly, so much so that it sounded like it could only ever have been sung by one man.

Most significantly, at the time of the Viper Room gig Cash had almost completed work on his landmark *American Recordings* album, made with Rick Rubin, the inscrutable, Midas-like hip hop and metal producer who had founded the Def Jam and Def American record labels. It would be released in April 1994, fanfared with a wave of MTV coverage and further 'tastemaker' shows at South By Southwest and the Glastonbury festival, each about as far from Southcoast World as it was possible to travel, culturally speaking, without falling off the edge of the planet.

The net result was that Cash was suddenly aligned with a new, young, cutting-edge demographic. From thereon until his death in 2003, and beyond into the ever-unfolding present, he became one of those rare artists who travel into old age without sacrificing an ounce of credibility or relevance. He was as critically acclaimed as he had ever been and twice as hip. He was, once again, Big Daddy Cool.

What happened?

The short, simple answer is Rick Rubin. The longer, more complex explanation lies between the covers of this book. It is the story of perhaps the most remarkable turnaround in music history. Cash's success with *American Recordings* wasn't as contrived or as premeditated as a comeback; it was, rather, both a return to something precious and deeply felt, and at the same time an entire reimagining of the creative possibilities open to a fragile, damaged man entering his seventh decade. At once an entirely new story and a profoundly satisfying conclusion to an old one, it was as though Cash's long black train of music had finally pulled back into the station after its 50-year trip through not just America and the world, but around the craggy coastline, over the dusty side-roads, and through the major tributaries of Cash himself.

And what a tale it told. The earliest work of most great artists contains, almost by definition, an expression of power and vitality that is unique to its circumstances. Typically propelled by years of struggle and pent-up energy, some elemental force is expended and wholly given to the music that can never be given again, resulting in an arrival which frequently becomes mythic the farther it recedes into the past. This is the work, often, by which an artist is measured ever after. It is both defining and limiting, for that combination of kinetic energy, wild excitement, enthusiasm, and surprise is a one time only deal.

It has been generally unfashionable to examine any artist in the context of their later years, because the mythology and energy of youth has been what the culture has demanded, of popular music particularly. But what happens to creative people toward the end of their lives, when they have stopped inventing themselves and know exactly what they want to do and how to do it, brings a whole other level of communication. Even as it burns at a lower heat and rolls at a slower pace, it carries a weight and depth of insight that can be as electrifying as anything previously created.

It happened to the artist Henri Matisse, who battled illness and loss of inspiration in his twilight years to arrive at his late-blooming paper cut-outs, known as the gouaches découpées. It happened to Beethoven with his late string quartets, and to Bach during his Leipzig Period. Perhaps alone among popular musicians we can add Johnny Cash to that list for what he achieved with his series of American records in the final decade of his life. They resemble the unflinching late-period self-portraits of Rembrandt, another artist who suffered indignities and struggled to negotiate a path through middle age and yet returned in the end to a point of courageous, visionary strength. These are not works that can be straightforwardly characterised as coming from a place of serenity, resolution, and reconciliation. They are more complex, turbulent, and troubled than that, but they all show the artist not only in mastery of his

21

craft, but also coming to an understanding of his own humanity.

In terms of Cash's life and music, this is a story that hasn't fully been told. His more dramatic derailments and epic exploits long ago passed into legend. The trouble with being declared a Legend is that it over-simplifies everything. The Legend, famously, demands to be printed, even if its means that history be rewritten in a manner that would make Stalin blush. The Legend, conversely, is not at all keen on the small, prosaic indignities that almost every artist has to negotiate and endure through a career that lasted half a century. The Legend isn't sure how to digest Southcoast World, or the mechanical grind of five shows a week at Branson, or an album as downright unfelt and unnecessary as *The Baron* and many more like it, or the rather too-frequent appearances on *Dr Quinn, Medicine Woman*, or the constant pain and indignity wrought by illness and old age. The Legend gets confused. The Legend wants the story of the man in black to be told in black and white, and so it quietly attempts to excise everything that doesn't fit the frame.

The Legend, of course, devours anything that pertains to scandal and personal demons: drink, drugs, sex, fame, and violence all feed the flames. Which is how we end up with a piece of entertaining but essentially reductive myth-making like the Cash Hollywood biopic *Walk The Line*. Heaven knows Cash's demons were real enough, and they were very much part of what made him the man he was from cradle to grave. They are part of this story, but there was much more to him than that. The over-familiar, gilded tales of his drugged escapades in the 60s and his tortured and ultimately redemptive love affair with June Carter have been smoothed into cartoon and caricature. Not only that, but they have served to diminish his talents as an artist and obscure a lesser known but no less remarkable period of his life: the gradual, quietly inglorious fall, post-1970, and the genuinely unprecedented renaissance in his later years.

Artists tend to do interesting things when they think no one's looking. In less exalted times, the true nature of a man is more likely to be revealed. The hiatus Cash endured in the 80s is as crucial to the path he plotted in his final decade as any of his earlier triumphs, or his bruising tussles with pills and booze. His considerable setbacks all but forced him to enter the 90s ready to follow his instincts, to once again endeavour to make music for himself without sweetening the pill for Nashville's money men. It brought him full circle, reconnecting him to the uncompromising pioneering spirit with which he started back in 1956 with 'Folsom Prison Blues', and which he poured into songs such as 'Big River' and 'Man In Black' and albums like *At Folsom Prison*. In the end, as in the beginning, Johnny Cash proved a master at articulating not just not his own dark, sweet, complicated heart, but something profound about us all.

American Recordings tacitly recognised the emotional connection between the prevailing genres in mid-90s America – heavy metal, grunge, and rap – and the country's old, patriarchal musical forms: folk, blues, and country. Cash attracted an entirely new audience grown up on a diet of Nine Inch Nails, Nick Cave & The Bad Seeds, Nirvana, NWA, Danzig, Slayer, Depeche Mode, Metallica, and Tom Waits, who could handle the dark stuff, cut raw and unadorned.

He did not regain favour in the 90s through the traditional rock'n'roll act of tactical evasion, pretending to be Peter Pan and hitching a ride on the latest bandwagon for as long as he could cling on. On the contrary, Cash reconnected with both his compass and his audience by emphasising his age, his experience, his frailties, his understanding and fear of mortality. He confronted his countless setbacks, missteps, and humiliations, large and small, and fed them directly into his music. He did it by acknowledging, rather than airbrushing, all his flaws and past misdemeanours. He didn't pretend to be someone different from the man he had always been; he did not attempt to 'reinvent' himself. He didn't ignore the shadow of his myth, but nor did he become a parody of what he once was. Instead, he simply became more. His vision become deeper, darker, straighter, *more* true, and in the process he created a new future for himself which set his entire career in a reconfigured, culturally relevant aspect and sustained him until the very end of his life with an intensity few could have predicted.

The quality of the work in that final decade is in itself is extraordinary. Given the circumstances under which the albums were made, it almost defies belief. Toward the end, as he had been several times before, Cash was a desperately ill man. He was virtually blind; each breath was an act of sheer will. And yet he would summon the strength to leave the Intensive Care Unit in Baptist Hospital, Nashville, to record at his home nearby in Hendersonville, and then return to his ICU room. "He was working right up until the very end," recalls his granddaughter, Chelsea Crowell. "Everyone was going: what on earth are you doing? But he knew exactly what he was doing – he was trying to get things done."

There is indeed a sense of completion on these albums, as though the circle of music and experience has travelled 360 degrees and can now be closed. It may be why almost every word Cash sings on the series of American records rings absolutely true, offered without pretence, judgement, malice, affectation, deference, apology, or guile. It is not easy music. Indeed, at times it seems hardly to be music at all. It is certainly a long, long way from that cold February day in Bognor Regis, when Cash seemed like nothing so much as an old boxer leaning heavily on the ropes, waiting for the bell to ring and the pain to stop.

And so we ask: how did it happen?

1

The Sound Of
Johnny Cash

ohnny Cash rolled into Madison Square Garden in New York on October 16 1992 to take part in Bob Dylan's 30th Anniversary Concert. He performed 'It Ain't Me Babe' as a spirited duet with June Carter Cash, his wife of almost 25 years, lover for considerably longer, and enthusiastic – if by now occasionally wayward – vocal foil. Cash had admired and then befriended Dylan back in the early 60s, and his sonorous swing through one of Dylan's most melodic numbers was enthusiastically received by a crowd drawn from a wide range of ages and backgrounds.

Brisk and businesslike, he was on stage for all of four minutes before being sucked back into the slipstream of the endless American highway, the thin, dark ribbon that almost every musician of Cash's generation was eventually forced to regard as home. Tomorrow, home would be Charlottesville, Virginia; then Sante Fe, New Mexico, and on to Colorado Springs, Lake Tahoe, and Denver. It had become a way of life that seemed as unending as the horizon stretching over the hill, leading him from town to town, song to song, year to year.

Both the show and the man were tiring. Although no one had quite seen the signpost yet, a fork in the road lay hidden just around the next bend. The night before the Dylan tribute concert Cash had appeared on *Late Night With David Letterman* to sing 'Blowin' In The Wind' with the relatively hip young house band. It had sounded good, but then Cash always sounded good launching himself at a great song without any fuss or frills. That was just a simple fact, although latterly it was one he seemed to have forgotten rather more often than might have been prudent. On *Letterman* he was announced on stage simply as a man who had "survived the test of time," which sounded like a rather polite way of saying that you might not want to play his latest album but, hell, at least the man in black was still plugging away after all these years.

On his next but one appearance on the *Letterman* show in June 1994, just after the release of *American Recordings*, Cash performed alone, dressed for a hanging. He played the old murder ballad 'Delia's Gone' in a new, brutally rewired version so menacing it made his previous recording of the song, cut in 1962 on *The Sound Of Johnny*

Cash, sound like a children's nursery rhyme. This time he was heralded by the host as the "walking definition of cool". Bend an ear to such subtle semantic shifts and you will hear the whisper of a career being disinterred, revived, and resculpted.

Rick Rubin played a pivotal role in this upgrade in the way Cash was perceived. The 29-year-old producer and self-styled record mogul watched him perform at the Bob Dylan concert on a bill that included other veteran performers such as Kris Kristofferson, George Harrison, Willie Nelson, and Roger McGuinn, none of whom were burning up the charts or the critics' hit-lists at the time. Alone among their number, Cash threw out a spark of some essential, undimmed spirit which caught light in Rubin's imagination. It wasn't anything specific or even intrinsically *musical*: Cash had never been a particularly skilful guitar player, nor was he an especially dextrous or versatile singer. "I don't sing very good, and I'm not that good at playing the guitar either," he bluntly informed recording engineer Sylvia Massey during the making of *Unchained*.[1] Cash was all about the bottom line. Nor was he airing some amazing new song for the first time, because this was a night for celebrating Dylan's music, not his own. In any case, as he was all too aware, he didn't have any amazing new songs at his disposal.

What captured Rubin's imagination was something less immediate and yet more profound than mere proficiency. It was simply a presence, an aura that lingered way beyond the rather unexceptional, pro forma context of his performance that night. Rubin stood and watched, and recognised Cash's eternal genius. He saw a vastness, a huge reservoir of experience and talent just aching to be filled again with the right music and words that conveyed some deeper meaning about who he was and what he felt as he limped, badly wounded but still intact, into old age. It had been many years since anything Cash had done had aspired to the level of true artistic significance, and Rubin was immediately energised by the prospect of helping Cash rediscover his connection to his music and himself. "I'd been thinking about who was really great but not making really great records," he said. "What great artists are not in a great place right now? And Johnny was the first and the greatest that came to mind. A unique character, kind of his own force of nature."[2]

Rubin had built his reputation producing the kind of music that, on the surface, seemed to exist at the opposite end of the spectrum to where Cash had found himself in the 80s and early 90s, as he churned out throwback country albums dressed up in ill-fitting modern clothes and recycled faded versions of his old personae with ever diminishing returns, all the while persisting with his sprawling, outdated live show.

An iconoclastic producer and label boss, Rubin initially specialised in rap, thrash metal, and libidinous funk-rock. Born in 1963 into a middle-class family from Long Island, he grew into his teens in the 70s on a diet of classic hard rock – Led Zeppelin, Aerosmith, Black Sabbath, AC/DC. After graduating from high school and beginning his studies at New York University in 1981, Rubin began combining nights at punk and hardcore gigs with an immersion in the clubs and block parties where the nascent hip-hop scene was starting to take flight.

Moving on from throwing DJ parties in his dorm room and playing shows with his college band Hose, in 1982 Rubin co-founded the Def Jam label, through which he released some of the earliest classic hip-hop recordings, including those by LL Cool J, The Beastie Boys, and Public Enemy. He wasn't just an unorthodox MD who brought swift and significant success to the label. Rubin also established himself as a visceral, unfussy producer from the less-is-more school.

"My first record, instead of 'Produced by Rick Rubin', it says '*Reduced* by Rick Rubin'," he later said. "I always wanted to take music down to its most basic and purest form. ... It's a natural part of me not to have a lot of extra stuff involved that doesn't add to the production, and getting to the essence of what the music is. [I] really feel like you want to feel like you have a relationship with the artist when you're done listening to their record."[3]

An emotional and sonic directness united all his early records, as well as a compulsion to honour the founding emotion and original mood that drove the music as it was being made. In rap and rock Rubin saw two pile-driving musical forms with an underlying kinship and several strands that could be entwined. He was responsible in 1986 for the hugely successful and lastingly influential pairing of Aerosmith and Run-DMC on 'Walk This Way', which not only made explicit a certain commonality of purpose and attitude between the two genres, but also led Rubin to start producing more of his beloved hard rock acts.

In 1988 he left Def Jam after a series of internal ructions and set up Def American. The label maintained a hip-hop presence through The Geto Boys and Sir Mix-A-Lot, but Rubin began to lean more heavily toward classic rock and metal in both his signings and the bands he produced, which included Slayer, The Cult, Danzig, The Black Crowes, Wolfsbane, and Red Hot Chili Peppers. By 1992 he was a household name in the parts of the industry where the legend of Johnny Cash may have been known but his music was seldom heard.

Rubin had reached the point where he wanted to break even further out of the box. Having just produced Mick Jagger's solo album *Wandering Spirit*, he was actively looking for a legend who had seen better days. No matter how few solo records Jagger sold – and make no mistake, copies of *Wandering Spirit* remained positively glued to the racks – the Rolling Stones singer was never going to fit the bill.

Rubin had already demonstrated that he could spot connections between artists and music from different genres. At the time when Def American was morphing into his new label, American Recordings – the 'Def' was, apparently, now seen as outdated and juvenile – Rubin identified a potential flagship artist in Cash, someone who simply by being himself could unify the core characteristics of all the acts he had already worked with.

"I think Rick was typecast as being this rap guy," says American Recordings' former creative director Martyn Atkins. "That was something he knew and understood from his time at college, but he was just into music. He really wanted to try and discover new stuff. He knew of Cash, knew some of his stuff, and thought he was a fascinating character. He was always drawn towards the more rebellious kind of musician. When Rick told me he was thinking about signing Cash he was excited by the idea but in reality he didn't have a clue whether Cash would go for it or not."

After Rubin spotted Cash performing at the Dylan concert the machinations of bringing these two singular men together slowly rolled into place. Rubin's label manager Mark Geiger made contact with Cash's booking agent Jim Gosnell, whom he already knew, and mentioned that Rubin was interested in Cash. Gosnell in turn contacted Cash's manager Lou Robin, who spoke with Rubin and then put the idea to Cash.

There was a significant amount of wariness. Cash had recently reached the end of his time with Mercury Records, a partnership which had began in 1986 with high hopes and expectations on both sides but which had quickly fizzled out into anger and disappointment. He still had a bee in his bonnet about the way his final Mercury albums had been handled, as well as harbouring a grudge about the manner in which many of his final releases for Columbia had been promoted, or rather the manner in which he felt they had been abandoned, to be savaged by the wild dogs of demographics and marketing strategies. He believed that if only these records had had enough time and money thrown at them they might have been hits, a notion that may have held a grain of truth but which was also an indication that he was fatally out of touch with an industry that had changed inconvertibly during the past decade.

Not only did Cash feel a weary distrust of record companies and their politics, at 61 he didn't readily have access to the cultural context in which Rubin made sense. "Dad didn't know who Rick was, and I was a little bit suspicious, too," says his daughter, the singer, songwriter, and author Rosanne Cash. "I thought: oh God, this is going to be another one of those things where they just exploit him and put this outfit on him that doesn't fit. I was really worried about it."

His son, John Carter Cash, then in his early twenties, filled in some of the blanks about who Rubin was and what he did and why he mattered; Cash's young grand-daughters bent his ear about how cool The Beastie Boys were. Even Dick Asher, an old friend of Cash's dating back to the 60s and the executive who had brought him to Mercury in 1986, got involved: "I spoke to [Rick]," he says. "They asked me what sort of feel I got for him, and I told John: I think this guy is going to be good for you. I think they were taking his temperature."

Lou Robin later recalled that they agreed to the meeting with Rubin "reluctantly, because we were without a record deal at that point and it was a very difficult time. All of a sudden all the labels that I talked to all thought, well, maybe his popularity has run its course."[4]

Given that no one else was rushing to snap up one of American music's most potent and powerful articles of faith, the Cash camp agreed to hear Rubin out. They finally met on February 27 1993, following Cash's show at the 600-seat Rhythm Cafe in Santa Ana, Orange County, California. It was not long after he had returned from the European tour that had included the damp, depressing lowlights of his stopover at Bognor Regis. Backstage, Cash gazed at this tall, chunky young man with long hair and a frizzy beard down to his navel. He looked, even to someone as open-minded and inclusive as Cash, like someone you might expect to find pan-handling for spare change outside a downtown bodega. He did not look like a man who could perform miracles on an ailing career.

Rubin gazed back. From his point of view and that of American Recordings, the man sitting in front of him was a walking, talking gamble. "I was always aware of how important he was," he said. "But no one under 40 who didn't live in the South knew much about Johnny Cash besides a few hits and his name."[5]

Despite his grumbles about Mercury's marketing budget and the number of albums they pressed (his claim that they printed only 500 copies of his last record, *The Mystery Of Life*, was a ludicrous exaggeration born from years of anger and frustration), Cash was far from exempt from blame at the way his career had floundered. He had lost most of his appetite for recording and was largely going through the motions. His torpor wasn't just down to the recent musical choices he had made, which had become unfocused and uninspired. His entire artistic eco-system, his wider creative habitat, had undergone a gradual process of stagnation. Martyn Atkins felt that his loyalty to his family, his band, his management, and his acceptance of a certain way of doing things had been holding him back for many years and had had an enervating effect on the way he saw himself and his music. Dealing with the Cash organisation was a little like stepping into an industry time-warp.

"My first feeling from meeting with Cash was that he was a cool guy, business-like, sort of friendly, but you could tell he had suffered fools for a long time in his life," says Atkins. "It was weird. He had all these people around him, he was like an industry to his family. He was the breadwinner. I guess that's a country thing. I'm not knocking that, but it was different to anything I'd come across before. He had all these people on the payroll to keep his tour afloat, because that's how he made his money. He was out of a deal, but no one really had a grasp on reality and no one was giving him any constructive advice on anything about his approach to making records. Knowing John, I'm not saying that anybody could have done that at that time. It's like trying to tell your dad what to do, if your dad was the greatest man alive. It's quite intimidating, because he was such an icon. How do you tell him?"

Rubin had no taste for such niceties. He put his cards on the table from the start and told Cash that he wanted to sign him. He caught more live shows over the spring of 1993 and the two men began to warm to one another and form a relationship based on a mutual, largely unspoken sense of kinship. With his loose clothes, solid bulk, and biblical beard, Rubin conveyed a slightly mystical aura. At first glance he looked like a Hell's Angel, but in fact he was the antithesis of the rock'n'roll archetype of the heavy drinker and drugger. A vegan who preferred not to wear shoes, an enthusiastic advocate of meditation who believed in magic, Rubin had stitched together a rather woolly belief system from a patchwork of new age philosophy, esoteric literature, the Bible, Buddhism, and eastern spirituality. He spoke softly and would listen to music with his eyes closed, as though weighing up some great cosmic calculation. Some found his guru status overplayed and somewhat affected, and believed he was more interested in the process and appearance of self-discovery rather than any tangible end product, but his quiet, calm, spiritual centre, his deep sense of self, certainly touched Cash.

The pair realised rather quickly that they liked each other. Trust followed. What sealed the deal was Rubin's complete lack of salesman's bluster and his recognition that he was dealing with a living, breathing artist rather than a museum-piece. Cash later recalled the moment the penny dropped. He had, rather guardedly, asked Rubin, "What would you like to do with me?" Rubin replied: "I would like for you to do whatever feels right to you."

"That sounded pretty good to me," said Cash. "Rick made me know that I could maintain my musical integrity, that I could do what felt right, and we would take plenty of time and all the money it took to do the album we wanted to do, and that the promotion budget was unlimited. And all of this sounded really good to me, after coming off several dry years where the record company just did not put up what it took."[6]

"They had a very common meeting ground," says Robin, "where Rick said: 'You don't need the singers and the orchestras. You just need to go and sing whatever songs you want to sing with your guitar.' And John [had] never heard anyone say that to him."[7]

It was a relief to know that somebody in the industry cared about the work rather than the numbers, but in the end it all boiled down to feeling wanted, and above all to feeling understood.

●●

Shortly after the release in April 1994 of *American Recordings*, Cash said something rather profound: "I've always wanted to do an album that was Johnny Cash alone — that's the concept."[8] It's a simple statement but it contains the essence of what makes *American Recordings* and the albums that followed so powerful, and begins to unwrap the means by which they cast their spell.

It might have taken the best part of 40 years, but Cash seemed finally to have realised a fundamental truth about his own work: he was *always* the concept. More than perhaps any other singer, he could turn a bare-backed rhythm, a handful of beginner's chords, and a half-page of bar-stool poetry into an unflinching piece of self-examination that, through being sung out into the world, became an intrinsic part of the evolving truth of who he was.

He was signed to Sun Records in 1955 by Sam Phillips, the man who also nurtured the early careers of Elvis Presley, Jerry Lee Lewis, Carl Perkins, and Roy Orbison. With his band The Tennessee Two, featuring Luther Perkins on guitar and Marshall Grant on bass, Cash embarked on an imperious early run of songs, encompassing 'Folsom Prison Blues', 'I Walk The Line', 'Don't Take Your Guns To Town', 'I Still Miss Someone', 'Hey Porter', 'I Got Stripes', and several more classic recordings.

These were epochal songs that spoke a new kind of personal poetry – raw, ravaged, with all the hurt and danger chalked some way above the waterline – but they travelled much further than mere self-expression. The combination of the words and skeletal music left the listener with a stark sense of something primitive on the prowl, of civilisation and humanity boiled down to its very bones: a railroad and a train; a river bisecting the land from south to north; the lawless open border of the west; women who spelled more trouble than good; the endless wastelands of a divided soul; the perennial, impossible choice between good and evil. 'Big River', perhaps Cash's greatest song, is an alternative national anthem that runs amok along the fluid spine of the nation, searching not just for the elusive essence of womankind, or the spirit of America itself, but also holding close to the light a kind of proud, defiant darkness, chiselled into lines of mordant beauty: "I taught the weeping willow how to cry / And I taught the clouds how to cover up a clear blue sky."

On these songs and early Americana albums such as *Songs Of Our Soil* and *Ride This Train*, Cash very quickly became mythic, aligned to all corners of the nation. Bob Dylan later called his best songs "perpetual, they always existed and they always will exist."[9] Like Walt Whitman, at his most engaged he sang as a transcendental artist through which everything and anything could be channelled. One of the legacies of Cash's music, from early Sun rising to slow, elegiac sunset, is to echo through the ages and across time zones and oceans Whitman's promise, in *Song Of Myself*, to: "Sing the body electric, a song of myself, a song of joys, a song of occupations, a song of prudence, a song of the answerer, a song of the broad-axe, a song of the rolling earth, a song of the universal ... I am large. I contain multitudes. I act as the tongue of you."

Armed with the right song and the right angle of attack, Cash was an entire world unto himself, a Babushka doll in mourning dress into which every aspect of humankind, in both its magnificence and tawdry failures, could be made to fit. As a result, there is no shortage of acolytes who hang their allegiances on the peg of his music, from neo-con right-wingers to the most liberal of peaceniks, from fundamentalist Christians to convicted murderers, from NRA goons to lesbian activists, from moonshine country boys to kohl-eyed indie girls. In a certain light he can be seen to represent them all.

It's easy to forget but important to remember that right at the middle of all this clamour stood a mere man, singing the puzzle of his own life as best he could. His reach was vast, his empathy almost limitless, but Cash was nobody's saviour. Certainly, he provided a conduit for his audience to see their own frailties and imperfections projected back at them. Like Nietzsche's abyss, look at him long enough and he'll look straight back at you, but only when he sang for himself – and *sang himself* – could that mysterious and powerful alchemy take place, enabling his truth to ripple out and connect with neighbours, countries, the universal. At these moments, and there are many in his catalogue, the gulf between the person we want to be and the person we truly are is illuminated by the music of Johnny Cash.

In his own case the chasm was wide indeed. Listen again to 'Folsom Prison Blues', a song in which freedom is cruelly contrasted with entrapment, the two ever-present poles connecting the threads of his music. The essential solitude of existence is presented as both liberating ("I shot a man in Reno just to watch him die") and confining ("Time keeps draggin' on"). It's a song of casual, pointless, eye-blink violence followed by an eternal penance. Cheap kicks and a punishing price. It's a song of bitterness and a song of acceptance. It's a song about being chained to the harshness of one world and being shown a fleeting glimpse of somewhere better. It's a song about being Johnny Cash.

Why would he need to sing about anything else? In the most elemental reckoning of Cash's career one might say that he really only ever sang one song, a great rolling epic that began in 1955 and still echoes today; and that song is about how it feels to be Johnny Cash before it is about – to quote from his own definitive list of obsessions, printed in the liner note to *Unchained* – "horses, railroads, land, judgement day, family, hard times, whiskey, courtship, marriage, adultery, separation, murder, war, prison, rambling, damnation, home, salvation, death, pride, humor, piety, rebellion, patriotism, larceny, determination, tragedy, rowdiness, heartbreak, love, Mother, and God".

Watching him on stage at the Dylan tribute concert, Rubin had recognised immediately this crucial aspect of Cash's artistry: he carried within him all these elements. He was his own subject, but he had lost the thread of his own song. Rubin understood that the historical reach of Cash's voice was his greatest gift, but that also in some ways the power and sense of drama it conveyed could work against him. It was a hungry muscle, it needed prime sustenance, it thrived on quality. Confronted with lesser material or battling with the wrong sound it could sound hollow, stiff, plain wrong. His was a voice and a vision constantly in search of a song big enough and wide enough to hold them and all they conveyed about both the man and the myth.

Rubin's genius was to see this. When the pair first began working together less than three months after their first meeting at Santa Ana, the great plan, the grand overarching ethos of this unlikely pairing, was simply to let Cash be himself. That remained the case for the next decade. "The way I picked songs for him would always be about what they said, not about the music," said Rubin. "I would ask myself whether it was something I could imagine him singing and it feeling right. ... All the songs we ended up with resonated with who he was."[10]

And who was he? A tangle of complications, a man defined by his contradictions, a perpetual work in progress: pride, humility, fear, strength, weakness, aggression, compassion, selfishness, piety, sentimentality, rage, love, wonder, silliness, mercy, gentleness, ego and reparation were all mixed into not just his soul but his music.

His duality was hard-wired. Born on February 26 1932 and raised in the cotton fields of Arkansas, Cash forever seemed both conflicted and old beyond his years. There is violence and sex aplenty in his music, but precious little mindless hedonism or youthful abandon. There is always a price to be paid for his kicks. By the time he had recorded 'Folsom Prison Blues' in 1955, Cash had already experienced overseas service with the Air Force and was married to his first wife, Vivian Liberto. His new-born daughter Rosanne would be followed in rapid succession by three more girls, Kathy, Cindy, and Tara.

He had responsibilities. He carried that weight. And he always sounded like a man. By comparison, his early label-mate Elvis Presley was loose-limbed and gangling, like nothing so much as an eager puppy scratching at the door to be let out to play. Like Elvis, Cash had already lost a brother. Unlike Elvis, whose twin died stillborn, Cash was nearing adolescence when Jack Cash died, in May 1944, at the age of 14. He had suffered a horrific accident with a table-saw in the high school agriculture workshop where he worked cutting oak trees into fence posts. His body was ripped open from his chest to his groin. After a week in which the family endured faint hope and deep heartache, he died in hospital. Cash later recalled how Jack, in his final moments, saw angels beckoning him and turned to his family and said: "What a beautiful place it is that I'm going."

Aged 12 at time, Cash grappled with the psychological consequences of Jack's death for the rest of his life. He never did quite shake off the sense of guilt, anger, loneliness, and sorrow that was wrapped up in it. It ingrained in him a kind of existential recklessness, as the premature and unexpected death of a loved one often does, a realisation that life is short and has to be grabbed and wrestled and fought and shaken until it yields. It also cemented, as he grew into adulthood, the overpowering sense he felt of his life running simultaneously along two very different paths. To Cash, Jack represented the road of reason: faith, family, and fidelity, those angels guiding him on. The other path, Cash feared, led straight to hell, and was the one on which his feet really felt most at home. Self-designated as the black sheep of the fold, shown little warmth or affection by his aloof, alcoholic father, part of him always felt damned.

This conflict was elevated to something powerfully dramatic in the best of his music, from even before he was aware it existed right up until his very last performances. When he started recording for Sun one could hear it immediately: the tension between the words and the music is woven into the fabric of 'I Walk The Line'. It's a terribly grown-up song portraying a man wrestling with his marital responsibilities. The lyrics are unequivocal in their demonstration of fidelity – "I find it very, very easy to be true" – and yet every note, every wobbling lurch from key to key, every wavering hum between verses, the aural equivalent of a drunken man stumbling in the darkness trying to find a light switch or reaching out drunkenly for a door handle to steady himself, speaks of the conflict he feels. He doesn't *sound* like he finds it very, very easy to be true. He can't even sing in a straight line, never mind walk it.

The man in black was never black and white. Conflict ran through him. Conflict between wired and straight; God and the devil; the Saturday night sin and Sunday morning hair shirt; loving patriarch and wayward son; country conformist and eternal rebel. Jack and John. And on it goes. He was always trying to resolve this essential contradiction in his music. Every testament of faith has a quiver of doubt; every hymn a whiff of cordite; every original sin comes with the certainty of an Old Testament bolt of judgement.

"These songs," he said in 1996, waving his hand imperiously over the great plains of his career, taking in everything from the peaceful whimsy of 'Memories Are Made Of This' to the vicious misogyny of 'Understand Your Man', "they're part of me, an extension of me."[11]

The thrilling see-saw of Cash's yin and yang remained key to his creative spark, the dominant tension that came to define him as both artist and man. The singing out of his internal battles was always the over-arching concept of his epic songs. Consider some other examples of his most enduring recordings: 'Ring Of Fire', 'Man In Black', 'The Beast In Me', 'Hurt'. Whether or not he wrote these songs, and whatever the specific lyrical details or cinematic symbolism, in Cash's hands they each became part of a kind of evolving autobiography, expanding and informing our understanding of the complexities of the man singing them. Bono from U2, who worked with Cash several times in his final years, once said that he feels he forever gravitates toward music that is either running directly toward God or running directly away from Him. Cash was much the same in his own creative instincts, except you could take that analogy further: he made music that was either running toward Cash or running away from Cash.

Rubin understood that Cash was an individual, not a symbol, and that his music was an attempt at completion, a fusion of all his disparate parts and opposing energies. Before they met that day in Santa Ana, Cash seemed to have lost sight of himself, misplacing his creative centre, losing his bearings, becoming so wrapped up in a kind of painful internal struggle that he failed to see – or refused to acknowledge – what was staring at him from the mirror. He forgot to sing himself for long spells of his career, or perhaps he just didn't have the resources of strength and fortitude spare to dig that deep.

When he faced up and grappled with his own nature he tended almost always to make enduring, meaningful work, but there were many times when he found it easier to avoid it. The result is that there are precious few truly bad Johnny Cash albums, but there are many that refuse to impart anything particularly meaningful about the man who made them. This wasn't dishonest. He was someone, says his friend, producer, and co-writer Jack Clement, "who would sing anything. He was a very silly man in many ways". He was also, says his daughter Rosanne, "the type of guy who, if you expressed enough enthusiasm about something, could be swayed into thinking it was the right thing at that moment".

Both of these statements partly explain why Cash encountered such dramatic swings in his artistic fortunes through the years. Eager to please and easily bored, he was a born fanatic who often leapt on a new idea with a child-like enthusiasm without really thinking it through, which may go some way to accounting for his more outré conceptual efforts in the 70s and 80s: weird stuff about hitchhikers and spacemen, pool sharks and chickens. It might simply have been displacement activity. At some point Cash became tired of looking into himself for inspiration. When you are your own concept, when the song is you, it makes a man terribly weary and perhaps a little afraid of looking too closely beneath the surface.

"I couldn't stand myself any more," he said in the mid 90s, looking back over these barren years. "I wanted to get away from me."[12] It would take some time before he found himself again.

2

Coming Down

How did Cash end up here, cutting backstage recording deals with someone he'd never heard of and who had recently produced a thrash metal album called *Seasons In The Abyss*? The somewhat eccentric, cagey negotiations with Rick Rubin that played out in the spring of 1993 were in stark contrast to where Cash had found himself as the 70s began. Then he could hardly have been more hip, high profile, or commercially successful; he could have walked into the open arms of any record company in the world had he not already been contracted to the most prestigious, Columbia.

It had been a slow descent. In 1969 Cash sold more records in the USA than The Beatles. His first live album, *At Folsom Prison*, had been released in May 1968 and proved an extraordinary triumph, shipping over 500,000 copies within a matter of months and reaching Number 13 in the national album charts. The album had given him his first Top 40 single on the *Billboard* Hot 100 since 1964 with a new, contextually hair-raising version of 'Folsom Prison Blues', although the highly charged recording later lost a little of its impact on the airwaves when that chilling, infamous "shot a man in Reno" line was edited out in the wake of Robert Kennedy's assassination.

He reprised the idea and built on the success of *At Folsom Prison* by recording *At San Quentin* in early 1969, another superb live prison album which didn't quite pack the visceral punch or element of surprise of the first but which consolidated his position as a huge star after several years in which his career had been yo-yo-ing from peak to trough. Released in June 1969, it gave Cash a Number One album on the *Billboard* chart and a Number One pop single with his hastily arranged, off-the-cuff rendition of Shel Silverstein's ribald 'A Boy Named Sue'.

Buoyed by these career peaks, he had entered the 70s at the head of a powerful second wind. There is a delightful irony in the fact that playing a concert in a high security prison made a mainstream pop superstar out of Cash; but relatively quickly it became apparent that, creatively, he was reaching the end of this particularly precipitous upward curve. If the pair of prison albums had the effect of re-establishing his reputation as both a vibrantly uncompromising artist and a commercially viable proposition, his two years fronting *The Johnny Cash Show* made him a national television star, hosting the kind of mainstream entertainment programme that families settled down to watch while digesting their TV dinners.

Taped in Nashville, *The Johnny Cash Show* was broadcast nationally on ABC and ran for 58 episodes from June 7 1969 to March 31 1971, first in its Saturday slot at 9:30pm, and later on Wednesdays at 9pm. Each week Cash would kick off the hour-long show by performing a song with his regular retinue of touring musicians, who had appeared with him since the early 60s and had played on *At Folsom Prison* and *At San Quentin*: The Tennessee Three, The Carter Family, which included his new wife June Carter, Carl Perkins, and The Statler Brothers.

Despite showcasing Cash's egalitarian approach and bringing together a genuinely groundbreaking and diverse range of guest musicians, *The Johnny Cash Show* had more than its fair share of hokey moments, whether it was The Statler Brothers' cheesy comic doggerel, Cash singing 'Everybody Loves A Nut' with an on the-wane Monkees, or the regular and rather wearisome horsing around with his wife. It started out as a relatively hip piece of programme-making, unique and unpredictable, but in time the wholesome shtick started to wear a little thin. Cash saw it himself long before the end: "It became too confining," he said. "I really didn't enjoy it all that much. The show lost its feel and honesty and consequently I lost a lot of interest in it."[1]

Nonetheless, the considerable leverage of having a hit TV show on top of a hit single gave Cash the power to indulge his pet projects. Indulging pet projects, of course, rarely results in great music. After making two tight, tough, terrific albums in *Hello, I'm Johnny Cash* and *Man In Black*, released in 1970 and 1971 respectively, the focus and energy in his music very gradually unwound, until eventually he seemed to lose his way entirely as he entered the late 70s and 80s. There was an increasing disconnect between him and his art. Something fundamental wasn't breaking through.

His penchant for the conceptual had been evident from early on in his career, on albums like *Songs Of Our Soil* in 1959 and *Ride This Train* in 1960, and again in the mid 60s, when he made a series of ambitious, far-sighted records: *Blood, Sweat And Tears*, *Bitter Tears* and *Ballads Of The True West*, each one an attempt to reflect and record various aspects of American history and the working man's place in it, one suspects as a subconscious means of personal self discovery. Today, these are largely forgotten masterpieces, but they are enduring evidence of Cash's ability to hold a mood and a theme together for 35 minutes.

Somewhere along the line, however, the concepts became overblown, eccentric, grandiose. In 1972 he put together *America: A 200-Year Salute In Story And Song*. It's a heartfelt affair, with Cash writing most of the songs, but it's an album notable more for oddities like the adaptation of the 'Gettysburg Address' and 'Come Take A Trip In My Airship' (a celebration of the moon shot rather than a personal invitation) than any of its musical accomplishments. 1974's *Ragged Old Flag* album found him preaching his equivocal brand of patriotism at the time of Watergate; however open-minded he could be when it came to certain social issues, Cash was unapologetic when it came to expressing his deep love of his country. In 1976, the Bicentennial year, he continued the theme with the single 'Sold Out Of Flagpoles'.

Into the second half of the 70s there were children's albums, covers records, and a strange, not-quite-there affair called *Look At Them Beans*. There was *Strawberry Cake* (an interesting pre-echo of the *VH1 Storytellers* concept in which Cash and Willie Nelson took part over 20 years later), recorded live in concert at the London Palladium in September 1975. In what might well be the only live album in history interrupted by an IRA bomb scare, *Strawberry Cake* featured Cash and his band performing a mixture of old classics, new original compositions, and other people's songs that he hadn't previously recorded. Between tracks he would give historical summaries of the background to each track.

It was interesting, original, and a little odd, but not as odd as *The Rambler*, the 1977 album in which Cash's perennial cowboy wanderer regenerates in modern America to play a more contemporary anti-hero, a rootless drifter ghosting his way across the country. Each song is interspersed with dialogue conducted between Cash and the 'hitchhikers' he picks up and the other transients he meets en route. It's a strange old thing, entirely self-written and fascinating in theory, but in practice almost impossible to listen to from start to finish, such is the disjointed nature of the concept and the less-than-compelling songs. Its lasting significance lies in the portrait it paints of Cash literally fleeing from any known point of reference, trying to shake off the ghosts of his past and the awkward questions thrown up by his present. Throughout many of these albums a hazy subtext emerged: as an artist, Cash was no longer holding his own attention. How could he expect to command anyone else's?

In 1975 Willie Nelson had turned the country music scene upside down with *Red Headed Stranger*, an Old West concept album of betrayal and retribution that sounded like it had been recorded in a dusty hole in the ground somewhere in the moonscapes of Arizona. Its unexpected success heralded the beginning of the somewhat contrived but rejuvenating Outlaw movement, which swept the likes of Nelson, Waylon Jennings, Jessi Colter, and Tom T. Hall along in its wake.

The taste was for minimalistic, tough guy narratives, cowboys and horses, God and guns. It should have been the perfect habitat for Cash, but he only caught a little of the reflected heat. He wasn't a dope smoker or a whisky drinker; he didn't have that laid-back, old time charm. He might also have considered that he was doing this kind of thing 20 years ago.

He returned rather wearily to Monument Valley with *The Last Gunfighter Ballad*, released in August 1977, only six months after *The Rambler*. Cash peered out from the album cover with his hat pulled low over his eyes, waving Hank Williams's six-gun into the camera lens. It was another retreat into the safety of a persona that was already well past its prime, as the album tacitly acknowledged. On Guy Clark's title song Cash embodies the scarred old gunslinger from another age, made foolish and redundant by progress, telling tales nobody believes and craving the "days of living by the gun" when the stakes were high and all this play-acting actually meant something: "When deadly games of pride were played / And living was mistakes not made."

Now such games seemed like mere tiddlywinks. Elsewhere on *The Last Gunfighter Ballad* he swings through 'The Far Side Banks Of Jordan' with his wife June Carter and invites his brother Tommy to duet on a tooth-achingly sweet version of 'That Silver Haired Daddy Of Mine'. It's a prime example of what *NME* reviewer Mick Farren called his "lordly macho sentimentality ... tired, beaten nostalgic and noble old gunfighter monologues. Heard one, heard the lot".[2] The production values are suitably faux-downhome and dusty (the sound of horses can be heard at one point), the playing is on the money, Cash sings with his usual grave aplomb, but it doesn't add up to all that much. The end result speaks volumes about a man trapped between the old and the new, looking for a fresh song to sing but unsure where to find it.

"He had been working so much, on the road constantly, the TV show, all this intensity, I think he was a little burned out," says Rosanne Cash. "He had no thought or desire to quit, but he hadn't had the chance to pull back and reflect and write, to go deep into a source of new inspiration. He was kinda pulling and looking for hits and ideas, but outside of that there was all this crazy stuff. There was some *wild* stuff. It was like he was distracted, and that kept adding on to itself."

In the mid 70s, several times comparisons were made in the music press between Cash and the still-living Elvis Presley. Both were former Sun artists who had begun their careers propelled by a kinetic primitivism, but who had steadily come to mistrust their most basic creative impulses. Cash never sank to anywhere near the levels of kitsch and bad taste that Presley plumbed, but he did seem to have lost his way.

"I think it's true that he lost touch with his instincts. We all were concerned about him at that time," says Bruce Lundvall, who in 1976 became president of Columbia, as well as president of the Country Music Association board. "It had become too homogenised; he lost the renegade factor. I never had that conversation with him, I wish I had, but if you have a true original you have to let them find their own way and keep your hands off. As I recall he had a lot of freedom in the company in terms of his recording activity. At Columbia I think he did the records that he wanted to do; they treated him with great respect. I think that was true of Billy Sherrill when he ran the A&R department down there. But he was getting frustrated with his music. It was less visionary in a sense."

These were not, by and large, *bad* records. Indeed, there is rarely such a thing as a really poor Johnny Cash record. It's always fine to hear him sing. That voice will rarely let you down. It has an in-built integrity that lends substance and clarity even if the rest of the picture is blurred. He brought a sense of essential *Cashness* to everything he did, a weight and earnestness that ensured some element of his greatness is almost always imprinted on every song. It could be as faint as a feather stroke, but it's usually there.

Occasionally it clicked, as it did in 1976 with 'One Piece At A Time', where the words and the rhythm and the carefree devilment in Cash's delivery caught light and fired everyone's imaginations, making it a hit both in the USA and the UK. A humorous rockabilly song, written by Wayne Kemp, about an auto worker who patiently assembles an entire car by smuggling stolen parts from the factory, it is an irresistible anthem to a renegade spirit of ingenuity and idiosyncrasy: "I've got the only one around," Cash growls with glee, which was true. He did. If only he had been gunning that engine a little harder and a little more often.

'One Piece At A Time' effectively marks the end of Cash as a singles artist. It was his last country Number One, and even then it veered perilously close to a novelty tune. It is also a fork in the road in another sense. From this point until *American Recordings*, he was forever lagging behind the pace, frantically trying either to chase the tail of progress or, as with *The Last Gunfighter Ballad*, plunging back into a version of himself both he and the world around him had outgrown.

❧

The annual Christmas TV Specials began in 1976, beamed in live from the splendour of his lakeside home in Hendersonville, 30 miles outside Tennessee. They portrayed the Cash family as an American classic, as wholesome as apple pie. Since their marriage on March 1 1968, Cash and June Carter had ascended to become the patriarch and matriarch of country music. As well as falling in love with her beauty and her many outstanding personal qualities, Cash valued June's connection to the first family of American music. The Carter Family were country royalty, the Grand Ole Opry's equivalent of the Kennedy dynasty, one of the great deltas of American roots music where the major tributaries of folk, gospel, bluegrass, and country converged.

The legendary Alvin 'A.P.' Carter wrote such mountain gospel standards as 'Can The Circle Be Unbroken (By And By)' and 'No Depression In Heaven'. He also collected and performed many obscure Appalachian songs, those haunting echoes of old, weird America that The Carter Family did much to introduce into the country songbook. Through marriage to A.P.'s brother Ezra 'Pop' Carter, June's mother Maybelle became part of the clan. Alongside A.P. and his wife Sarah, she was one third of the biggest act on country music radio in the 30s and early 40s, selling hundreds of thousands of records. When A.P. left the group, Maybelle continued touring as The Carter Family, with her three daughters, June, Anita, and Helen.

Cash never regarded himself as better than any other human being, but part of his power as an artist was tied up in ego and image and stature. It was downhome and rootsy, but it was also imperious and all-enveloping. There was an in-built grandness to Cash that sat comfortably alongside his down-to-earth, man-of-the-soil credentials, and his marriage to a scion of country nobility sealed the deal.

He and June had big personalities and star quality in spades. They lived large by instinct rather than design. One British newspaper interviewer visiting Hendersonville in the 70s described them rather deliciously as "benevolent Borgias".[3] Set in almost 200 acres, the interior of the house was about as far from the stereotypically taste-free American ranch-style furnishings as one could imagine. There was gilded classical French furniture, carved German dressers, elegant Italian pieces, light, airy rooms with heavy brocade and oyster shades. Away from home there was an apartment at 40 Central Park South in New York and suites at the Savoy when he came to London.

There were also the bizarre excesses and the ingrained, almost imperceptible detachment of the privileged. An obsession with exotic animals was made manifest in Cash's private zoo, where Waldo the Ostrich later attacked and nearly killed him. Meanwhile, in a mansion on the land at Hendersonville, they set up the House Of Cash, a museum with private rooms cordoned off with regal red rope. Only royalty lives with its personal history so carefully curated on its own doorstep.

Everything about Cash operated on a vast scale, more easily measured from outside rather than within its boundaries. London-born singer and songwriter Nick Lowe first found success in the 70s with Brinsley Schwartz and later Rockpile. He became Cash's son-in-law when he married June's daughter Carlene Carter in 1979, and recalls that when he was first summoned to meet his prospective father-in-law he was shown straight into the great man's bedroom, like a cat before a king. "I had my first meeting with him while he was lying in bed eating his breakfast," he says. "His presence was so overpowering he seemed to suck all the air out of the room, until you got used to it. He was the most charismatic person I ever met."

Nobody stood on ceremony, but even when Cash and his wife came to visit Lowe and Carter over the Christmas period in 1979 in their "pokey" terraced house in Shepherd's Bush, London, it had all the pomp of a state visit.

"Three taxis turned up," Lowe recalls. "One had Johnny and June in and was full of luggage, and the other two were just full of luggage. There they were, on the pavement in this not-very-salubrious neighbourhood. John would wear the stuff he wore on stage all the time, the full black, double-stitched shirts and suits, and June was swathed in fur with a mink hat, all the things you're not allowed to wear any more. All our Irish neighbours were shouting out the window and they were waving back. Everybody loved them, it was like a royal show."

Cash presided over his own feudal court, a sprawling entourage of family, employees, and musicians who were all dependent in one way or another on his success and munificence. He was a loyal and extraordinarily benevolent sovereign. "He was generous beyond a fault;

he never said no to a friend," says David Ferguson, who engineered all the *American* records. "If somebody needed some money he was there." This was a very American form of nobility: it saw the best in people; it gave them any number of second chances. Once you were in the fold it was very hard to be thrown out.

Rodney Crowell, the celebrated Texan songwriter, became another in-law between 1979 and 1992 through his marriage to Rosanne. Cash and June were "charming and elegant; they knew how to make you feel like you were the only person in the world", he says, but they were also used to calling the shots. "When Rosanne and I started living together out in Hollywood [before they were married] John wasn't happy. We were summoned to sort out what we thought we were doing. I was smashed drunk and showed up at his place in Jamaica with his daughter thinking I was going to sleep in the same bed with her. That turned into a bit of a confrontation. Of course I backed down, it was his house, but I think he decided he liked me after that."

Cash's live show became an extension of this grand, extravagant, simplified, and perhaps rather compromised vision of family and fealty. In time it grew as tired and out of touch with the reality of both Cash's life and the state of the music industry as his records. He had begun touring in the mid 50s with The Tennessee Two, perhaps the most pared down, bare-boned band in history. Now the show had grown into an ungainly undertaking.

Over the years W.S. 'Fluke' Holland had arrived on drums, transforming, with incontrovertible logic, The Tennessee Two into The Tennessee Three. June Carter and The Carter Family came onto the scene in the early 60s, which certainly changed the mood. They were resolutely old school, rooted in the traditions of the past and more than a little twee, qualities that seeped into the stage show. Shortly afterward vocal trio The Statler Brothers also joined the troupe. Bob Wootton – June's brother-in-law, married to her sister Anita – replaced the deceased Carl Perkins in 1968, and later Cash added a second guitarist.

In 1971 a piano player climbed on board, often sporting a new face and name with each tour, and in 1978 a two-man horn section further augmented the line-up. By the late 70s, with the exception of The Statler Brothers, who had left to pursue their own career, each of these elements remained integral parts of the evening's entertainment, with each artist given their own mini-showcase on stage before Cash came on as the main act.

He always brought June back out for an encore, the pair mock-sparring their way through 'Jackson', the reformed wild man and his undaunted woman playing their story for laughs, before duetting tenderly on 'If I Were A Carpenter'. Holding hands with his wife, Cash would then lead the congregation of family and friends in a damp-eyed rendition of 'Were You There When They Crucified My Lord?' until the curtain fell. Factor in frequent appearances by Cash kin such as Rosanne, Carlene Carter, or Laura Cash and you had a big, hokey, family-orientated throwback to the 50s and 60s. It was a thoroughly professional show, great value for money, but it had very little flair and looked increasingly like old hat.

"It was an extension of his television show, a kind of wholesome cabaret affair," says Lowe, who saw more than his fair share of Cash concerts and was often dragged on stage to participate. "I actually didn't care for it all that much. It was a big, unwieldy thing, cousins and aunties and a big band. He was still touring that but the times were a-changing, not just in pop music but also in country and western. The old order was going, country was trying to reach for a much wider audience and he was on a treadmill. Audiences were starting to drop off."

"I think they'd played that show out," says Rodney Crowell. "The show was the whole schmeer, this overblown production. The audience had lost their bearings, and John was probably doing a few things by rote." Crowell's earliest musical memories involved seeing Cash at a "hillbilly show" in 1958 at Magnolia Gardens in East Houston, and hearing 'I Walk The Line' on the radio around the same time. But he had also grown up on Dylan, The Beatles, Willie Nelson, and Gram Parsons, and made his breakthrough as part of Emmylou Harris's Hot Band, so he was able to view Cash and his career with the same outsider's objectivity as Lowe.

He was struck by two things. Firstly, that the portrayal of the wholesome, all-American family that underpinned his live act was at best one dimensional and at worst hypocritical. June had been married three times. Cash had been an absentee father for most of his life, and although he loved his children deeply and tried hard to atone for his past mistakes when his son John Carter Cash was born in 1971, it remained a struggle. The children had been raised in unstable, confusing environments, and as they grew into adulthood the Cash homestead was frequently a troubled nest: there were multiple marriage breakdowns and widespread issues with alcohol, while many members of the family – including Rosanne and Carlene, and throughout the years several more of the extended clan – experienced serious problems with drug abuse.

"There's a certain thing with Southern country music culture, based on that myth of a perfect family that doesn't really exist," says Crowell. "First and foremost John and June were artists and performers. We know the Picasso story: you follow the muse at all costs. Most great artists have a certain amount of selfishness. I loved them both, him and June, but you know what? They weren't as great parents as they were selling to the world. Any of the children would go with that. They were the grandparents of my children, and I took a bit of an issue with the patriarch-matriarch thing, because it was schmaltzy and not true. I knew their kids, I'd married one of their children, and I knew that they weren't parenting their kids, and hadn't, so I bristled at that. John painted himself into a corner with that patriarch image. Sometimes it will blind you about yourself, and maybe he didn't see it."

The second aspect that seemed obvious to any slightly detached observer was the clear disparity between the reduced circumstances of Cash's career in the late 70s and the grand manner in which he and June continued to deport themselves.

"Rosanne and I were living in LA and so went up to see a show in San Francisco," says Crowell. "John and June went out and it wasn't even a quarter attended. There were about 3-400 people in a 1,500-seat theatre. I was walking around watching this, thinking: oh my God, this has gotta be hard, but when the show was over they were whisked away in a limousine. I remember thinking: God, they're out of touch with reality. It could have been Madison Square Garden sold out! I was just stunned. Years later it dawned me that it *wasn't* that they were out of touch with reality. I know now that John knew exactly what was happening, and I know it was hard, but his way of dealing with it was: Fuck it, I'm a big star and I'm going to carry on 'as if'. That period was a deep valley, but they didn't back off from their status at all. They were like those members of the British aristocracy who no longer have any money. There was a bit of that. They *were* royalty, you know."

It was all symptomatic of a wider malaise. The TV show was the first agent of change altering the way in which Cash was perceived. As the months wore on and the format began to atrophy, the frame that the television series threw around Cash was ultimately that of a former pill-poppin', margin-hanging bad-ass being folded into the cosy bosom of the ad-selling entertainment industry. Folk singer Phil Ochs, an old compadre of Dylan's and a firm believer that the guitar was mightier than the sword, went so far as to say that Cash "now stands as proof that television can kill".

Cash's renewed faith also became a more prominent part of his public life. Having actively embraced Christianity in the late 60s, he began writing a book about the Apostle Paul and became close friends with the Christian evangelist Billy Graham. Graham was to all intents and purposes a decent man, an ally of Martin Luther King and a vocal supporter of the civil rights movement in the 60s who had campaigned for desegregation. However, he seemed to belong to a world that was an awful long way from the gates of San Quentin. Cash swung into his orbit just as Graham was beginning to lean toward the right, forming a rather too-close allegiance to Republican president Richard Nixon, which involved Graham leading private church services in the White House and Nixon appearing at Graham's Christian crusades. His morning phone calls offering spiritual guidance to Nixon became the stuff of legend and often ridicule.

Cash came to be seen as part of the same axis of orthodoxy. He performed for Nixon in the White House, and although he made a point of playing a deliberately confrontational song, 'What Is Truth', and of putting on record his disagreement with the war in Vietnam, his mere presence was perceived as an endorsement of Nixon's presidency. He even spoke to him on the phone, at Graham's behest, after the Watergate scandal had disgraced and unseated him.

Cash's Christmas Specials frequently featured Graham as a guest, and in 1978 and 1979 he and June returned the favour by taking part in the *Billy Graham Christmas Special* and showing up at the preacher's huge outdoor crusades in Florida and Tennessee, high profile appearances they had been making for most of the decade. The same year Cash released a double gospel album, *A Believer Sings The Truth*.

These factors – God, TV, June, the pumpkin-pie family jamboree – seemed to conspire against his complex creativity. Cash gained a huge amount of traction from being, and being seen as, an outsider, even if the price he paid personally was often high. In the 70s he became sucked into various incarnations of The System until it looked as though he had begun to conform to a role that limited him terribly. He used to possess a sense of danger so palpable that even now its long shadow was still clearly visible, but his contrarian edge had been worn down into something more avuncular, more conservative, more conciliatory.

"The hardest context to take him out of was that of the Nashville establishment, which he never really [belonged to], but people would see him as part of that," says Rosanne Cash. "This narrow, regimented, establishmentarian country royalty, which is a really suffocating mantle to put on him and the exact antithesis of who he was, yet even now it still exists. That corporate aspect. At some point in those years, it's not that he became that image of the corporate, God, country, family thing, but he did play along with that a lot. The Billy Graham crusade, taking June and The Carter Family on the road, all that Holy stuff. Oh my God, it was horrendous."

●●

There was a palpable and not unrelated drop in pressure in his work, which proved difficult to reverse. Cash entered the 80s having made only one Top 10 country album since 1974. His subsequent attempts to stir up some commercial heat were by turns lacklustre, bizarre, and plain embarrassing.

Cash was still just about powerful enough and had enough traction within the record company to be able to pursue most avenues; and he did. He veered from an album of Christmas carols to one in which he collaborated with Christian schoolchildren; from an album of retro rockabilly to the synthetic modern pop-country sounds of *Silver*. He didn't know what he wanted to do. He underwent the classic directionless person's pursuit of new projects with great but fleeting enthusiasm, before retreating into disappointment. "He was the type of guy who, if you expressed enough enthusiasm about something, he could be swayed into thinking it was the right thing at that moment, and then later on he could see that it wasn't," says Rosanne Cash. "I think that's what happened: '*This* is a great idea, *this* will recast you, blah blah blah,' and he goes in and does it and it doesn't turn out well. There were a lot of conceptual things in that era that didn't quite make sense or fit." He was waiting for some miracle to strike from without, because he was unsure of how to make it happen from within.

Even when he was misfiring, Cash at this point still cared deeply about what he was doing. In 1980 he contributed to the concept album *The Legend Of Jesse James*, written by English songwriter Paul Kennerley, who was married at the time to Emmylou Harris and worked regularly with Cash in the 80s. He had made his breakthrough in the industry in 1978 with *White Mansions*, a country-rock song-cycle set during the Civil War which had dovetailed with the mood music of the time: the South was in vogue due in part to the TV series *Roots* and Jimmy Carter's presidency.

The Legend Of Jesse James was another conceptual affair. The musicians included Levon Helm as Jesse James, Emmylou Harris as his wife Zerelda, Charlie Daniels as Cole Younger, as well as cameos for Rodney Crowell and Rosanne Cash. But who would play Frank James? Eric Clapton and J.J. Cale were considered for the role, until Harris suggested Cash.

"I'd like to say the whole thing was written with him in mind but he was just sort of off the radar," says Kennerley. "I laughed. I only saw him as one of the founding fathers. [Producer] Glyn Johns thought it was a great idea and through Emmylou someone got in touch with [him] and told him what it was about."

Cash was keen. It appealed to his love of American history and outlaw mythology. He was playing a State Fair in Cheyenne, Wyoming, when Kennerley and Johns went to visit him and June at their motel the following day. "I'd printed all the lyrics out and we had two Walkmen with all the songs, and they sat down and listened," says Kennerley. "I can't imagine anything more boring, but they seemed to get totally absorbed. He was banging the lyric sheet in time with the tracks we'd recorded and the ones we wanted him to sing. June was really excited as well. He took his headphones off at the end and said: I'd love to do this. We felt very lucky. I remember Glyn and I giggling when we left his motel room, because it seemed so obtuse that we had been in the company of this amazing man."

A matter of days later he came in to the studio in Nashville to record his part. It was a Sunday. "He was with his bus driver, he'd been out deer hunting," says Kennerley. "There was a black-on-black shirt on a hanger in case there was going to be a photograph. [Cash's guitarist] Marty Stuart was there and John said: Have you been to church, son?"

This was not an epochal point in Cash's career, nor was it a particularly astonishing collection of songs, but what impressed everybody present was how much he put into the job at hand. "We were just overdubbing his voice," says Kennerley. "He'd hung on to the cassette we'd given him and he'd learned the melodies. One of the songs was slightly gospelly, and he just grabbed hold of it and roared through it. This rich, joyous voice. It was just fantastic, he was such a presence. He just did one or two passes at everything and that was it. Every occasion he sang a song of mine, much more so than other artists, he really took the song seriously, even when the song didn't deserve it. That's what he was interested in. He did it right."

His signal was intermittent at this time. Almost everything he did came down to attempts to either recapture past glories or awkwardly fit in with the times. He tried to keep pace in 1981 via the sleek, over-produced, pedestrian sound of *The Baron*, with producer Billy Sherrill sweetening every note and Cash virtually sleep-walking through the entire thing. The cover is laughable, with Cash decked out as a bad daytime TV character, and there is some awful schlock on the record. The title track is a slick gospel-country number that labours over the metaphor of a pool duel as a gunfight, while 'The Greatest Love Affair' is a big, patriotic, sloppy, sentimental kiss planted on the liver-spotted cheek of the Reagan regime. The tell-tale cortege of multiple composer credits, rarely a good sign, trailed behind several songs.

The Baron didn't work, so Cash tried nostalgia. *Rockabilly Blues*, released in October 1980, is one of his better albums of this period. Indeed at the time it was rather optimistically hailed as that double-edged sword, the return to form, harking back to his uncomplicated, direct Sun sound after the over-worked *Silver*. The production from Cash and Earl Ball is understated, rendered clean and with a kick, but ultimately it's a stiff-legged, broad-shouldered, middle-aged version of those early Tennessee Two cuts, gruff and solid rather than spectacular. It bore only scant resemblance to Cash at his peak.

He tried even more nostalgia, reconvening the old gang on *The Survivors – Live*, which documented a night on his 1981 European tour when Carl Perkins and Jerry Lee Lewis joined him on stage. It was loose, spirited, and fun, but essentially passé. It was better than the later *Class Of '55* album, which reunited Cash once again with Lewis and Perkins as well as Roy Orbison, and saw them recording at the old Sun Studios in Memphis. Even the writers who contributed material had the decency to be a little ashamed.

"Marty Stuart sent my song 'We Remember The King' down to those sessions and they recorded it," says Paul Kennerley. "When they sing that white gospel on that last chorus, right at the bottom is Johnny Cash's lead vocal, and it's great, but it's a miserably terrible song and a real 80s production. Unfortunately, these aren't great records."

More telling than the fact that he wasn't having any hit records, or indeed making any particularly good records, was that *Silver* in 1979 marked the first in a run of five studio albums, up to and including *Johnny 99* in 1983, on which Cash, previously a highly prolific writer, contributed in total only seven songs. "It was symptomatic of everything else," says Rosanne Cash. " Being a bit burnt out, desperate, floundering. I'm sure he was using [drugs] during a lot of that time, and he was constantly in motion, which makes it hard to write."

But as past classics such as 'Ring Of Fire' and 'Sunday Morning Coming Down' had shown, and *American Recordings* eventually proved beyond dispute, he didn't need to write to connect. He merely needed to inhabit. The one standout album of this period is undoubtedly *Johnny 99*, from 1983. Shaken into action by the bleak emotional power of Bruce Springsteen's *Nebraska*, which in itself had been inspired by the monochrome majesty of Cash's Sun recordings, he covered two songs from the album. The quality and ambiguity of Springsteen's writing, the way he captured the nuances of moral ambivalence, seemed to bring something back to life in Cash. He did a fine job with both songs.

The title track twisted together the personal and the political. The drama was enacted in a familiar internal landscape of conflict and despair, in which a working man finds himself backed into a corner by his circumstances and ends up with "debts no honest man could pay". He takes the law into his own hands – the price is 99 years in jail. The line about taking a man's life for the thoughts that are in his head could hardly have resonated more profoundly with Cash in his earliest incarnation, and one can hear him pick up the thread with relish.

The other Springsteen cover, 'Highway Patrolman', is simply spellbinding, as good as anything Cash recorded in his final decade. At 50, he sings it somewhere between a confession and a prayer, with an underplayed sorrow at the centre of the performance that only the weight of experience brings.

'Highway Patrolman' is a tale of brotherhood, crime, small town loyalties, and the price of staying true to bonds of love and blood. There's nothing quite like hearing Cash get to grips with life's complexities, and here he rattles down those parallel rails once again, singing of liberty and entrapment, mining the grey areas. Unlike the overcooked modern gloss he had daubed all over *Silver*, this time producer Brian Ahern teases out a sparse, sympathetic arrangement. Everybody is listening, everyone cares, Cash more so than anyone. He empathises with both the conflicted cop and the brother who strayed over to the wrong side of the tracks. It's a terrific piece of work and a clear – though at the time largely overlooked – signal of where Cash could and should have been heading with his art.

It's not surprising that he later returned to Springsteen. He sang '(Further On) Up The Road' during the sessions eventually released posthumously on *A Hundred Highways*, and in 2000 he recorded 'I'm On Fire' for the tribute album *Badlands*. With its tick-tock rhythm, humid menace, out-of-control psychic freight train and unresolved sexual torment, the latter was Cash *in excelsis*. Why he didn't cover it in the 80s, when he still had the vocal power and physical presence to really capture the potency and sense of danger in the song, is a mystery. In the 2000 version he wasn't on fire, merely smouldering.

What else could he have been singing during this period? It would have been wonderful to have heard him take a walk through Dylan's 'Every Grain Of Sand', or Elvis Costello's 'Different Finger', or Townes Van Zandt's 'Marie'; perhaps even Tom Waits's 'Gun Street Girl' or 'Blind Love'. There were numerous songs that would have made for interesting times, perhaps sparked up Cash's sense of himself. Most of them passed him by.

He was excited by *Johnny 99* but he didn't have the strength of focus to drive it through to its logical conclusion. Aside from the Springsteen covers, the other eight songs on the album are punchy and fresh sounding, but they don't fulfil the potential of what might have been.

"He had that *Johnny 99* record and leading up to it he was really, really enthused about it," says Rodney Crowell. "I remember the conversation: 'You could do this really stripped down with a three-piece band.' I was always lobbying for what Rick Rubin actually succeeded with. In general he would be prone to being very enthused and inspired about something he wanted to do: what do you think about this, what do you think about this? But then nothing would come of it."

'Highway Patrolman' is the best solo recording Cash made between 1979 and 1993, and certainly the one most alive with possibility. It illustrates once again just how important the raw meat of a song was to him. All that rigmarole about pool sharks, sheriffs and the Wild West meant zero if it didn't connect with some essential part of him. Here was Cash singing as a contemporary artist, with something to say not only about where he was at this moment in time, how he felt, what made him tick, but also about America in 1983. He could feel it, and therefore so could everyone else.

Jon Langford, who co-curated the 1988 Cash tribute album 'Til Things Are Brighter, remembers seeing an otherwise fairly humdrum Manchester show in the mid 80s. "The best bit was when he sang 'Highway Patrolman' on his own," he says. "Just his voice in this huge concert hall, it was really amazing. I thought: he's really got something going on here. He was still thinking about himself as an artist, trying to make a statement."

There was nothing diminished about his core talents. His charisma, his reach, his ability to step inside a performance remained entirely intact. It was only his instincts that were letting him down. Rodney Crowell had a similar epiphany on seeing Cash display his power up close.

"I remember being on tour with him in Switzerland," he says. "We were standing watching him and just mesmerised by his stage presence and body language and the way he performed for that audience that night. Look at it intellectually and that's part of the down period, but here's a night in 1985 when he was just absolutely captivatingly *on*."

What makes it all the more frustrating is that 'Highway Patrolman' is one of the few recordings from this period that really captures what Johnny Cash could be. One might reasonably claim that many more of his songs achieved the opposite effect, forming the soundtrack to a gradual process of reduction. There is very little that expands our understanding of the man and, as the natural, Whitmanian concomitant to that, ourselves. It sounded like he was avoiding the issue, dodging himself, trying not to dig too deep, skimming the surface with these odd-ball conceptual affairs and albums cobbled together from material coming off the Nashville conveyor belt, fine but rarely truly engaged. For a man who had to sing himself to really cut through, too often in the 70s and 80s he sounded unsure of who he really was.

Cash's artistry ran deep rather than wide. His cultural frame of reference was vast, particularly for someone who was, nominally, a country singer. He read everything from Jewish history to James Joyce. Who couldn't love the moment in his 1971 *Times* interview with Philip Norman where he said he was looking forward to his forthcoming trip to London so he could get back to rummaging around in Foyles bookshop? You never heard George Jones say stuff like that. Yet he distilled it all into something that, musically and sonically speaking, was tight and narrow.

We were never going to hear Cash start swinging with a Big Band, or making electronic music, or tackling the Great American Songbook, or dabbling in anything *too* leftfield or esoteric. Even with *American Recordings*, which greedily gathered songs from all over the landscape, Cash enveloped them in his very own style, chopped and chipped and cut them down to size. There's a musical template to which the majority of his songs conform, except it's more than a template. It's a patent, and with its increasing familiarity came the challenge to bring something extra to the words, the power, the performance. This is the aspect that faltered most frequently during this period. The songs had become archetypal, almost interchangeable; too often it seemed that we had heard them already, too often they sounded like an echo of some former echo of an earlier glory. The music had crossed the line from signature sound to cliché.

Johnny 99 didn't do any business. The album made no impact on the charts, and nowadays it is largely forgotten. Which is a shame, because within its grooves can be heard a faint precognition of something that Rick Rubin understood: even in his doldrums, if Cash was singing the right words and listening to the beating heart of the right song, he very rarely went wrong.

3

Sin And
Redemption

Throughout most of his life Cash grappled with two enduring obsessions. Each was a kind of love affair, neither was easy, and in combination they graphically illustrated the division running through his soul.

The first was his commitment to his religious faith, the second his addiction to drugs. His pursuit of these two very different forms of solace, pain relief in spiritual and chemical form, forever altered the way in which he was publicly perceived and rewired his instincts as a writer and a performer. Attempting to honour and acknowledge the conflicting parts of his nature, to sing them out with one authentic, unified voice, was perhaps the defining battle he faced as an artist.

One of the less celebrated highlights of *American Recordings* is the stark, stunning 'Redemption', Cash's song of grim gratitude to a God who saved him. The language here is extraordinary – soaked in blood and vines, the imagery is built from wood and chains and cross-hatched with light and darkness – but the story it tells is deceptively simple, recounting the path that led from the crucifixion of Jesus Christ to the personal salvation of John R. Cash. "And a small inner voice," he sings, "Said 'You do have a choice.'"

'Redemption' is about Cash's very personal relationship with Christ. It lasts three minutes and it took a lifetime to write. He had written frequently in the past about his relationship with his saviour, but only with 'Redemption' does he allow himself to convey a tangible sense of struggle and price. It's a visceral admission that the serenity which is often supposed to accompany faith was always an aspiration for Cash rather than a realistic attainment.

A little earlier on the same album he sings 'The Beast In Me'. It is a song about a very different relationship, this time between a man and his primal negative image. A portrait of someone condemned to spend his life wrestling with his inner animal, the song was in some respects about its composer, Nick Lowe, who despite a rather wry and urbane demeanour had plenty of his own demons to contend with. In another very clear sense it was a comment on human nature in general and the many and nameless monsters lurking just below our surface collective civility. It was, however, a song specifically written for Johnny Cash. "I though it was a really great title for him," says Lowe, who consciously took on the voice and characteristics of Cash – "I inhabited it" – on the night he first began writing the song.

Lowe writes that the beast is "caged by frail and fragile bars". Cash was ever on guard. He sometimes gave the impression of a man being eaten away from the inside out. Never truly at peace in his own mind, he had a twitching, stalking, palpably nervous outward demeanour that seemed to suggest a more solid threat, almost as though there was something with real and tangible physical dimensions trapped inside him wrestling to escape. 'The Beast In Me' is a song written to size, made to measure Cash's complex dimensions, and his performance on *American Recordings* fills every part of it. He was sufficiently self-aware to recognise it as a poetically astute portrait, a mixture of man and myth, that fitted him like a glove.

*

'Redemption' and 'The Beast In Me'. God and Gollum. The Bible and the Brute. These are the two poles, Cash's emblematic North and South, yet they frequently met and merged in myriad forms. He became very fond of the cover image on *American Recordings* and one can see why. When Andy Earl, the photographer who took the picture, visited Hendersonville in 1996 he spotted a print of the picture on the wall next to Cash's studio, beside a classic black-and-white portrait from the 50s. Although the photograph of Cash – looming over the land like a hellfire preacher with a guitar case for a staff, flanked by two dogs – was a snapshot of a brief moment that was not and could not have been planned in advance, it captured something intrinsic about the man. Cash understood symbolism, especially of the biblical variety, and took comfort in it. He saw something of the human condition and a whole lot of himself in the picture of a black dog with a white stripe and a white dog with a black stripe. He called one Sin and the other Redemption. And there he was, as ever, standing right in the middle.

His notions of sin and redemption weren't neat or defined. One was intrinsically bound up in the other, no more so than in his life-long struggles with drugs. For Cash, the affirmation of his Christian faith was inextricably connected to his pledge to kick the addiction to amphetamines.

He had first taken pills in 1957. The use of Benzedrine, Dexedrine, Dexamyl, and similar variations of speed was rife among the touring musicians of Memphis and Nashville, who routinely played upward of 300 dates each year. Known colloquially as 'LA Turnaround' on account of their ability to get a troupe of travelling minstrels to California and back without having to pause for anything as rudimentary as sleep, uppers were legally available without prescription until the late 50s and even afterward were liberally handed out by accommodating doctors. They seemed practically essential to anyone who wanted to burn through the punishing number of miles required to maintain what might tentatively been called a 'music career' and still have sufficient energy at the end of the day to play a show.

When an exhausted Cash first took amphetamines, in Florida in the summer of 1957, it felt like a bolt of lightning was crackling through his giant frame. Not only did this essentially shy man feel alive, energised, and endlessly talkative, but his on stage persona seemed to expand to fit his voice. He was always a charismatic presence and a highly strung performer; the pills heightened his nervous energy into something weirdly compelling and immensely magnetic. His eyes flared. He couldn't stand still. He would twitch, twist, and contort, as though his muscles were in serial spasm. He would sling his guitar behind him as though it were a pirate's cutlass, running his fingers up and down the blade with menace, at the same time tossing back his head in something between a seizure and a snarl, like some prize stallion stamping at the dirt. It was immediately apparent that this was a man battling to keep fearsome internal forces at bay.

The pills brought it all to the surface. Of course, the more Cash took, the more he had to take next time to get that kick, and the longer he had to keep going to avoid the inevitable crash. These drugs were the equivalent of a daily onslaught on his nervous system, snapping at the synapses, twisting the body and the brain into strange shapes.

"I once told him: the unfortunate thing about your generation is that you guys came in on uppers and downers, the stuff that killed Elvis," says Rodney Crowell. "It was so much gentler 15 years later when everyone was smoking grass and drinking. Amphetamines and barbiturates are so hard on your body."

By the early 60s, Cash was well and truly hooked and would remain so for almost the entire decade. The fall-out has been well documented, parcelled up in a kind of reductive glamour and shrunk to fit a narrative of convenience. Suffice to say that it was far from pretty. He missed numerous concert dates, either because his voice was shot, dried up, and parched into little more than a croak through the ravages of speed, or because he simply didn't show up. His recording sessions, too, could be fraught affairs. "He'd be stumbling around in the studio, falling through guitars," says Nashville guitar legend Norman Blake, who played on numerous Cash sessions in the 60s. "Take his knife out and rip the furniture. Maybe it doesn't show in what you hear, but nobody knows how many hours went into some of those cuts. And angst and paranoia."[1]

He was wild. He lost his temper and then lost control at the Grand Ole Opry, smashing up the footlights by dragging his microphone stand along the front of the stage. He had several run-ins with the law, although none resulted in anything more serious than a night spent in the cells to cool off, until his high profile arrest in El Paso in October 1965 for smuggling hundreds of illegal pills over the border from Mexico into the USA. Found guilty, he eventually escaped with a suspended sentence, but it looked very much like the kind of spiralling decline that killed Hank Williams. By his early thirties it had turned Cash into a haunted husk of a man who, in Kris Kristofferson's memorable depiction, was often seen by his peers stalking through the neon wilderness "like a panther".[2]

By the mid 60s he was estranged from his first wife Vivian, finally acquiescing to a very public divorce in 1967 on the grounds of 'mental cruelty'. Far from his first infidelity, his affair with June Carter had begun not long after The Carter Family had joined him on tour in 1962. His projected professional profile was of Nashville's family man, in theory happily married, living in California with four young children, and dutifully singing the gospel. In reality he was helplessly addicted to amphetamines, a heavy drinker, an absent father, and an adulterer.

The guilt at his hypocrisy seemed to drive Cash to even greater extremes. His behaviour became more and more unhinged, his fear and paranoia almost inconceivable. There was nothing heroic about this. It unleashed a form of insanity. "I first met him in the 60s; he'd just finished the [*Ballads Of The True West*] album, and he was not in great shape in those days," says Bruce Lundvall, who at the time was working in Columbia's marketing department. "He was bone-thin and he had issues with drugs at that point. He was out of control. The one or two times he came [into the Columbia office] in New York it was really frightening. He was so paranoid with pills he would walk through the hallway with his face to the wall, and slip into the office with whoever he was going to meet with. It was very scary."

The intense pain he endured is dreadful even to contemplate; it would take almost 30 years until he was finally able to fully face working through it in his music. In the interim he turned to God with an almost desperate devotion.

After a decade of addiction, Cash recognised in 1967 that he was reaching a critical point. Again, he saw the two tracks laid out before him. One route promised almost certain death and desolation; the other, life, love, faith. His resolution was bound up in his commitment to June, who was a devoted worshipper and vehemently anti-drugs. With her persistent persuasion, Cash attended a service at the First Baptist church in Hendersonville and offered himself to Jesus. He aligned himself in particular with St Paul, someone who had come to a literal fork in the road and had chosen the way that led toward the light; a man who transformed himself from Saul, a "violent persecutor", into the Apostle Paul, God's servant.

'Redemption' returns to this moment in 1967 when he had heard the "inner voice" offering him a choice. It had whispered to him for almost as long as he could remember, certainly since the moment his brother Jack had died. Raised a Baptist, Cash had conducted a long running, on-and-off, occasionally passionate but ultimately rather casual affair with religion since childhood. He subscribed to the 'Saturday night sinnin', Sunday morning salvation' school, taking refuge in the church and taking comfort from the songs of his childhood when, as it frequently had, the weather turned dark and he sought instant shelter. Soon enough he would cut loose again. Religion existed in an easily accessible part of his heart where it could be dusted down to provide comfort; but there was no real commitment in thought, and certainly not in deed.

He always loved singing spiritual songs and hymns, perhaps more than he loved singing anything. It was honest and heartfelt, part of the beautiful mix of influences in his music. He came out of a Southern gospel background, playing with The Carter Family and The Statler Brothers, and spirituality was very much a part of his music from the start, but it was always a struggle to adapt it into a mainstream career. One of the reasons Cash left Sun in 1958 was Sam Phillips's refusal to let him make a gospel album, while at his very first Columbia session in July 1958 he insisted that he recorded his own song 'It Was Jesus (Who Was It)'; the 1959 album *Hymns From The Heart* swiftly followed. He continued singing, writing, and recording music in that style for the rest of his life.

Cash did not hide his newfound dedication to Jesus Christ when he began recording *The Johnny Cash Show* in 1969, a fact that caused the TV network some discomfort. God is rarely good for (show) business. Cash was undaunted, promptly recording a television special in 1970 with Billy Graham. As the decade wore on his expression of his faith became more explicitly evangelical. He was baptised in the Pentecostal Assembly of God in 1971 and began worshipping near his home at the Evangel Temple in Madison, Tennessee. Shortly afterward he said: "I don't have a career any more. What I have now is a ministry. Everything I have and everything I do is given completely to Jesus Christ now. I've lived all my life for the devil up until now, and from here on I'm going to live it for the Lord."[3]

As if to prove the point, in November 1971 he travelled to Israel to film *The Gospel Road*, a rambling biopic of Christ, for Twentieth Century Fox, and then worked on the soundtrack, which was released as a double album in 1973. It provided further evidence of Cash's commercial decline: peaking at Number 12 on the country album charts, it didn't even make the *Billboard* Top 200.

He performed in Dallas at Explo '72, a huge evangelical conference organised by the Campus Crusade For Christ, a kind of Christian Woodstock intent on reclaiming the ethos of peace and love from the clutches of what Merle Haggard called "the acid takin' dopies" and bringing it back to God. Billy Graham spoke, Cash played and speechified. He attended a similar concert at Wembley in 1973 and showed up at countless gatherings all over America. He would appear at Billy Graham's rallies in front of crowds of 100,000 people and in the company of prominent televangelists such as Oral Roberts, Tommy Barnett, and James Robison.

There seemed to some a lack of discrimination about where Cash chose to express his beliefs. Graham's personal credentials were unimpeachable, but there were others who were not so adept at practicing what they preached.

"He was very good friends with Billy Graham, and one or two other less reputable types," says the resolutely agnostic Nick Lowe. "He had a few questionable friends. It was June who got him into it, but he went for it. Religion is so much a part of those people, demonstrating your religious observance. It was all 'Praise Jesus.' I got used to holding hands and saying Grace before meals, which is something we don't do in Brentford very much. There's actually something delightful and charming about it. I felt rather privileged."

In 1975 Cash enrolled in an intensive Bible study course with the Christian International School of Theology, graduating in May 1977, and was later ordained as a minister. As his faith became more devout, so it began to impact on his work. He wrote, at Graham's instigation,

'Matthew 24 (Is Knocking At The Door)', an odd, apocalyptic ditty sung over a syrupy saloon-bar country track. It warned against the Cold War and the Russian threat: "The great bear from the Northland has risen from his sleep / And the army ranks in red are near two hundred million deep."

He bargained with Columbia, who were becoming alarmed at his diminished commercial clout. God might be Great but He didn't sell. "The importance of a hymn was minimised by so many in the record business that it had lost some of its importance to me," he said. "Still, I had pledged to 'tithe' my music."[4] In order to release another gospel album, 1975's *Sings Precious Memories*, Cash agreed that the company could take a firmer rein on the content of some of his mainstream albums. By 1979 Columbia had run out of patience with his devotional music and refused to release the double gospel album *A Believer Sings The Truth,* so it "came out on some oddball label", says Jack Clement.

His commitment to sing out his love of Christ was commendably honest and heartfelt, but it had clear consequences. It re-enforced the perception, already encouraged by the television show and his marriage to June, that he was part of the establishment. To the largely liberal music press and the rock fraternity, who had once felt Cash was as much theirs as he was Nashville's, it was an uneasy mix. After all, everyone knew that God was both a conservative and a Republican. His detractors pointed out that where once he had played to the killers of Folsom and San Quentin, now he was more likely to be found singing for moneyed gamblers and hard-nosed hookers at the Las Vegas Hilton. He justified the decision by rather loftily quoting the Apostle Paul: 'I will become all things to all men in order that I might win some for Christ now'.

In attempting to express a deeply complex, ever-changing, troubled and almost overwhelming passion for God, he often lapsed into forms of expression and stances that emerged at the other end looking simplistic and reductive.

"I think he was trying to make amends on a grand scale, I really do," says Rosanne Cash. "It was his way of tithing, his way of making some kind of redemptive gesture for all of the damage of his past, even for the death of his brother: this grief and guilt at the centre of it all that he's trying to mitigate. It was an honest gesture but the way it played out didn't really appeal to me. He had a deep mysticism at his centre, and it was kind of reduced to this form where it played out in public in this one-dimensional form."

This rather orthodox depiction of his faith seemed to polarise his work, which became not only increasingly stodgy and uninspired but somewhat confused. His 1971 album *Man In Black* opened with 'The Preacher Said, "Jesus Said"', a song that features Billy Graham orating some corn-fed homilies from the Bible, and ended with the self explanatory 'I Talk To Jesus Every Day'. In between were bandit songs like 'Ned Kelly' and the brilliantly realised and socially engaged 'Man In Black' and 'Singin' In Vietnam Talkin' Blues', both extraordinarily wide-reaching and empathetic pieces of writing.

It was a fearsomely slippery tightrope walk: the anti-Vietnam, pro-American, gospel-preaching, outlaw-loving, Bible-reading, counter-cultural libertarian, patriotic country icon. Cash was all these things, and many more, but it confused people, perhaps even the man who was singing the songs. "John was intellectually dedicated to [religion]," says Rodney Crowell. "It wasn't a smokescreen at all, but then again he was a man of appetite, too. He was on the high road and low road at the same time."

It was a central conflict he rarely addressed in the 70s and 80s. He sang gospel songs and he sang outlaw songs, but there was little sense in his music of how he resolved those two parts of his character in his own mind, no suggestion of the pain and difficulty that process involved, precious little indication that the one could not exist without the other. Indeed, after the late 60s and early 70s, arguably Cash did not again attempt to confront his conflicted soul – the beast walking in his clothes – until *American Recordings*. On 'Redemption' he allowed everyone to see the darkness that existed at the centre of the light, revealing how he had "clung to the tree". By singing this song, a white canvas with a big black stripe down the centre, he finally conveyed what a desperate battle it had often been for him to keep his faith.

It was always a struggle. It always would be. In all, Cash was baptised three times in the 70s, the last in 1979. It was as though he regarded each immersion in holy water as a protective force-field which would only last so long before it needed to be renewed in order to continue warding off evil spirits. There was an underlying sense of desperation to his faith, a definite sense of God keeping the beast at bay.

"I heard at the time that he would just take off once in a while," says Bruce Lundvall. "He was missing some of his freedom. I think he still had a wild streak in him at that time, actually, but he'd gotten religion. It was pretty obviously June's influence; she was more the one who had seen the light. We'd often have a nice Sunday dinner at his house in Nashville, and I remember one time him asking if we'd like something to drink. I think I asked for a Bloody Mary, and the answer came: no, we don't serve spirits in this house! Down in Nashville at his home on the lake, before we'd eat we'd have a moment of prayer, which I found to be unusual. Cash with his head down praying."

Religion undoubtedly became the rudder that steered him through the choppy waters of sobriety and fidelity, but finding a way to reconcile his devotion to the complexities of his artistic vision became a long running problem. "I think the conflict between religion and music confused him at one point," says Lundvall. "I heard that and felt that at that time. Probably saved his life, though, by the same token."

Quitting drugs was no easy task. Initially Cash preferred to portray it as a black-and-white affair – he was wired up, then defused – but it was not, and never would be, an easy road. 'Redemption' tells us that he was constantly at the mercy of temptation: "My old friend Lucifer came," he sings. "Fought to keep me in chains." Cash later said that the concert at San Quentin, recorded on February 24 1969, was among the first he had ever performed without the aid of drink or drugs, but for at least the next 18 months, possibly longer, he still used pills. The frequency and quantities gradually diminished until he felt he was fully in control.

He subsequently managed to keep the beast under lock and key for most of the 70s, with Jesus and June as the round-the-clock jail-keepers, but it was always there, pacing the floor, searching for weak spots in the defences, keeping up its incessant chattering.

Whether the trigger was a decline in record sales, or uncertainty about the way his career was going, or a cooling in his religious ardour, or simply the "suffocating mantle", in the words of Rosanne Cash, of trying to present himself as a God-fearing paragon of virtue when the truth of his own nature was always much richer and more complicated than that portrayal allowed, it's hard to say. But by the late 70s Cash began using drugs again.

In an interview in the mid 70s, he recalled the shame he felt back in the early 60s, when he was recording *Hymns From The Heart* for Columbia and yet was already in the mire of amphetamine addiction. "I was a little ashamed of myself at the time because of the hypocrisy of it all." he said. "There I was singing the praises of the Lord and singing about the beauty and the peace you find in Him, and I was stoned and miserable. I was climbing the walls."[5]

A similar scene played out in the late 70s and early 80s. In public, to most people's knowledge, he remained the peace-preaching, deeply religious family man they saw on the Christmas Specials and on Billy Graham's crusades. In private he was wired, distracted, detached, and in his own way wreaking just as much havoc as he had during his first bout of addiction.

The fall-out was less obvious than it had been back in the 60s. There was no public admission until he entered a clinic late in 1983, and many of his friends and colleagues were barely aware of the fact that he was using again during this time. "I never noticed any of that," says Jack Clement, who worked with him during this period on *The Adventures Of Johnny Cash*. "I'm not sure he was into it that much at that time. I worked with him some when he was at Columbia [in the 60s], I did a lot of sessions when I was just playing guitar as a sideman, and he was kind of wacky during some of those times. But most of the time we worked together it was a fairly normal situation, as far as I knew. I always kind of ignored [the hell-raising stuff]. When I worked with him he was never a rogue or anything."

"I never had any problems with him then at all," says Bruce Lundvall. "I found him to be a very gracious man."

Others were forced to take closer stock of the situation. In the late winter and spring of 1979, at Columbia's instigation, Cash went into the studio in Los Angeles with Brian Ahern and Rodney Crowell to record a new album. *Silver* was an attempt to jazz things up a bit. Billed as a 25th anniversary event – this was pure marketing desperation; Cash had started making records in 1955 – it was intended as a reinvention of sorts but ended up as a lukewarm compromise, uneasily updating his traditional sound by pasting on modern production overdubs: mushy keyboards, disco drums, and cheesy synthetic trumpet riffs. A tilt at something a little more contemporary, it was at least an acknowledgement that a change in approach was required, but there was no sense of kinship between Cash and these new sounds.

Released in May 1979, *Silver* gave him a hit country single in '(Ghost) Riders In The Sky', and the three Cash originals were strong, particularly 'I'll Say It's True', an archetypal bar-room country number which he sang with George Jones, and 'I'm Gonna Sit On The Porch And Pick On My Old Guitar', but making the album was not a happy experience.

Another of the tracks, 'Lonesome To The Bone', was first recorded for *John R. Cash* in 1975, when it sounded like a decent attempt to rewrite Kris Kristofferson's 'Sunday Morning Coming Down'. Back then the line about "sweatin' poison out" was delivered as a painful memory. The fact that it had become a reality again might have been one of the reasons Cash chose to dust down the song and re-record it in 1979. 'Cocaine Blues' may have been resurrected for similar reasons, although it is a markedly inferior version to the one on *At Folsom Prison*, a tired old warhorse that only stops plodding when it starts limping.

Cash later recalled that he "squared off in the studio" with Crowell, who had worked with Ahern in the past on several Emmylou Harris records and was helping out on production on the album. In what he calls "a sea of sycophants", Crowell prided himself on giving Cash straight answers to straight questions. "God knows, he and June were surrounded by a lot of people getting money out of that machine, kissing their ass, so I made a decision to shoot the truth as much as I can, in as much as it was any of my business. I think he actually appreciated that. I busted him about his drug use. I never judged him on that, but we used to argue a little bit about it on *Silver* and later. I let him know I'd been around the block and I knew what was going on."

While his first battle with pills was a hellish descent into fear and paranoia, the second bout was, in many respects, far worse. There wasn't a lot of public wildness. "I never really saw him cutting loose," says Nick Lowe. "[He was] not exactly tame, but there was no shooting of streetlights or anything like that going on." There was none of that terrible panache, but it was somehow more painful, more shameful, than it had been previously, and it took twice the toll on a body that was already less than pristine. "Chemical dependency is a progressive disease and it hit me a lot harder the second time around because I was older," said Cash.[6]

With Cash now nearing 50, it looked even more like everything around him was falling apart. *Silver* was the last album to feature long-standing Tennessee Two bass player Marshall Grant, his sidekick since 1954. Grant's acrimonious departure from the band sparked a lawsuit and counter-lawsuit. It was suggested at the time that Cash felt that Grant had somehow become too powerful since taking on the role of tour manager and was not always acting in his interests. He also later said he felt that he needed to absent himself from a sound, and a band, with which he had been associated for so long. If he had followed this through and hired an entirely new group of musicians that idea might have carried more weight, and indeed might have proved rather effective. However, it's also likely that Grant's frank distaste for Cash's drug habits and his weariness at clearing up after the singer contributed to their split. It was further evidence that Cash's judgement in personal matters was badly out of kilter.

"June couldn't do anything with him and no one else cared," said Grant later. "He was at his worst at that time, even though they tell me that after I'd left the show he got even wilder."[7]

When Cash toured Europe with Carl Perkins and Jerry Lee Lewis in April 1981, his drug use had become even more obvious. "I saw a few things happening where he was like: OK, you caught me with my pants down, so to speak," says Crowell, who was recording the shows for the 1982 live album, *The Survivors – Live*. "We talked a bit about that and the fact that I was his son-in-law, and how did we square that with the way I could see him behaving? That record was when we had a lot of conversations about [drugs]. I'd been married to his daughter for two years and he started opening up and talking about the dark side a little bit."

The dark side encouraged the re-emergence of the demons – so vivid you could practically touch them – that haunted Cash when he was in the throes of addiction. Fate didn't do an awful lot to help him. In 1981, in one of the great tragi-comic incidents of his life, he was attacked by an ostrich called Waldo in his animal park. He broke several ribs and was taken to hospital for treatment. The painkillers he was prescribed only exacerbated his drug problem. "The whole thing just snuck up on me again,"[8] he said, finding himself addicted to those as well as amphetamines.

He wrote a bizarre latter to Nick Lowe, dated February 25 1982 and sent from New York. The envelope had 'From Johnny Cash' written for all to see on the back, but then this was the man who throughout his life insisted on checking into hotels under his own name: "What name would I be under?" he asked. "I mean, who cares?"[9]

The letter to Lowe ended on a peculiar note which seemed to suggest a mind in an altered state: "Is it possible we'll all be together around Christmas at least?" wrote Cash. "I think everyone has decided it's OK to be weird. You'll be comfortable in my home. If you aren't, I'll burn it down. Sincerely, John."

During his European tour in November 1983, having overdosed on Valium, Percodan, and alcohol after a show in Nottingham, Cash lashed out repeatedly during a vicious hallucination in which he became convinced that there was a bed hidden somewhere in his hotel wall. Shortly afterward he returned to Nashville and was treated over several days at Baptist Hospital for the damage to his hand, which had become infected. It was discovered during his stay that he had internal bleeding and would need an operation to remove some of his intestine. He was given morphine, which only further intensified and complicated his chemical dependency.

Matters had reached a head. The family felt obliged to stage an intervention right there at his bedside, during which his teenage son, John Carter Cash, told him he was embarrassed when his friends came around to visit and saw his father stoned. "It was a huge decision," says Rosanne Cash. "He was ready for it, though. He was so quiet and humble when it happened, he wasn't shocked or confrontational in any way. He was very sweet about it." Exhausted and defeated, Cash checked into Betty Ford Clinic in Palm Springs and sought help. He emerged in February 1984 after 43 days of treatment, clean, sober, and lucid, but the beast never left him alone.

You can listen as closely as you wish to the music Cash was making throughout this period but you will struggle to hear a whisper of these upheavals. The story of Cash's musical decline is not that the beast broke free and began to wreak havoc in his life again, distracting him from the task in hand, although to an extent that is indeed what happened. The wider problem lay in his inability to express his conflicted nature in his writing and his performances. His struggles were an integral and indeed a valuable part of who he was, but there was no serious attempt to grapple with these complexities in the albums he made in the 80s. His life was endlessly complicated; his work was often parodic and simplistic. The two failed to connect.

But these experiences were being stored up. On *American*

Recordings Cash came to terms with the punishment he had inflicted on his mind and his body throughout his life and filtered it through grace and redemption. There is a cumulative depth to that record and the ones that follow which speaks volumes about a man who, as Lowe plainly wrote, "has had to learn to live with pain".

Recognising and working through that pain brought a huge weight of reckoning to those last songs. When we hear Cash sing 'Redemption' or 'Why Me Lord' he is not just idly hymning. When we hear him singing 'Like A Soldier' or 'The Beast In Me' he is not reconnecting with some spurious sense of rock'n'roll savagery enacted in his youth. He is reflecting on his immediate circumstances, his daily battles: his ambivalent and ongoing relationship with drugs, his equally complex relationship with God, his bewildering trials with his health, his wearying bouts with both himself and the people who never seemed to quite understand him.

The darker side of the *American* albums is where Cash articulates a life of acute struggle. It is the sound of physical and psychological pain being borne, but only just. It is the sound of those two wild dogs, Sin and Redemption, given free rein at last.

4 I'm Leavin' Now

hen *Unchained*, the second album in the *American* series, won a Grammy in 1998 for Best Country Album, Rubin's American Recordings label took out a $20,000 full page ad in *Billboard* magazine. It featured the classic image, taken in 1970 by rock photographer Jim Marshall, of Cash looming into the camera with his middle finger raised in a blur of righteous anger and his mouth forming an unmistakable plosive in the key of F. The accompanying text, deeply ironic in intent and strategically positioned directly above Cash's rigid digit, read: "American Recordings and Johnny Cash would like to acknowledge the Nashville music establishment and country radio for your support.'"

Although it was a piece of mischief-making clearly orchestrated by the image-massagers at the record label, Cash would hardly have been human if he hadn't thought back to the events of the previous decade and struggled to suppress a smile at the way things had turned out. If he'd thought about it a little longer he might also have counted his blessings that Nashville turned its back on him when it did. Their indifference proved ultimately to be a catalyst for him to re-evaluate his own status as an artist.

Rick Blackburn will forever be demonised by some as 'The Man Who Dropped Johnny Cash'. As president in the 70s and 80s of Columbia's country-music operation, he was the industry executive who donned the black cap and let Cash's recording contract lapse in 1986 after 28 years in which he had been a central pillar of the world's most prestigious record label.

It was a decision regarded as heresy by many of Cash's family, friends, and fellow artists. "It hurt him," says Rosanne Cash. "I mean, he helped to build that fucking company."

Rodney Crowell agrees. "I think he felt he'd earned that place that Bob Dylan has earned with Columbia, that he was someone you'll never let go," he says. "They made a mistake, they should never have done that. You can renegotiate and continue to make records and it would have been good for everybody."

Dropping Cash, says Blackburn almost a quarter of a century later, was a decision based entirely on "the business of the business". The business of the business, it transpires, has nothing to do with what an artist has done for you and your company in the past, and everything to do with what they can do for you starting from today. The business of the business doesn't like it when the numbers don't stack up; it feels even worse when the suddenly powerful medium of country radio displays no love for your act. The business of the business is the big, brash bottom line. It laughs in the face of anyone who believes the music industry has truly ever been about anything other than making money.

Blackburn recounts a short parable concerning the laws of commerce, which says a mouthful regarding the context of Cash's fall from grace. When the wave of the Outlaw movement eventually broke, the country music industry found itself at an impasse. Blackburn wanted "to take the temperature". In 1983, he hired as consultant a man who had been instrumental in relaunching onto the market the US pain-relief drug Tylenol, following a scandal the previous year in which seven people were murdered in the Chicago environs after being given Extra Strength Tylenol mixed with cyanide. Sidney Furst, an expert in business and marketing affiliated to Columbia University, was employed by Blackburn to set up focus groups and engage in consultation in areas where Columbia's country artists were performing sluggishly, with the sole aim of establishing what it was young people wanted from their cowboys.

"We were stagnant, and we didn't know where country music was going to go," says Blackburn. "We tried to marry the music to a lifestyle; we learned that from Madison Avenue. There was a hunger for something new even if it was someone like Ricky Skaggs, who was doing really traditional, old-school stuff but with a young face. Once we'd discovered video and how to do mass market there was a real hunger for it. We moved in that direction as an industry and out of that evolved country music radio, which became huge, whereas before that it wasn't so much.

"When all that happened there was this big sucking sound and people like John were just displaced by younger artists coming in: Clint Black, Ricky Skaggs, Randy Travis. Add that to country radio and there was a movement afoot for younger people, so that's what we set out to do. That whole sea-change rocked Nashville, and it had a displacement effect for some of the real traditional artists who had built the industry. John was searching for direction, but everybody was. Our business in the 80s shot up more than you would think. We had a younger demographic saying: what have you got that's new? If we mentioned people like Johnny they'd say: my dad likes them."

It would be fanciful to suppose that the fate of Cash's recording career lay solely in the hands of a Jewish academic from Brooklyn, but Dr Furst's research studies were a sure sign of the times. Cash would later be heard spitting out phrases like "new market profile" as though they were the vilest and most depraved of all expletives. "If I hear 'demographics' one more time I'm gonna puke right in their faces" just about summed up his attitude.[1] He bemoaned the fact that "country has gotten to the age now of electronic, push-button, TV, video, and all that. I'm a traditionalist".[2]

This was not his world. Cash still measured his worth as an artist largely by trusting the evidence of his own eyes every night at show time. "I'll tell you about a conversation we once had," says Blackburn. "We were sitting out at his house one time and I said: John, we're not doing the units and yet the industry is growing. He said: 'My biggest fear is going on stage, the curtains open and nobody's there.' That was almost like the ultimate rejection for him as an artist, that someone doesn't show up when you're going to sing. He didn't look at sales figures as much as some of the others."

Perhaps he should have. By the mid 80s he was playing to a diehard audience who were more interested in hearing 'A Boy Named Sue' and 'I Walk The Line' than anything he had produced in the past decade. Nobody disputed Cash's legendary status, but legend was a tough job description. It didn't leave much room for a sense of humour, middle age, ill health, boredom, plain old bad calls. The music industry is by nature cyclical, and when you've done what you do for a certain length of time people think they can live without it. You might even agree with them. Plenty of people loved what Cash had once been, loved the *idea* of him, but precious few of them were interested in what he now was.

And there was a lot of music, probably too much. Within a year of the tantalising promise displayed on his exemplary version of 'Highway Patrolman', he was approaching his nadir. By the time producer Billy Sherrill laid the less than appetising prospect of 'Chicken In Black' in front of him in 1984, Cash was near enough past caring about his recording career, and his audience had dwindled to a fraction of what it had once been.

'Chicken In Black' was in many ways the logical destination of where his career had been heading over the past few years. It's a moment of symbolic significance, albeit one rarely mentioned in dispatches. The one blessing, after all, about reaching the bottom of the barrel was that precious few people tuned in to hear the scraping sound.

Released as a single in October 1984, it was a long way from the austere majesty of 'Big River' or the empathetic socially conscious sweep of 'Man In Black', or even the beautifully nuanced ambivalence of 'Highway Patrolman'. You might say some bloodthirsty foxes were running amok in the creative hen house. It may have the shape and sound of one of Cash's archetypal three-chord chicka-boom affairs, but the lyrics fly off into less traditional territory. Hold on tight. The premise of the song, its inspired narrative conceit, is that Cash, suffering from a persistent headache, has been advised to undergo the rather drastic remedy of a brain transplant. The fact that he agreed to do the song in the first place suggests that it might not have been such a bad idea.

The organ in question was taken from the body of a recently deceased criminal mastermind, and thus post-op Cash unwittingly becomes Manhattan Flash, the "best bank robber in town". When he asks the doctor for his old brain back he is told that it's been transplanted into a chicken that has subsequently been signed to a ten-year recording contract. This, it will by now be clear, is not a song where Cash is summoning up the spirit of Walt Whitman, or indeed even Slim Whitman. In the video – this was 1984, and everyone was starting to kneel before MTV, which was part of the problem – he hams it up as both Manhattan Flash and Johnny Chicken, portrayed by Cash as a superhero fowl in flowing cape, a yellow tunic with an 'M' emblazoned on the front, and big black boots into which he has tucked his baggy blue trousers. As a joke it wasn't terribly funny; as a satire it was dire; as a career move it was emblematic of a man who had almost entirely lost the plot.

Cash later attempted a spot of revisionism regarding 'Chicken In Black', dismissing it as an "intentionally atrocious" burlesque, a wholly conscious act of self-sabotage, as if by recording something so awful he could display his simmering contempt for Columbia, which was showing less and less inclination to promote his product, and force the company to either back him or bin him.[3] It was a nice try, but Cash was not the kind of man naturally inclined to play those kinds of games with his music; and even if he were, it only illustrated how bereft he was of any hope by this point. One thing is for sure. He was recording and releasing a song that he actively despised. "I hated it from the first day and I refuse to admit that I even know the words to it anymore," he later said.[4]

Despite the persona that tended to precede him, Cash had always displayed a sense of humour in his life and in his music (perhaps his greatest work-related pleasure at this time was appearing on *Sesame Street*: "I really would like to do it about once every six months,"[5] he said). Running as a counter-melody to its austere, rough and ready top note, his best-selling album, 1968's *At Folsom Prison*, featured such broad, corny musical gags as 'Flushed From The Bathroom Of Your Heart' and 'Dirty Old Egg-Sucking Dog', both written by Jack Clement, who defines Cash primarily as a clown "who would try anything, the sillier the better sometimes".

These songs were included in the Folsom set as fire-breaks, designed to ease the tension and also – in their bawdy, macho, slightly childish way – to suggest that between Cash and the inmates there existed the fraternal bond of the locker-room.

'A Boy Named Sue', taken from *At San Quentin*, remains his biggest hit and is a humourous shaggy-dog story. But there was a world of difference between these tracks – well-judged, and sung from a position of great artistic strength – and 'Chicken In Black', on which Cash later admitted he had made "a mockery of himself".[6] It was more than simply a bad song. Any artist who has been recording year in and year out for over three decades will eventually release a record that, on reflection, makes their cheeks scorch with shame. Cash had cut his fair share of turkeys, never mind chickens, over the years. That wasn't really the problem. The issue was one of wider perception: here was a man who no longer seemed to know the value of what he had done in the past or what he still had to offer, who was prepared to take an axe to everything he represented up to that point in a song that made him blush even as he was singing it.

As 'Chicken In Black' faded into a kind of terrible post-apocalyptic silence, he even parodied the legendary hum that lent 'I Walk The Line' a considerable part of its strange fascination. The result was a record that succeeded only in telegraphing Cash's weakness and confusion, giving the impression that the last career move he had left to make was to sacrifice his most significant asset: the sense of dignity and poise that came wrapped up in his 'man in black' persona.

"The nadir was 'Chicken In Black', where he was kind of mocking and dismantling his own legacy," says Rosanne Cash. "There was an undercurrent of desperation in it. It was painful. Everybody [realised it was a big mistake], but that was it. Pretty much the end of [him with] Columbia."

The fact that 'Chicken In Black' crawled into the Top 50 of the country charts – a modest feat which nonetheless not one of his previous half dozen singles could claim to have achieved – was cold comfort. It wasn't anything so bold as a hit; it was only less of a flop than he had become accustomed to having. Yet even if the song had reached Number One it would have given only the brief illusion of resurgence. A song such as 'Chicken In Black' could never be a success by the artistic standards that Cash had set himself. It was simply another blind date between artist and material (Cash, mercifully, did not write the song) in a career that had lost all semblance of shape or discernible pattern.

This is where we find him on the map in the 80s, having ping-ponged between styles and half-baked concepts for the best part of a decade, chasing something he didn't necessarily want and probably couldn't quite define, writing hardly any new material and yet frustrated by the lack of decent songs he was being offered. All around him Nashville was changing beyond recognition. So was his record label. Bruce Lundvall and Dick Asher, both friends and powerful allies, had gone. Asher, who had risen to deputy president, left Columbia for Polygram, whose label roster included Mercury Records, in 1983, in a putsch orchestrated by Columbia's combative chief executive Walter Yetnikoff. Label president Lundvall had left a year earlier to join Elektra. Neither was particularly enthused by the way the wind was blowing.

"I was very frustrated at what was going on at Columbia. It became politicised," says Lundvall. "I was like an umpire trying to direct traffic. Rick Blackburn was a sales and marketing guy, but he had good ears and good skills. He was very aggressive in going after artists. There was a certain conflict between he and Sherrill, one being a creative guy and one being a commercial guy."

The unyielding demands of the "business of the business" were all very well, but Cash was hardly exempt from criticism. He had lost focus, lost momentum. He had nothing much of interest to say and in many ways had no one to blame but himself. "The last time he had to convince [Columbia] was probably *Folsom*, where he really went in and had to make a case," says Rosanne Cash. "After that, I think he was floundering a little bit."

In mitigation, he was quick to point out that his spirit had been sapped by the lack of interest from the people releasing his records. "There were times when I didn't care," he later admitted. "It was, like, complete apathy from the record company and I guess I got that way, too."[7]

Rick Rubin: "I think he was almost at the point of giving up. I think he'd probably made a hundred albums, and making an album wasn't a big deal to him. It wasn't important to him. It was just another one: 'Eighteen months roll by, put out another one, doesn't really matter, no one really cares. I'll either do it or not, it doesn't make a difference.' I think that's where he was at, where the record-making part of his artistry didn't matter so much to him … I don't think he was emotionally invested in the record-making process."[8]

Cash's 1985 album *Rainbow* was the final straw. Not especially loved by the man who made it and barely registering on the radar of its paymasters, it was, Cash complained, simply born and then starved of all affection and sustenance until it died a quick, quiet death. This is true, in so far as Columbia had effectively given up on him as a commercial proposition.

It's an album that illuminates both sides of the argument. There are good things about it. 'I'm Leavin' Now' is a decent recording of a song he would reclaim on *Solitary Man*, although the ghostly echo of the spicy horns from 'Ring Of Fire' reeks a little of last chance saloon. And there are some good song choices in Kris Kristofferson's 'Here Comes That Rainbow Again' and John Fogerty's 'Have You Ever Seen The Rain?' The former, however, is a terrible muddy plod, while the latter is perfunctory. With the assistance of producer Chips Moman, Cash was striving for the smooth country radio sound that was all the rage at the time, but he seemed stiff and ill at ease.

This was his great dilemma: if he did what he'd always done he sounded old hat; if he tried to adapt he sounded forced and diluted. It would take seismic shifts in time, age, and perspective to resolve that problem and realise that the trick was to cut the country-music industry out of the equation altogether; he had to drip-feed his music entirely off his own instincts, supported by a producer whom he could trust to let him be himself. That resolution took more guts and imagination than either Blackburn or Cash exhibited at that point. Nobody was playing the long game; nobody saw that he really didn't belong in this environment at all.

Instead, he had to content himself with bellyaching about Columbia's refusal to get behind each of these albums and therefore give him a platform, as though all his music needed in the 80s was to be placed in front of an audience in order for it to be lapped up and loved. But it was more complex than that. There were bigger cultural forces at play than advertising budgets and promotional windows.

Asked 25 years later why he didn't pull out all the stops to get Cash's career back on track and help him make a splash again, Rick Blackburn is resolute. "Tell me how to pull out the stops?" he says. "Please, tell me. Let's say I take out big, big ads in all the trade magazines. OK. What else? When I go to a 28-year-old music radio director in Houston linked into two dance clubs, doing remote broadcasts, who's a big deal, and he asks: what have you got new that's doing boot scootin' boogie, buddy? What do you say? *Johnny Cash*?"

The question hangs in the air. It wasn't a popular view then and it isn't today, but Blackburn has a point. Times had changed, tastes had changed, the faces had changed. Cash had changed, too, but either too much or not enough. His live show was creaking in all the wrong places, and he didn't seem to recognise that it took more than simply pointing people toward his albums to make them successful.

If Cash thought, as many of his friends and colleagues did, that his stature and legacy was such that he would be immune from the axe chopping the Nashville old guard into dead wood, he was mistaken. 'I'm Leavin' Now' proved a prophetic statement. It was his swan song for Columbia. "Finally, we both agreed that we weren't entertaining each other any more," he said.[9] And that was that.

Blackburn remains ambivalent about how he dealt with Cash, and is the first to admit that "I didn't do anything to further his career. Can you imagine how someone like him felt? It was awkward. You'd meet him in a restaurant or somewhere and it was definitely awkward, but it was a natural progression. He was gracious about the whole transition, more gracious than some, I remember that. Some of them were like: I built this and you owe me more, but it was what my job was. The numbers didn't stack up, and he understood that better than you might have thought he would. After Johnny went to Mercury we maintained a good relationship, actually. I'd call him from time to time, and he'd call me. It wasn't a hostile thing, it didn't go down that way at all."

There was an added twist in these upheavals. Rosanne Cash had been signed by Blackburn to Columbia in the late 70s and had gone on to enjoy tremendous critical and commercial success with her albums *Seven Year Ache*, *Rhythm & Romance*, and *King's Record Shop* and her 1985 Grammy-winning single 'I Don't Know Why You Don't Want Me'. One of the most difficult aspects about being dropped by Columbia was having to face up to the fact that, if he wanted to measure the fortunes of the old guard against the new guard, all Cash had to do was stand back-to-back with his daughter.

"Rosanne was selling a million copies and John was selling less than 30,000," says Blackburn. "That's the sucking sound right there, that's the displacement I'm talking about. It was a good time for some and a sad time for others. But he was also very proud of his daughter."

Rosanne Cash: "It was unspoken, but it was painful. More painful for me than it was for him, because he was in the role of proud parent. He was very proud of me, all the letters he wrote to me at that time told me how proud he was, but there was a wound that was in there, too. I felt a little awkward about it, I didn't want to flaunt it in any way or make it worse for him. It was tricky. Just before Columbia dropped him, he called me and asked me what my royalty rate was. I told him, and he kind of harrumphed and hung up the phone. Shortly afterward he was dropped."

Checking up on the dollars and cents doled out to the company's prestige acts was tied into feelings of wounded pride and professional self-worth. Nonetheless, Rick Blackburn claims that Cash was not, strictly speaking, dropped from Columbia. Rather it was the case that his contract was not renewed because they wouldn't pay him what he was asking.

"His contract was up and he had had an offer from Mercury," says

Blackburn. "My old boss at Columbia, Dick Asher, was at Polygram and he offered Johnny a pretty big deal at that time based on the number of units he was selling. I couldn't match it, not at those numbers, and I told Cash and Lou Robin that. They went ahead and did the deal. It becomes a numbers game. I'm not going to get into his deal, that's a privacy thing, but we were so far apart."

Dick Asher: "I don't remember it that way at all. I don't think it was a big [money] deal, I think it was relatively modest. I didn't have to break the bank or anything. He wanted a deal with us. He somehow didn't like the way he was treated [at Columbia]. Maybe that was to do with the negotiations, that he felt they were insulting in view of what they had done in the past. I think after it happened it was an embarrassment to Columbia."

The manner in which it was announced that Cash and Columbia had parted was also something of an embarrassment. It was July 1986, and Blackburn had agreed that Cash's camp could make the public statement that he was moving to Mercury, to make it appear like a positive, proactive move rather than a decision that, which ever way it was sliced, was being foisted upon him. In terms of its roster, history, and profile, Columbia was a considerably more illustrious label than the one he was joining.

"The agreement was that Cash would make the announcement that he was moving to Mercury," says Blackburn. "That was fine. That would put the light on it that Johnny has moved on to better things, as opposed to we just don't want him any more. I was doing an interview with a reporter from *The Tennessean*, Bob Oermann. I was called away on a phone call and there were some papers on the desk, including the current roster of artists to be circulated to lawyers and staff. Bob read that, and three days later he printed in his paper that Columbia had dropped Johnny Cash. It was picked up by *USA Today* and it created a firestorm. It caused me to look like I broke my word that Johnny and Mercury were going to make the announcement, and I thought that was unfair."

Regardless of how it played out, members of the country music community and the record industry were, to varying degrees, stunned by the news. "It was a very big surprise when Columbia let him go," says Bruce Lundvall. "I had the same situation with Miles Davis, when Walter Yetnikoff said: 'He's too expensive, let Warner Brothers have him.' Miles was a one-of-a-kind artist, and you don't let them go. Same with Johnny Cash. He's the kind of career artist you never let go. It's a big mistake to lose a one-of-a-kind artist."

Paul Kennerley: "I remember the shocked feeling in Nashville, talking to Emmylou [Harris] and friends; the idea that the living moral compass of country music was dropped by Columbia yet the kind of crap I was writing was selling. The charts never actually recovered. There was a lot of nonsense going on."

Cash wasn't entirely surprised, but it was a blow to his ego. "I think he saw it coming," says Rosanne Cash. "But he was hurt, really hurt. Oh, I was furious, I was so angry. It doesn't matter if they're selling records or not, you don't drop Johnny Cash. Bruce [Lundvall] is one of the few people who realises that. When I went back to renegotiate my contract I asked for a wildly inappropriate amount of money to re-sign because I was so angry at what they had done to my dad. And they gave it to me!"

"He was disappointed about it but we didn't sit around moping," Jack Clement recalls. "It was stupid, you don't go around dropping Johnny Cash. He was an institution. Just to have him on the label was worth keeping him for the name value, the prestige. I thought it was dumb and so did pretty much everyone else. It was a very short-sighted decision. His career at Columbia was really in the dumps at that point, and they just didn't do anything with him. Bunch of young idiots."

It's very easy to portray Nashville as the big, bad bogey man in all this. The common conception is that when Columbia dropped Cash in 1986 it was an act of rhinestone regicide. They deposed a king. "I was maybe one of the first not to continue with a bellwether artist," says Blackburn. "But when you're running a business it's about everything moving forward. It's not 'What have you done for me?' but 'What are you going to do for me?' It's a debate that will go on, and it's a good debate."

Nobody at the time really saw the bigger picture: namely that, as Crowell points out, "because he got dropped it set off the dynamic where he could eventually find a new audience". Cash badly needed to leave Columbia for the good of his creative health. At some point in the 80s he must surely have looked around at where he had pitched up. On one side he saw his lacklustre albums and the blatant indifference of his record company; on the other he saw his band, his family, and his long legacy. He found himself trapped. He needed a jolt, a change of scene, a new perspective.

"I think he knew things were changing and he didn't know how to get with it," says Nick Lowe. "He never whined, he definitely wasn't a whiner. It was everyone else who was outraged, like Dwight Yoakam: 'Fucking Columbia, they built their entire operation on Johnny Cash, how can they chuck him out?' But John didn't express any anger to me, although I know he *was* [angry]. The one time when we did discuss it, he said that things weren't great right now, but it was more resignation. He was supporting this huge operation, the show and the family. There was no way he could stop, really, he was funding it all, but of course the more he did it the more not-very-good it was, in a way. He did occasionally talk about these things over a glass of red wine, maybe being a little indiscreet, perhaps. When we got a little more friendly he told me [about his frustrations]. And of course it was making him ill."

The cruellest of ironies was that after coming to grips with his drug addiction the second time around, Cash was forced to endure a catastrophic chain of health-related problems from the age of 50 onward. They may have been connected to the punishment he had inflicted on his body by years of heavy drug use; they could just as easily be attributed to the unforgiving lifestyle of being on the road almost constantly for nearly 30 years, or to his diet and his smoking, or to fate, to chance, to God's will. They seemed somehow connected to his ceaselessly tormented inner nature. He was not a man who found it easy to relax; he had an excess of nervous energy, he worried about people, and he was acutely aware of his responsibilities to his fans, his band, and his family. It was little wonder he suffered from high blood pressure.

Even before the final few years of his life, when his health declined to the point where it seemed all that kept him going was sheer cussed will-power, he had to contend with a dreadful litany of setbacks which took a heavy toll. He had put his body through an immense amount of suffering, and it all caught up on him rather rapidly when he hit middle age. To fully understand where much of the weariness and many of the shadows in Cash's final decade of music came from, and also to understand how many obstacles had to be overcome in order to make it, one simply has to trace the outline of the variety of health problems he faced. "He was an old man even when he was a middle-aged man, to tell the truth," says Rosanne Cash. "Physically and spiritually."

He was forced to take a month off in the summer of 1987 when he fell ill on stage in Iowa, discovering suddenly when he tried to address the audience that he couldn't talk properly. He cut short the show and was taken to the local hospital, where he was diagnosed with an irregular heartbeat and told to rest.

Over a year later, in December 1988, it was discovered that his heart problems were in fact extremely serious. During a check up at the Baptist Hospital in Nashville, a place that was to become almost a second home to him over the next 15 years, doctors found that he was suffering from a severe blockage of his arteries which required an immediate heart bypass procedure. Following the two-hour operation on December 19 Cash developed double pneumonia and became critically ill. Over the Christmas period his life hung in the balance. He very nearly died and spent two weeks in hospital before finally being discharged. He later remembered undergoing a near-death experience, when he felt himself slipping away, only to be pulled back from the brink. He always sounded rather ambivalent about his return to the living world.

In 1990, following what should have been a relatively routine operation to remove an abscessed tooth, Cash was beset by a bewildering confluence of complications. The wound didn't heal properly, with the result that a cyst formed on the jawbone. The operation to remove the cyst was badly botched and Cash was left with an infection that caused him almost unbearable pain. Further unsuccessful operations left his jaw in such a weakened state that he managed later to break it while eating dinner, a fact he didn't discover until long after it happened.

He not only had to cancel one European tour but also the rescheduled dates. The long-term physical impact could be seen in the obvious alteration in his features. From this point on, one side of face looked constantly swollen and drooped slightly; several people thought that he had suffered a stroke. By 1996 he had undergone 34 separate operations to reset his jaw, but none was successful. The pain was excruciating and unrelenting, although he refused to make a big deal out of it. "It's my pain, I'm handling it," he said. "Once I get my face down on a soft pillow for about ten minutes I can go off to sleep."[10] His predicament put yet another spin on that line from 'The Beast In Me' about learning to live with pain.

These debilitating setbacks were routinely punctuated by further scrapes which most people would regard as serious but which to Cash in his heightened state of disrepair seemed like only minor ailments: bronchitis, laryngitis, respiratory infections. A meeting in London in May 1989 with Marc Riley and Jon Langford, co-creators of the Cash tribute album *'Til Things Are Brighter*, revealed much about the various sources of aggravation and illness which afflicted Cash almost constantly.

"He was playing at the Royal Albert Hall and we were invited to be his guests," says Riley. "So me and Jon went. After the show we were told Johnny wanted to meet us. We waited for an hour. We weren't disgruntled, we just thought he had his family here, he'd had a big night. ... Just when we were thinking of going the door opened and this big booming voice came out: 'Marc, Jon.' He shook hands and talked to us for a while, he was gracious about the album, and then he went away. Afterward [promoter and drummer] Hugh Waddell came up and said: 'We're really sorry to keep you waiting, but before the show he had a blood clot and they had to give him some [anticoagulant] Warfarin. Then they gave him some more Warfarin after the show and told him he had to lie down for an hour.' Talk about a humbling experience. It was unimaginable that someone in that state would go to such efforts to see two guys who had made this little record."

A surprising and rather poignant aside emerged from his frequent bouts of ill health. "When I had bypass surgery in '88 I sold the [publishing] company [Song Of Cash, Inc] because we needed the money," he later said. "And then I fought to get that company back. I got every song back and I'll never give it up again. I don't give a shit what happens financially, I'll never give up my songs again."[11]

"It was a tough time for Johnny then," says engineer David Ferguson. "You've got a lot of overheads and you need to make money, a lot of money."

As Nick Lowe points out, Cash was a man with deep and perhaps inescapable commitments to his family and his band. Here was a reminder of the cost – physical *and* financial – not just of being forced off the road during a dry spell in his career, but also of keeping almost 50 people in gainful employment through thick and thin.

It's hardly surprising that in the 80s Cash wasn't testing himself. He was battling a bewildering array of foes. Another major consequence of these illnesses and operations, aside from the immediate symptoms and the effect they had on his health, was the fact that they pumped more and more painkillers into his system. In November 1989 he had quietly sought treatment over two weeks at Cumberland Heights Alcohol and Drug Treatment Center in Nashville for what was termed "relapse prevention therapy", but which was more likely intended to address the problem of weaning him off whatever pills he had been taking.

The legend of Cash's life has tended to be written in binary form. His duality was rarely that clearly defined, and when it came to drugs the boundaries were never cut and dried. The accepted narrative is that after Cash's second brush with addiction ended in 1984 he remained clean until his death, but it was a lifelong struggle with many grey areas. "There weren't strict lines of demarcation between: dad was sober, dad was not sober; dad was clean, dad was using," says Rosanne Cash.

"There weren't those clean lines. It was kind of like: oh, I think he's using painkillers again, or something's going on."

He was in so much pain in the last 20 years of his life that he sometimes would use whatever it took. "In truth, John never kicked that stuff," says Rodney Crowell. "I'd see him on the Larry King show saying how he was clean, and then three days later he'd be zonked out."

"He really went in and out," Rosanne Cash continues. "This was a life-long struggle. It was varying degrees: it was better, it was worse, it got better, it got worse. This was something he always struggled with. People think: oh, June 'saved' him, he got clean and that was it for the rest of his life. Isn't that a great story? No, that's not what happened. People love the Hollywood version, but that's not what happened."

5

**Against
The Wind**

ust how far from the centre of things Johnny Cash had spun is captured in a humiliating little one-act drama that played out in the summer of 1986. Jimmy Bowen was a hot-shot Nashville producer and industry man who had just taken an executive position at MCA records. Cash had the rather brave idea that an old-fashioned Tin Pan Alley-style audition – taking his guitar into Bowen's office and singing his songs to him, just as he'd done to Sam Phillips 30 years earlier – might give Nashville *du jour* a taste of the kind of rich and unique fare they were missing out on. It was essentially a premonition of *American Recordings*, Cash again presenting himself as the ultimate concept. He went in and played his best game for half an hour. "What do you think?" Cash asked when he had finished. "Let me think about it," Bowen replied. And Cash never heard from him again. "Not a phone call, not a note, not a peep," he later recalled.[1]

One suspects this display of blatant indifference toward a man who would have felt he deserved a little more respect may have hurt Cash even more than being dropped by his record label. "Nashville has a very short memory," he said. "And it's crazy for jumping on trends."[2] It was almost as though he was being punished for not conforming to the cliché of living fast and dying young, for not allowing death to smooth him into something less awkward, less complicated. "Nashville's hell on the livin' but it sure speaks well of the dead," says Steve Popovich. "That great Shel Silverstein lyric ['Rough On The Living'] sums up a lot of what went on here. When you're hot, you're hot, when you're not, you're not. It's real simple."

Popovich had worked closely with Cash in the past as assistant to the head of pop promotion at Columbia. He had left the company in the late 70s to set up his own record label, and was now heading up the Nashville division of Polygram, whose stable included Mercury Records, working under label boss Dick Asher, another old ally from Cash's Columbia days. Asher had taken over Polygram's office in New York with an edict to either get rid of the country stable, which was floundering badly, or knock it back into shape. He opted for the latter. "Polygram's Nashville office had been a bit of a shambles," says Asher.

"And I thought Steve would do well there in helping to rebuild it. But it was a challenge."

Contrary to Rick Blackburn's recollections, Asher says it was only after they became aware that Cash was no longer wanted at Columbia that Mercury became involved in negotiations to sign Cash. "After a while Steve said he'd heard from John that he was loose and he was sort of feeling around to see if we wanted him," says Asher. "I guess John was a little reluctant to come right out and ask and I don't blame him."

Steve Popovich: "Columbia, quite unceremoniously I thought, had dropped him. I spoke to Dick Asher and said Dick, this is disgraceful, we need to make a lot of noise down here and I think it would make a great addition to our roster. I became reacquainted with John, went down to Hendersonville to meet him. He didn't show any sense of being sore but we talked about it and you could tell he was kind of hurt by the whole thing. Life has a way of taking the wind out of your sails and that's where he was at that point.

"There was a major shift in Nashville in the record companies and then in country radio, and these people became too old for radio to play. For current radio you needed an ongoing succession of hits, and John hadn't had those in a few years prior to leaving Columbia. A lot of the people who built these companies, once they cease selling it becomes a very cold business. A bean counter decision: 'We're not making any money [on new records], we have the best of the catalogue, why are we even fooling with this artist?'"

Within a matter of weeks Cash and Mercury had agreed a deal. Asher, perhaps thinking with his heart rather than his head, says that he "didn't consider there to be any risk at all" in signing Cash. "It was like stealing money," he says. "He was a tremendous talent, wonderful writer. Those kind of people eventually have something good come to them, even after low periods. When you get the chance to sign an artist like him, you take it. We did some nice things, and he was a wonderful magnet for our offices in Nashville."

Cash coming to Mercury was supposed to be a fresh start for both the label and the artist. He signed the deal on August 21 1986 and went into the studio almost immediately. It was a much happier creative environment than the one he had latterly endured at Columbia. Jack Clement, the trusty lieutenant who had worked on and off with Cash for 30 years and often got the best out of him, was roped in as producer. Working with men he knew, liked, and respected gave Cash a bounce he hadn't had for some time, but there was more than a suspicion that he still wasn't quite firing on all cylinders creatively. "I was just trying to get some really good records out of him like I always did," says Clement. "I don't know if I had any particular theme or anything. I felt like he was a little bit bewildered and confused at that point. He didn't know exactly what to do, so we would try a bunch of different things."

Released on April 13 1987, his comeback album was called *Johnny Cash Is Coming To Town,* a suitably imperious-sounding title intended to throw a little of that famous Cash swagger out into the world. It's a good album. Clean, direct and fresh sounding. It opens with a funky, horn-driven gallop through Elvis Costello's 'The Big Light', released on Costello's *King Of America* record the previous year, the inclusion of which demonstrated that someone was at least keeping their eyes and ears open. The lyric, a wry tale of a hangover so palpable it "has a personality", humorously aligned Cash to the right side of the wrong side of the tracks once again. His writing hadn't caught fire, however. There were only two Cash originals. 'The Ballad Of Barbara' was a reprise of an old, though admittedly fine song from *The Last Gunfighter Ballad*, and the other was the somewhat average 'I'd Rather Have You'.

But the reviews were decent and everyone at Mercury had high hopes that the album would put Cash back on the map as a force to be reckoned with. With the aim of appealing to the increasingly powerful Country Music Television (CMT), the country equivalent of MTV, he made videos for his cuts of Guy Clark's 'Let Him Roll' and Merle Travis's classic 'Sixteen Tons', famously a hit for Tennessee Ernie Ford in 1955. Despite all the bustle and good intentions, the album didn't have anything close to the impact they had all hoped for. *Johnny Cash Is Coming To Town* reached only Number 36 in the country charts, the kind of damp squib, nowheresville chart position he'd been racking up at Columbia for years.

"We did pretty well with that, but not as well as everybody had expected," says Popovich. "*Water From The Wells Of Home* was the one that I was real disappointed with the low sales on."

Cash's second Mercury album, *Water From The Wells Of Home* was indeed expected to do brisk business. An album of all-star duets, it includes contributions from Hank Williams Jr, Emmylou Harris, Tom T. Hall, Waylon Jennings, Glen Campbell, Jessi Colter, as well as June, John Carter Cash, and a pregnant Rosanne.

The star attraction from out of town was Paul McCartney. Cash had a fine old home in Cinnamon Hill in Jamaica, where he would customarily spend the winter. The tradition became to celebrate Christmas early in Nashville and then head for the Caribbean with his family, dispensing plane tickets to a revolving group of good friends so they could fly down. Cash would put them up, feed them well, and generally give them the full blast of his hospitality.

Cash and McCartney were neighbours in Jamaica, and when they discovered they were both on the island over Christmas 1987, the two ended up having dinner together. Tom T. Hall popped in and the night ended in a 'guitar pull' lasting until three in the morning, during which time they wrote a new song called 'New Moon Over Jamaica'. It was recorded in McCartney's studio in England when Cash was touring the UK the following May, only weeks before the album was released. Most of the rest of the album was recorded at Jack Clement's home studio in Tennessee.

Released in May 1988, *Water From The Wells Of Home* limped to only Number 48 in the country charts, a hugely disappointing result. The lead single, a duet with Hank Williams Jr on 'This Old Wheel', which everyone at the company thought was going to be a smash, didn't even reach the country Top 20.

"I was proud of that record, it had everybody on it," says Clement.

"I think someday the world might rediscover those things, or discover 'em for the first time. The goods are there, I believe, we were just on a down part of the cycle. It was just a bad time. The label was kind of soggy at the time and so was Johnny Cash's reputation, and I think it just got lost in the shuffle."

But the album is soggy, too. Its smorgasbord of cameos was intended to bolster Cash's position, prop him up, recontextualise him for an 80s audience, but in the end achieved the opposite, smacking of overkill and a lack of focus. The endeavour wasn't helped by the fact that not one of the artists – aside from Rosanne Cash – could charitably be described as hot property at the time; even Paul McCartney was enduring something of a slump.

After the non-event of *Water From The Wells Of Home*, the realisation quickly dawned that, despite the best efforts of everyone involved, it wasn't going to happen with Cash and Mercury. "In the end we just didn't have the magic record," says Popovich. "Elvis had to die to get a hit, and he was in much the same situation as John before he did: radio wouldn't play him. People get tired, and maybe that's the way it should be."

The initial optimism that Cash had felt on arriving at a new label quickly dissipated, particularly when Dick Asher left Polygram shortly after the second album. Cash's final two releases for the label, 1990's *Boom-Chicka-Boom* (hardly a title to attract a new audience; his reliance on the old signature sound was one of the problems) and 1991's *The Mystery Of Life*, were major flops. His claim that they only printed 500 copies of his final album seems absurd. *The Mystery Of Life* reached Number 70 in the country charts which, while hardly spectacular, suggested sales figures at least into four figures.

However, Dick Asher claims that "anything is possible with his last album. After I left I think the company was taken over by people who thought they knew a lot more than they did. One was a lawyer and one was Alain Levy [appointed executive vice president in 1988], who had come from Europe. They got it wrong on a lot of things. They did some terrible things and got rid of some fine people. The atmosphere changed completely".

The Mercury albums marked the first time Cash worked with David Ferguson, who had been engineering for Jack Clement since the early 80s. "He got back together with Jack and they had a lot of fun making those records," he says. "They're good records, but they didn't promote them right and nobody really knew what to make of him. He'd kinda done it all. I think Mercury let him down a bit. Steve Popovich had the right idea and his heart was in the right place, but the company just wasn't behind him. That was disappointing to John."

"It was a very transitional time in Nashville," says Dick Asher, "and we just couldn't break John to the point where I was thrilled that we'd done a good enough job. It was an uphill battle. I was not so happy with Mercury's performance, we weren't really so expert in country music and we had a ways to go. Some of it is attributable to that; and also that he wasn't pulling that much of an audience at that time. The albums to a certain extent were orphans out there."

Cash became openly hostile toward the company and began singing a familiar lament. "I became very happy for a little while, we all were," he said. "Then the power at Mercury/Polygram in New York shifted and I became, again, an artist the company weren't interested in promoting."[3]

By the end, his career was in a worse fix than it had been even at Columbia. The quality of the output might have been more consistent, but there was absolutely nothing happening. All Cash's initial optimism seeped away, and he began to feel isolated, bordering on irrelevant. "I've never looked at the charts and grieved because my name wasn't in there," he said, but he also acknowledged that he missed the days when people were eagerly waiting to hear his latest music.[4] He was a big man with big appetites and a big ego, and even if he no longer expected to be tearing up the pop charts, the fact that his albums were released into a chasm of indifference smarted.

"[Success] was important to him," says Rosanne Cash. "He liked playing on a big field, he liked playing at the top of his game, and he liked people seeing that he was at the top of his game. He liked being competitive. He wasn't one of those guys who was like: I'll just work here in a quiet room and that's enough for me. No. He needed a big field. He was used to that and it's hard to give up once you're used to it." Steve Popovich adds, succinctly: "Very few people walk away and say: I've had enough hits."

What Cash was missing, what he craved more than anything, was to be at the centre of things, to have people listen and digest what he had to say. The big question, when you stripped away all the talk of promotion, lack of support, demographics, was this: what *did* he have to say? The point seemed to have escaped him that, no matter who was at the helm, whether it was Columbia or Mercury, whether they were hard-nosed business executives or close friends, his records hadn't been selling for a considerable number of years. It wasn't just a matter of promotion.

Jack Clement was a trusted ally, Popovich and Asher were fans and loved everything he did. Cash was in creative control of all these albums. He was able to do virtually anything that he wanted. Take a closer look at some of the song choices on *Water From The Wells Of Home* and you can see not only the problem with the album itself, but also a sense of the more endemic problems underlying Cash's time at Mercury. Everyone was out of touch. One of only two Cash originals on the album, the other being the title track, the corny 'A Croft In Clachan' is described by Popovich as "a wonderful song, a great lyric". It's neither. Who exactly this strange, sentimental lament was meant to appeal to in the modern market wasn't clear. In an interview conducted to promote the album, Cash said: "We really believe it's going to pay off, we've come up with some commercial now sounds." If he really believed that he was making 'commercial now sounds' it's no surprise that his career was in trouble.

All the factors that made Cash's arrival at Mercury look so appealing initially were, in many respects, the problem. At the time some critics heralded these albums as the start of an "artistic renaissance", which compared to 'Chicken In Black' they perhaps were, but on a wider level they were self-evidently no such thing.[5] They may have contained reminders of Cash's vibrancy, they were sturdy *echoes*, but they weren't taking him or his music to a new level. Revisiting 'The Ballad Of A Teenage Queen' as the opening track on *Water From The Wells Of Home*, hooking up with The Everly Brothers, rerecording 'Hey Porter' on *The Mystery Of Life* – it all spoke of the dread hand of nostalgia hanging over his work.

The fact that the people who were instrumental in bringing him to the label were friends he had worked with previously at Columbia may not have been the boon it first appeared to be. Everyone at Mercury was intent on helping him recapture former glories, an impossible task, rather than thinking about how to realign his core genius to better fit the times. The problem was that nobody there really wanted Cash to change at all. The success of Cash's time at American Recordings was partly attributable to sheer calculation. There was no such clear-eyed calculation at Mercury. They had all known him for years, and believed, in the words of Steve Popovich, that he "was always dangerous to have a hit. As big a star as Johnny Cash is only one step away from selling a million records, because he's pre-sold. I always felt he could have a world-wide hit and I loved the challenge of trying to bring him back".

Popovich is right about his latent potential, but nobody at Mercury, including Cash, had any idea of what was required to tap into it. It wasn't about going back to some Platonic ideal, dusting down a version of who he used to be and what he used to sound like. It was about using all those past experiences, distilling them down to their essence, and presenting Cash's music as something radical, relevant, and resonant. He wasn't quite there yet.

*

The Highwaymen provided a welcome antidote to feeling ignored. His anchor point throughout this period, in many ways, was his stint in the country supergroup that featured Cash, Waylon Jennings, Kris Kristofferson, and Willie Nelson. Musically, the union tended toward the solid rather than inspired. To an uncharitable eye it looked like four horsemen unceremoniously unseated in the Nashville apocalypse riding into the sunset; a quartet of has-beens huddling together for warmth and emotional sustenance through a long, hard winter. To the less cynical it was a once-in-a-generation meeting of four writers and performers who had each, in different ways, challenged the status quo in Nashville and reached out far beyond the confines of the country genre.

The idea for the collaboration had come about in November 1984, when Nelson, Jennings, and Kristofferson all travelled to Montreux in Switzerland to take part in Cash's annual Christmas TV Special. Why Switzerland? "Because that's where the baby Jesus was born," deadpanned Jennings. They batted songs back and forth in the hotel room, including Jimmy Webb's 'The Highwayman', and at the end Jennings suggested they might develop the theme further in the studio. Kristofferson in particular wasn't so sure it would work: too many egos, he said, too many choices.

Events gathered their own momentum. Back in Nashville the following month, Chips Moman was producing a duet between Cash and Willie Nelson called 'They're All The Same', earmarked for his forthcoming and ill-fated final Columbia album, *Rainbow*. Jennings and Kristofferson were in town and dropped in. Cash was no doubt glad of the distraction. They quickly recorded 'The Highwayman', which became the theme song to the whole enterprise. It told the tale of a daring, creative soul passing down the ages, finding transient form in the shape of the highwayman, the sailor, the dam builder, and the astronaut. Each one was an incarnation of this deathless American spirit, weaving through history, forever on the move.

It was a masterstroke of a song choice, as Cash's guitarist Marty Stuart pointed out: four verses, four souls, and four great American icons in the band to sing it. Indeed, 'The Highwayman' proved an all-too-rare example of a track big enough and built in such a way as to be able to accommodate them all. Topped off with Peter Israelson's lavish black and white video, which helped enhance the myth-making that inevitably surrounded the coming together of these four musicians, it became a country Number One in 1985, a welcome shot in the arm for

Cash's career. Their first album, *Highwaymen*, also gave them a Number One and included a couple of old Cash numbers. They all traded lines on 'Big River', now with a new verse that took in Nashville, and sang 'Committed To Parkview', Cash's touching, blackly comic, and all-too-knowing song about being in a psychiatric institution, which had first appeared on *One Piece At A Time*.

Although it was a lot of fun, artistically the band was only intermittently successful. Theirs was not a particularly comfortable mix of voices, and there was the added issue of four powerful individuals each with a substantial ego trying to carve out space within the group. There were arguments over which musicians to use from whose band, and which songs to sing. "It was like four big stallions trying to pull together in one direction," says Jennings's wife Jessi Colter. "I think Waylon had a lot to do with that. They found a way to do it."

Unlike the first, the second Highwaymen album, begun in March 1989 and released a year later, lacked a killer track to pull it all together. "It could have done with a little more time spent on it," said Waylon Jennings. "We ran in and out too quick, and we didn't have that one great song. It's hard to find material that goes over with four people, each with strong, let-it-all-hang-out opinions."[6] It did, however, once again give the group a country Number One and a *Billboard* Top 100 album at a time when Cash was otherwise almost completely off-radar.

The second album also provided the opportunity for the group to tour for the first time. They had played a one-off show at Willie Nelson's Picnic in 1985, but the short US stint in March 1990 was their first time out on the road. It gave Cash the chance to play large arenas at a time when he was generally booked into small, modest venues, and the sets were exemplary, each man including some of their own classic songs as well as songs they had recorded together as The Highwaymen.

They each had their own bus, travelling in convoy through the night after each show, like some chrome-plated wagon train. Times had changed. Cash and Jennings had both recently undergone bypass surgery; the former was extolling the virtues of a new fruit protein drink while Jennings had finally kicked cocaine. There was a feeling of hard-won survival in the wind, an air of gruff romanticism.

Although they came together only sporadically, The Highwaymen boosted Cash's public profile, and his ego, and gave him a sense of place throughout a difficult time. "Familiarity breeds respect," said Kris Kristofferson. "I never lost that sense of awe."[7]

Cash enjoyed hanging out with his friends and they made some good music, some of the best of his output in the 80s and early 90s. It allowed him to feel that he was still relevant, still at the forefront of something. "It was the one place where he still seemed to be centred," says Rosanne Cash. "The thing that was most true to his nature, and where he seemed he felt the most relaxed during that period. He was with his friends, the music was good, he loved that."

They toured America again later in 1990 and visited Europe, Australia, and New Zealand in May 1992. Their final shows were in the Far East in the winter of 1995, by which time they had completed their third and final record, *The Road Goes On Forever*. It was an album too far. By now the novelty had well and truly worn off and the momentum of the project had run its course. 'It Is What It Is' ("but it ain't what it used to be") was supposed to be a wry comment on getting older, but it simply sounded like a shrugged act of indifference, particularly compared to the taut, utterly relevant music on Cash's *American Recordings*, which had come out less than a year earlier.

In hitching his train to other country musicians struggling to adapt to the changing climate of the 80s and 90s Cash found a haven, but he also reinforced the impression that he was part of a travelling museum of music, a troupe of gnarled veterans collectively trading on former glories. By the early 90s he had reached the point where an artist is rewarded for his longevity rather than any recent dazzling feats of creativity. In 1991 he was given a Grammy Living Legend Award, and the following year he was inducted into the Rock And Roll Hall Of Fame, a much deserved accolade which quite rightly recognised his influence on several generations of musicians and his status as something much more than just a country singer. These were welcome baubles, sincerely felt tips of the hat, but more than anything they were acknowledgements of Cash's long shadow and his physical tenacity; they echoed the sentiment of David Letterman's comment in April 1992 about Cash seemingly having been around forever. "Nobody knew what to do with Johnny Cash," says David Ferguson. "But everyone loved him." That's a less pleasing place to live than it might sound.

Coming on the heels of the desperate disappointment of his time at Mercury, Cash seemed to be paying close attention to the mood music. The impact of his industry struggles and his increasingly poor health prompted him to reflect on his lifestyle and his career. He became involved in the development of Cash Country, a multi-million dollar, 100-acre entertainment complex in Branson, the small Missouri town that had become an all-year-round country music theme park, where tourists were bussed in daily to watch veteran performers going through their old routines at the dozens of purpose-built theatres scattered around the town.

Cash Country was the brainchild of property developer David Green, and was intended to be a self-contained world of entertainment, including amusement parks, a museum, a hotel, a shopping complex, and a go-cart track. There would be three theatres. Cash officially put his name behind Cash Country. He agreed to open the complex and to play at least 75 nights a year at one of the theatres, well over half of his current touring schedule, beginning in May 1992.

"It was an impulse," says Rosanne Cash. "Like *Strawberry Cake* and *The Baron*, like 'Chicken In Black'. All impulse. He was having a very big mid-life crisis, all that stuff was his version of a 20-year-old girl and a Corvette. It's what middle-aged men do when they don't know what to do. He was floundering a bit, there was something desperate about it and confused. He was trying to find his centre. I think he realised that. I have a letter from him where he asks me to come and play at his theatre in Branson, and I remember when I got it I just kind of groaned. 'How long is this going to last?' I wasn't afraid to say those things to him."

It looked very much like he was cutting his creative losses, pulling in the wagons and coming in to pasture, but fate had other ideas. Green's huge investment fell through, the founding company went into insolvency, and Cash Country was never built. He lived to breathe another day. "It was divine intervention," says Rodney Crowell. "I remember that. That would have been it for him – go there and die. I was talking to Mel Tillis and he told me John would have hated it, he wouldn't have lasted 15 minutes. He was a huge star and entertainer, but above all that he was an artist first and foremost. His sensibilities were those of an artist, he was smart and interested and curious, it wasn't just about raking down the money and staying booked. And, subconsciously, realising that must have been what led him to do *American Recordings*."

6

Still In Town

Far from the hermetically sealed confines of Branson, something interesting was happening. Despite his recent trials, Cash had always been an honorary member of any musical constituency defined by its vaguely alternative stance, its outsider status, or its lack of conformity. As he found himself drifting, not entirely through choice, beyond the attentions of the country-music establishment, a loose, less ritualised coalition of artists threw a welcoming arm around his shoulder and once again began taking an active, and audible, interest in him and his work.

It seems incongruous for such a quintessentially American artist, but many of the scattered seeds of Cash's revival were sown in the unlikeliest places: not just Hendersonville, California, and New York, but in the pubs and clubs of Leeds, Manchester, and West London, and in the recording studios of Berlin and Dublin.

Cultural contexts tend to shape-shift when viewed from the other side of an ocean. Cash still had a reputation in the UK and Ireland, where many of his less noteworthy exploits and less winning records had passed by essentially unnoticed. In the States he was an old, ornery country star with an outmoded stage show and an erratic recent history of albums. His last great record was decades behind him and he was arguably as well known for attending Billy Graham's crusades and for his TV appearances as he was for his music. He was revered but dismissed as culturally irrelevant. A man more inclined toward self-aggrandisement and self-pity than Cash might have reflected that only in his own country is a prophet without honour. It's not too fanciful to see him as a kind of country King Lear, an enormously powerful and influential man locked out of his own kingdom. There was bit of that going on: a sense of exile and a palpable narrowing of his domain. From certain angles he looked like a preacher without a pulpit, a singer without a suitably powerful song.

Overseas he was viewed differently. Although the last time Cash had troubled the UK charts had been with 'One Piece At A Time' in 1976, in Britain, Ireland, and Europe he still had considerable cultural kudos in the contemporary musical community. He came over on average at least once a year to play to his diehard fans, but beyond that a new generation of artists who had no connection with traditional country music were championing Cash as a kind of spiritual father-figure. It was, admittedly, the Cash of 20 years past who was being exalted, the one who had smashed the footlights at the Grand Ole Opry and sung uncompromising songs of truth for men heading toward Death Row, but it didn't take long for some musicians to start joining the dots and realise that the man was still around, still working, still the man in black.

It is from this source that we see the earliest context emerging for his 90s revival. Like a vintage car lacking sufficient horsepower to compete with younger models, he was partly reliant upon the efforts of others to get his motor running again. "The rock'n'rollers have always been fans of Cash because he was a fascinating mix," says Steve Popovich. "Deeply religious, very patriotic, but having his own devil in the bottle. And he always spoke out for the voiceless."

In the autumn of 1987, *New Musical Express*, the weekly British music bible covering the spectrum of cutting-edge news, reviews, and features, offered *The Tape With No Name* as the latest of the many excellent cassette compilations it regularly gave away with an issue. It was a sequel to its 1984 compilation, *Neon West*, which had featured everyone from Waylon Jennings and Gram Parsons to Rodney Crowell and The Judds, but rather pointedly, during the age of 'Chicken In Black', hadn't found room for Johnny Cash. This time, newly signed to Mercury and on the back of positive notices for *Johnny Cash Is Coming To Town*, Cash alone among the founding fathers of modern country music was showcased on *The Tape With No Name*, singing 'The Night Hank Williams Came To Town'. The rest of the artists featured were the young pretenders of new country, including Rosanne Cash, Steve Earle, Randy Travis, Lyle Lovett, Ricky Skaggs, and Reba McEntire.

It was a small but significant acknowledgement that he was not considered yesterday's man, at least not in the UK. Long before the alt.country movement began to take hold in the USA, the cassette reflected a general interest in Americana among British musicians, which seeped into everything from the cow-punk scene to the fringes of goth and rock.

Nick Cave was one of the most prominent of the new breed keeping the flame alive; more accurately, he had been relentlessly mining the darkness in Cash's songs and beating it until it bled pure black. An Australian singer and songwriter, he made his name leading the abrasive, post-punk gothic assault of The Birthday Party, and then, after their demise in 1983, formed The Bad Seeds. Cave was explicitly influenced by Cash. Indeed, his music sounded almost like the final flurry of brutal blows in a fight Cash had started back in the mid 50s.

"I lost my innocence with Johnny Cash," he said. "I used to watch *The Johnny Cash Show* on television when I was about nine or ten years old. At that stage I had really no idea about rock'n'roll. I watched him and from that point I saw that music could be an evil thing, a beautiful, evil thing. ... There was something that struck me about him, and about the way my parents shifted around uncomfortably. I've always been interested in him from then on, always known him and known his stuff. I've covered several of his songs."[1]

On *Kicking Against The Pricks*, the 1986 album of covers by Nick Cave & The Bad Seeds, Cave recorded the little-known 'The Singer', co-written by Cash and Charlie Daniels, which as 'The Folk Singer' had been the B-side of the live version of 'Folsom Prison Blues' released in 1968. It was an obscure but oddly fitting choice. The original is a rather self-consciously doomladen Gothic oddity, its slow, ominous tread portraying the singer as a tortured loner "born 200 years too late and 200 years too soon". There are storm clouds lurking in Cash's version, but they are orchestrated. Cave's version brings them nearer to the ground, ramping up the meat-hook guitar riff and slathering on the Hammer Horror tension, plumbing the implied depths of the original. A year earlier, on *The Firstborn Is Dead*, Cave had recorded 'Wanted Man', the tongue-in-cheek travelogue of a lady-killer on the lam, written in Hendersonville in 1969 by Cash and Bob Dylan and recorded a matter of days later on *At San Quentin*.

The two men slowly wound their way toward each other. Cash, of course, later covered Cave's classic song 'The Mercy Seat' on *Solitary Man*, ensuring the circle had a pleasing symmetry. He would use the phrase "to kick against the pricks", a Biblical term that first crops up in Acts 26:14, in one of his last songs, the suitably apocalyptic 'The Man Comes Around'. Even at somewhere close to Cash's lowest ebb, in 1993 at Bognor Regis, the odd Nick Cave fan lurked in the audience, brought into his orbit – and a less hip orbit it would be hard to find at that point – thanks to Cave's patronage. The pair would finally meet in 2002 and make their connection explicit, singing together on 'I'm So Lonesome I Could Cry' and 'Cindy', like two old war-scarred galleons rolling back into port after years at sea.

Cave's endorsement in the 80s not only joined the dots between Cash and cult artists like Lee Hazlewood, Sanford Clark, The Velvet Underground, and Duane Eddy, it made explicit his affiliation with a crop of loosely alternative artists who may not have been selling bucket loads of records but who were critical and cultural bellwethers. Many of them appeared on the very first Johnny Cash tribute album, *'Til Things Are Brighter*, put together by two British indie musicians, Jon Langford of The Mekons and Marc Riley, formerly of The Fall and The Creepers. In their mid twenties at the time, they were both Cash fans of long standing, although when they attended his concerts they often felt that they were the sole representatives of their generation who were interested.

"He wasn't on the radar for most people who grew up listening to Bowie and The Stooges," says Riley. "We were just big fans. I had grown up listening to him as a really young kid, and it had stayed with me. We'd go and see him through the 80s, at the [Manchester] Apollo, or in Blackpool, and you'd have to say that 95 per cent of his audience was the purple-rinse brigade. We were the only young people there. It was closest to cabaret, nostalgia. There was no credibility associated with it; he was probably at his lowest point of cool. He was still a hugely impressive man, but he wasn't courted at all by anyone under the age of 45, which at that time seemed very old."

"Cash to me was like Elvis," says Jon Langford. "I had no

perception in my head that he might have ups and downs in his career and that this might be a really bad time for him. He wasn't unfashionable to us but he was to everyone else. He had June and all the Carter sisters with him, and his son coming out and singing Kris Kristofferson songs. It was the whole show. There was no youthful hipsters. Me and Marc were definitely the youngest people there."

The tribute album the pair put together was not a lavish affair. The house band consisted of Riley and members of The Mekons (Langford on guitar, Simon Taylor on bass, Steve Goulding on drums, Brendan Croker on lead guitar), and they cut all the backing tracks in a single day at RikRak studio in Leeds. The selected singers came in to Berry Street in London over the next few weeks to add their contributions.

Marc Almond, who sang 'Man In Black', was the one proper pop star taking part. Around him were musicians from many other spheres: punk, rock, indie, indie-country, alternative. *'Til Things Are Brighter* featured contributions from the vocalists of bands such as The Triffids, That Petrol Emotion, Buzzcocks, Fatima Mansions, and Cabaret Voltaire, groups that featured regularly in *NME* and *Melody Maker* and were established figures on the independent charts. It placed Cash's music into an entirely new, slightly subversive, and wholly contemporary context. Just as importantly, it features some fine performances.

Michelle Shocked's breakneck gallop through 'One Piece Of A Time' – by far the most recent Cash song on show – is absolutely fantastic; The Triffids' David McComb croons convincingly through 'Country Boy'; Buzzcock's Pete Shelley's very English yelp transforms 'Straight A's In Love' into an oddly vulnerable thing, while Mary Mary, from psychedelic grebo rockers Gaye Bykers On Acid, rips through 'A Boy Named Sue' with psychotic relish. It probably didn't hurt that at the moment of climax he strategically deployed "motherfucker" instead of "son of a bitch".

Cathal Coughlan of The Fatima Mansions sings 'Ring Of Fire'. In his previous band Microdisney he would often perform Cash's 'Cocaine Blues' live alongside a version of Merle Haggard's 'The

Fighting Side Of Me'. He always regarded Cash as being above and beyond notions of cool.

"It was like night and day," says Coughlan. "'The Fighting Side Of Me' is a great song but we did it with irony. When we did 'Cocaine Blues' it wasn't ironic at all, it was straight-down-the-line rebellious. Someone had done me a mix tape in 1982 of the Sun stuff, 'Big River', 'Cry, Cry, Cry', and it just blew me away. I knew him since as this kind of cabaret figure; he had faded definitely, but I still had a lot of regard for him. Doing 'Ring Of Fire' wasn't one of my more storied studio sessions, but the album seemed to get him into some interesting places."

Not all of 'Til Things Are Brighter is terribly good. It might have been an idea, for instance, to check that the vocalists could all sing in the selected key before the band recorded the backing tracks: this applies particularly to Cabaret Voltaire's Stephen Mallinder and his tilt at 'Cry, Cry, Cry' or The Mekons' Sally Timms' on 'I Walk The Line'. But it struck the right balance between respect and wayward abandon. It wasn't frivolous but it was fun, and unafflicted by the grim sincerity of some of the more portentous musical tributes later directed toward Cash. 'Til Things Are Brighter had enough love in its heart to laugh just a little at and with its subject.

Cash got wind of the project long before it was released and was thrilled at the idea of a new generation of musicians interpreting his songs. "He always said he could learn more from a 19-year-old than he could from someone his own age," says Rosanne Cash. "He loved young people, and he loved to find out what young musicians were doing. It was really energising to him. He didn't have any rules about that kind of thing."

When he toured the UK in May 1988 he hooked up with Riley and Langford backstage at Manchester Apollo before his show that evening. "We asked if we could take a photograph for the album cover, which he was happy to do, so we did it on stage after the sound check," says Riley. "He was so lovely, such a presence. It was a humbling experience. He was so gracious and interested in what we were doing."

Aware that the idea of releasing a Cash tribute in the rather inauspicious year of 1988 seemed "a bit gratuitous", the pair had decided to make the album a benefit for The Terence Higgins Trust, the campaigning British charity which raised money and awareness for HIV and AIDS, at the time still widely perceived as an issue which almost exclusively affected the gay community. "You might have thought that a lot of the country fraternity would have run a mile from a disease associated at that time primarily with homosexuals, but he said it was great that young people were doing his music for a cause that hadn't really been dealt with at that point," says Riley.

Country Music People magazine took a rather different tack when the album was released in August 1988 on the independent Red Rhino label. After claiming in their review that "many Christians abhor homosexuality", it pondered whether Cash, as a Christian, was aware that money from the album was being spent on "a controversial disease's victims". But Cash had already chosen his side. "We didn't know what his reaction would be when we told him it was a benefit for AIDS, but he was very cool about that," says Langford. "He told us it was something he was quite keen on, because he and Waylon Jennings had both had open heart surgery and their surgeon had died of AIDS. There was that thing in the papers in Nashville when the album came out: does Johnny Cash know that his money is being used to combat AIDS? He responded really quickly to that!"

'Til Things Are Brighter caused a stir in the kind of places Johnny Cash's name hadn't been heard for quite some time, including college radio and alternative music magazines. Much the same places, in fact, that embraced *American Recordings* a few years later. "Its profile was quite high and it got good reviews," says Riley. "Cash hadn't yet been rediscovered as a cultural icon but he still generated excitement. There were The Mekons, Marc Almond, elements of The Fall, all choosing this country star with not very much credibility. It was a good story. I'm not blowing our trumpet, but I'd imagine it introduced Cash to an audience who hadn't been aware of him or perhaps just thought he was [uncool]. What Rick Rubin achieved with him obviously dwarfed what we did, but I'd like to think we played our part and were a bit ahead of our time."

"Some people didn't really get that Cash was a serious artist," says Jon Langford. "They thought we were indulging a bit of kitsch. I remember one critic in *Melody Maker* dissing it along those lines, but we just thought of it as showcasing these great songs. It was like a pre-echo of his stature, that he wasn't forgotten, that he wasn't Tom Jones, that he hadn't gone off to Vegas. There was an artist in there who was troubled by complacency. So I think we managed to stir up a bit of interest about him. He told us it was a morale booster; he was very flattered and supportive. I later learned from Marty Stuart that he felt ignored and irrelevant around this time, and when you hear the Gaye Bykers On Acid covering your songs I guess you know you're not irrelevant."

Indeed, Cash took great delight during a BBC interview in listing the names of many of the artists involved, and seemed to particularly enjoy slowly and mock-sombrely intoning the name Gaye Bykers On Acid. He stayed in touch with both Riley and Langford, and was genuinely peeved when he discovered that the album launch – at the less than stately venue of the Old Pie Bull pub in Islington, north London – was to be held just days after he was already scheduled to leave the UK. "He would have done it," says Langford. "Sharing a dressing room with Frank Sidebottom ..."

"He felt a real connection with those musicians; he felt very validated," says Rosanne Cash. "It was very good for him. He was in his element. He absolutely understood what they were tapping into and loved it. It was re-energising for him."

A short while later, in March 1989, British band The Godfathers released their UK Top 50 album *More Songs About Love And Hate*, which featured a song called 'The Walking Talking Johnny Cash Blues'. It was both a musical tribute – a furious garage punk update of the boom-chicka-boom sound – and yet another evocation of Cash the outlaw: "I took some speed / I thought it was what I need," growls vocalist Peter Coyne, who later described Cash's music as "mother's milk"[2] while drawing a clear line between Cash and the band's other influences, "people like The Stooges or MC5".[3]

The Godfathers were a US-influenced British rock band. In the States, Bruce Springsteen had made his affiliation with Cash clear on *Nebraska*, but the only significant statement occurring away from the mainstream came from One Bad Pig, a Christian thrash-metal band based in Austin, Texas. Described by singer Carey Womack as "a medium-sized fish in a small pool", the band had worked up an arrangement of 'Man In Black' and had decided, as a long shot, to get in touch with Cash's management to see whether he would like to sing it with them. To their surprise, the response was positive. They were invited to John Carter Cash's 21st birthday party on March 3 1991, a shindig out in the Tennessee woods featuring performances by everyone from Bill Monroe to The Oak Ridge Boys, and shortly afterward Cash agreed to come and sing with them at Bennett House studio in Franklin, Tennessee.

Sensing the potential for some A-grade publicity, the band alerted all the major country music and Christian media outlets. "[Country TV show] *Crook & Chase* were supposed to send out a film crew, and another TV channel, as well as some print journalists," says Womack. "We thought we'd spread our message on nationwide TV, but they all cancelled. We were disappointed."

Cash, it seemed, was no longer news. It was a difficult time personally for him. His mother, Carrie, was dying of cancer and he came to the session direct from her bedside. "We had gathered in the main room to pray, holding hands, and Johnny walked in," says Womack. "He approached the circle and apologised for being late: 'My mother is on her death bed,' he said. 'We're having a death watch, and I just had to get away.' We invited him to join the circle and pray with us and he did. We prayed for him and his Mom in a circle, that he'd have a peaceful heart while he was away from her. That eased everything out and we had a great time doing it." Carrie Cash died, aged 86, on March 11 1991, just days after the recording session.

The song itself is hardly earth-shattering, a fairly tepid exercise in pantomime punk. Cash gamely elbows his way into the room and strides through it. "I don't think he had any idea what kind of sound we made beforehand, but he was up at the mike dancing around," says bass player Daniel Tucek. All the band were amazed at how powerful his voice was up close. There's a neat touch during the fadeout, when Womack ad-libs a self-deprecating line about Cash being the 'real man in black'. Cash didn't like the implication and added his own ad-lib. "He said: that's not what I want to put across," says Womack. "He said: we're all in this together if we're in it at all." As if to prove the point, they squirted him with silly string after the session, and by God if he didn't squirt them right back.

'Man In Black' by One Bad Pig featuring Johnny Cash became a Number One single on the Christian rock charts. "It was a very popular song on the late-night Christian rock shows back then," says Tucek. "People who didn't know that much about him in recent years became new fans. A friend of ours picked him up at an airport a year or so later and he said: man, I'm Number One in the charts with 'Man In Black' and One Bad Pig! He was real excited about it. I think it caused a few ripples in areas that he hadn't featured in for a while."

"I do think it was important," says Carey Womack. "Just remembering some of those conversations between his people and our people, we heard back that he was in a place in his career where he felt pigeonholed and not as relevant as he would like to be. He wanted to renew his career and reach young people as well as his established audience. So I think this was a small step in that direction, finding his way back to something. I think he may have felt: this isn't really what I had in mind, there's something better I can do – which is what the *American Recordings* became, but it was one of the steps leading that way."

These were all relatively low-level, marginal acts of patronage, but they helped build a cumulative momentum that proved significant. The coming together of Cash and U2, however, had a much more direct and obvious impact on his career. The Irish rock band were at that point the biggest group in the world, having released the globe-strafing album

The Joshua Tree in March 1987. Born out of punk in the late 70s, they had recently began to explore roots music. They were not alone. In the mid 80s a kind of collective panic attack gripped some of Britain and Ireland's most declamatory rock bands. Raised with Bowie, Roxy Music, and the New York proto-punk of New York Dolls, Patti Smith, and Television as their Year Zero, they'd grown bombastic on a staple diet of production gloss, layered atmospherics, and lyrics exhorting every passing stranger to "walk on by". A sudden identity crisis afflicted them all, and like a be-mulleted shower of waifs and strays they began to wonder where exactly they had come from.

Strange things occurred. Simple Minds wrote 'Belfast Child', a six-minute dirge plundered from an old Irish air, and took it to Number One in the UK singles charts. Mike Scott of The Waterboys headed off from his London base to Dublin, thence to Galway, to immerse himself for three years in traditional Celtic music, resulting in the landmark *Fisherman's Blues* record. And U2, a band whose hinterland had previously stretched back no further than glam rock and punk, began to lose themselves in Americana. *The Joshua Tree* had overt touches of gospel, blues, country, and early rock'n'roll. For their next album, the half-live, half-studio effort *Rattle And Hum*, they went even further. Bob Dylan appeared on a couple of tracks; they buttonholed B.B. King for a duet; and even recorded in the old Sun studios in Memphis. The engineer on the sessions was Cash's old buddy Jack Clement, who had worked on those early recordings at Sun and had recently tried to help Cash salvage some semblance of dignity at Mercury. Through such serendipitous connections do two generations of seemingly unconnected musicians find themselves edging toward one another.

U2's attitude to Cash perfectly captures the contradictory way in which he was perceived at this stage of his career: he was simultaneously residually hip and a bit passé. "We would have been aware of him from earlier than *The Joshua Tree*," says U2 bass player Adam Clayton. "My first forays into learning to play guitar and singing a tune would have been based on Kris Kristofferson tunes and Johnny Cash tunes because they connected with rock'n'roll, they weren't straight country. At 13 or

14 I was aware of Johnny and the prison gigs and that sort of thing, but when The Sex Pistols came along you couldn't admit to that. It wasn't a reference point that was even helpful."

Now, slowly and almost imperceptibly, Cash was becoming a relevant reference point again. Sun hadn't been operational as a studio since 1969, although Cash, Jerry Lee Lewis, Carl Perkins, and Roy Orbison had recorded parts of their *Class Of '55* album there in 1985, which may have been the only truly authentic and auspicious thing about it.

When U2 arrived during the *Rattle And Hum* sessions to cut 'Angel Of Harlem', 'When Love Comes To Town', 'Love Rescue Me', 'She's A Mystery To Me' (later recorded by Roy Orbison), and a version of Woody Guthrie's 'Jesus Christ', much of the original recording equipment was still in place. Jack Clement engineered the sessions and recalls that the band were struck by the sense of history in the room, amazed that these were the same microphones that Cash and Elvis had once used, that the sound of those original Sun sessions was still in the building, soaked into the bricks and the linoleum. "We were right there in Sun studios and I'd maybe say that [Elvis or Johnny] had stood right there," says Clement.

Here was a tangible connection being made between the ghosts of America's historic musical past and rock's living present. U2 wanted to seal the deal. When the sessions for *Rattle And Hum* were complete, Adam Clayton and singer Bono decided to delay their return home to Dublin and instead stay on in America to embark on a road trip, travelling in a Cherokee Jeep from Los Angeles to New Orleans. According to Bono: "We filled the car up with Johnny Cash and set off."[4] It was a further exploration of the roots of a country that now fascinated them.

The road led, inevitably, to Nashville, where they spent several days as the guest of Jack Clement. "Of course, one of the first things they wanted to do was meet Johnny Cash, so we went over to the house and had a big dinner together," Clement recalls.

"We came across a table with this enormous spread of food which we thought was in our honour, but in fact it was for June Carter's cookery book," says Adam Clayton. "They were shooting the cover. We had been invited for lunch but it wasn't to have *that* lunch; we had something much humbler. Then Johnny showed us around the house. We were 27, 28-year-olds, still wet behind the ears and it didn't make a whole lot of sense to us. It was quite an odd house, built on many levels and curved in a strange way. It wasn't furnished how you'd expect. It wasn't American ranch style, there was a lot of classical French furniture and Italian pieces.

"He showed us a little bedroom off the master bedroom, like a little box room, and kind of admitted that that's where he'd end up when he was on the pills and couldn't sleep. There were lots of books in there. It was a bit like having separate bedrooms when you're on the piss, I suppose. He took us off to the private zoo, where I think an ostrich had nearly killed him. When we were back in the house he gave Bono and myself one of his black stage shirts, just enormous. Neither of us could fill it, but it was a very sweet thing to do and it does still hang in my wardrobe, so in a way I feel like I see the man in black quite regularly."

Cash was vaguely aware of U2 but it wasn't really his kind of music. Nevertheless, a mutual understanding between the two camps soon developed. "We realised that he was rooted in a roots format, and particularly coming from Irish music we realised how deep and what a full tone there is in that," says Clayton. "If you're a punk rocker from London you just won't know that, and you won't understand the form and the culture: that in America you can tour for a year and not play the same place twice. So it was understanding all of that."

Bono was the most in-your-face, unguarded, emotionally eloquent member of the group, and he began to invest in people like Cash a mythical quality, something that spoke opaquely but profoundly about America and faith and struggle and humanity. He had a similar obsession with Elvis. Their roots were far enough in the past to be historical, connected to something primal and monolithic, but they were also part of the present day landscape, close enough to touch, literally in Cash's case.

In Cash, Bono saw a troubled, divided quality he instinctively recognised. With the exception of Clayton, who has no strong religious faith, U2 had always worn their Christian beliefs on their sleeves, and had been candid in recounting the conflicts it had brought into their lives as young men in a rock'n'roll band. The constant struggle between faith and sin, good and evil, piety and humour, conservatism and rebellion was one Bono acknowledged also existed in himself, albeit played out on a far less dramatic scale. "I've had a lot of father figures in my life," he said, "But somewhere near the top of them has got to be Johnny Cash."[5] Jack Clement says, "It was a natural attraction for both of them. Especially Bono to him."

Bono identified Cash as one of life's seekers, rarely at peace with whatever course he chose. He recalled how, during that first visit to Hendersonville, Cash had said Grace at the table and then winked at him and added: "Sure do miss the drugs, though."

These observations would be made explicit in 1993, in 'The Wanderer', the song Bono wrote with Cash in mind. Back in 1988, they bonded over another song, 'Ellis Island', which they attempted to write the first day they met at Cash's house.

"That would be Bono's opening line to most people he met at that time: I've been thinking about you and I've got this song in my head," says Adam Clayton. "That's his way of connecting with people quickly. Bono will always talk songs with his heroes, and he's always got something that might suit them."

They agreed to finish the song by fax, but never did. "It got to a certain point, but it's probably still in Bono's head somewhere," says Clayton. However, the important part was that the connection had been made. The two camps stayed in touch and would get together whenever Cash was playing in Dublin. One such occasion occurred in February 1993, just five days after his concert at Butlin's Southcoast World in Bognor Regis. U2 were working on a new album. When they heard Cash was in town, Bono, drummer Larry Mullen, and guitarist The Edge went to see the show. "I got them out on stage with me at the end to sing 'Big River'," Cash later recalled. "That was really quite a party.

Bono wrote down his verse on the palm of his hand, he was singing looking at his hand. After the show he asked me if I would come by the studio next day and listen to a song he wrote for me. And we put down the track that day."[6]

Lyrically, 'The Wanderer' must have appeared to Cash as an eight-course meal might appear to a man emerging from a month-long fast. Its suitability was no accident. Originally called 'The Preacher', it dug into the heart of what made him tick as a man, a myth, and an artist, and was based on the biblical book of Ecclesiastes, in which a preacher strives to discover the meaning of life, walking various, often contradictory avenues in search of spiritual fulfilment.

"He tries knowledge, educates himself, reads every book, but that doesn't work," said Bono. "He tries travel, sees every sight, but that doesn't do it. He tries wine, women and song, that doesn't do it. ... And the most extraordinary line is: 'There is nothing better for a man than that he should eat and drink, and that he should make his soul enjoy good in his labour.' Love your work. That's what it is."[7]

Bono was openly in thrall to Cash's mythical status and the words he wrote for 'The Wanderer' vividly dramatise the image of him as the last great American. It captures the sense of restlessness Cash was feeling at this point, a good, deeply flawed man in search of meaning in a ruined world: "I went out there in search of experience / To taste and to touch and to feel as much as a man can / Before he repents."

"Bono had written this song and very much inhabited the soul of Johnny in terms of the lyric and his own performance," says Adam Clayton. "And then, lo and behold, Cash is in town. Bono invited him down to Windmill Lane and he came in and listened to it. It was quite traditional in its changes but Edge and Bono worked it up into something a bit more intriguing. We were doing quite extreme stuff, we'd just done *Achtung Baby*. Even though musically it's like a sci-fi band at the Holiday Inn and it's not sonic territory he'd be comfortable in, Johnny understood it and inhabited it. He knew his part in it. Bono always identified with these somewhat misfit, biblical characters and I guess Johnny fits into that. I can only surmise that there was a handshake going on in there. Cash was a pretty cute fella. There was an acknowledgement that this was relevant and not gratuitous, that it had some gravitas to it."

Perhaps more than anything that happened subsequently, 'The Wanderer' put Cash back on the map. U2, never the coolest of bands, were nevertheless at their most critically acclaimed and experimental in the early 90s, but Cash could get far hipper credits elsewhere. What the album – which sold over three million copies in 1993 alone, and more than double that in total – offered him was a powerful platform from which he could reach people who had, mercifully, no idea about 'Chicken In Black', but also had no knowledge of 'I Walk The Line'. All they heard was something akin to the voice of God singing, "I went out walking with a Bible and a gun …" What was there not to love?

After U2 had recorded with B.B. King and Dylan on *Rattle And Hum*, it's easy to dismiss the inclusion of Cash on *Zooropa* as evidence of a kind of post-ironic, evangelical desire on U2's part to rehabilitate some of their favourite legacy artists. It wasn't, however, as premeditated as that. There was little sense at the time that 'The Wanderer' was going to be on the final album.

"You acknowledge that that ends up being a part of it, but at the time you're just trying to do the work and it's very hard to think where it will end up in [a cultural] sense," says Clayton. "At that point we were just having him down to sing on a tune that we felt needed a little X factor to it. In some ways it's our own fandom that overpowers that kind of situation. You don't necessarily think that most of your audience are going to particularly enjoy Johnny Cash. You hope they will, but you do it because you want to do it and not so much because you think it's good for them."

In other words, it was an organic musical meeting rather than anything cynically contrived with an eye on bridging two opposing demographics. This seems important. The experience of recording with U2 didn't make Cash consciously try to align himself to a new audience, although, as he subsequently discovered, it certainly placed him in a context where others could market him much more easily. More important than any of those things was the fact that the experience reaffirmed certain core traits about him as a man and an artist. 'The Wanderer' can be read as a comment on Cash's creative predicament in the early 90s: "They say they want the Kingdom / But they don't want God in it" is the kind of line that speaks volumes about where he was at that time, as is the portrait of a man "looking for my own name". Bono's words spoke to him of his own outsider status and, as Clayton says, absolutely correctly, "informed his own sense of isolation as an artist". In other words, the song helped him realise something fundamental about where he belonged, and it was not inside the country music establishment, or indeed inside anything at all except his own vision.

●●

This was perhaps the key realisation that stemmed from all these essentially extracurricular activities, which in terms of the quantity of music he made during this period constituted a mere drop in the ocean. They weren't simply about reminding the public at large that Cash was, as Jon Langford says, a serious artist and not some limping cowboy who belonged in the pasture. More significantly, they worked subliminally on Cash's own sense of self, reminding him of his own power as an artist, of his responsibilities as a writer and performer, and where his loyalties ultimately lay: always happiest on the outside, riding the blinds, paying no mind to those who sought to fence him in. Worn out, uninspired, physically reduced, commercially forsaken, he had become forgetful of many of these traits in the 70s and 80s. It took, it seemed, too much energy to constantly live up to the expectations of being Johnny Cash. Who could blame him if he stopped trying too hard? It was useful to be reminded that, as he put it, "if you got it, you always got it".[8]

As a piece of music, as a set of words, but most of all as a representation of Cash himself, 'The Wanderer' tapped into an unsparing and uncompromising self-image that would very soon drive *American Recordings*. "It would be very hard for *me* to claim that, but if you want to join the dots there may well be a connection," says Adam Clayton. "He may have felt he needed to recontextualise himself to get to music fans, and that's generally the younger audiences. It's a frustration of many artists. They get to a point where they look like people's parents, and people write them off, even though their skills may be greater than they were as teenagers."

"The U2 collaboration in particular was very significant," says Rosanne Cash. "It was a regrounding thing for him and he was very proud of it. It centred him. It was a musical decision, he realised [the connection to a new audience] after the fact."

The same is true of 'The Beast In Me', the song Nick Lowe had finally finished after a decade's work and had recently sent to Cash, and which, like 'The Wanderer', was specifically written to be "inhabited" by him. Hearing these songs, and hearing Nick Cave's take on Cash, or hearing it from artists as diverse and confrontational as One Bad Pig and Gaye Bykers On Acid, had a similar effect. Through the prism of other people's perceptions, he saw himself more clearly and saw the importance of once again singing himself.

Whether he was consciously aware of it or not, each of these experiences repatriated Cash, the king in exile. They formed a gathering wave of momentum that swept him away from the seasonal concerns of Nashville and toward something much more relevant and pressing, a reinvigorated notion of who he was as an artist and what the possibilities were. He was accelerating imperceptibly toward something. He was also aware that his own writing, so neglected in the past decades, also had to measure up. "I work harder on my songs now than I ever did," he said. "I'm aware of the great writers ... that we have in the business and I want mine to be like theirs."[9]

A matter of days after his return from recording 'The Wanderer' with U2, and a mere couple of weeks after that rather bleak stop-over at Southcoast World in Bognor Regis, Cash finally met Rick Rubin.

7

**Outside
Looking In**

e stand on the cusp. Looking a matter of months into the future, Cash has begun making *American Recordings* and things will never be quite the same again. Gazing backward, we see the great sweep of his career, already almost 40 years deep, stretching away into the far distance. One can't negotiate a straight line through it all. Cash certainly didn't. Too much of the surface noise, as well as the more ambient evidence, is contradictory, confusing, scrambled. He frequently veered off track, and in trying to be all things to all men he often failed to do much of any note at all. One can, however, take readings from point to point, and you don't need to be a weatherman to see which way the wind blows.

At this pivotal point it feels important and necessary to establish Cash's credentials as an outsider artist, someone who in his ideological and artistic leanings, major studio collaborators, subject matter, and song choices always excelled when he was permitted, or permitted himself, to roam beyond any perceived boundaries.

However unexpected and idiosyncratic they appeared at the time, the *American* records were the oddly logical culmination of a life spent in conflict with conformity. These albums picked up and tied together several of the most significant threads of Cash's career: singing songs from well outside what many people regarded as his natural habitat; engaging with social issues and shining a light on corners of society in a manner that aligned him far more with the liberal rock fraternity than with country music; and, perhaps above all, working with unconventional men who pushed him hard, who understood his innately strange and special qualities – combining his vast, iconic scale with something flawed and deeply personal – and cleared a path that allowed them to be expressed without compromise.

Rick Rubin was not the first industry maverick to step into the studio with Cash. The input of the man with the shades, the biblical beard, and long hair only seemed incongruous on the surface – a surface which made him seem to all the world like someone auditioning for an understudy role in ZZ Top – and within the context of what Cash had been doing for the past few years. Taking the longer view, not only did Rubin's participation have precedents, it made perfect sense.

Up until the point that he and Rubin began working together, Cash had made his most culturally potent, enduring, and arguably most creatively successful music in conjunction first with Sam Phillips and then with Bob Johnston, two men who recognised his unorthodox status and did their utmost to facilitate it.

Like a great athlete, he thrived on confidence. He was the kind of musician who went on a hot streak when he had an empathetic coach on the sidelines. The three outstandingly potent peaks of his career – 1955–58, 1968–71, and 1994–2003 – are the times when he sounded least like a member of the establishment and most like the conflicted man he was. They are also the times, not coincidentally, when he formed alliances with producers who were artists too, and who allowed him to follow his muse without trying to make it fit into a preconceived box.

"I never did like musical bags or categories," Cash said in 1993. "We busted out on our own at Sun Records in the 50s, with our long hair and sideburns and black clothes, and they called us every name under the sun, from 'rockabilly' to 'white nigger'. I took it with pride, because they were telling me: you're different."[1]

Sun boss Sam Phillips, an eccentric individualist if ever there was one, produced Cash's stunning 1957 debut album, *With His Hot And Blue Guitar*, as well as his earliest singles. It's easy to forget now how primitive and deeply unusual those early records were, and how akin they are in many ways to *American Recordings*. Even before one takes into account the similarities in mood and theme, and the fact they were cut live, there's only the breadth of a barely audible upright bass line and those clean tremolo guitar notes separating 'Folsom Prison Blues' from 'Delia's Gone'. Both are essentially all about the empty spaces, with Cash's looming voice filling the speakers. There are no drums, no strings, no fiddles, no pedal steel. Nothing frivolous. Nothing unnecessary.

"When you heard the Sun stuff you knew you were listening to the real deal; it was more stripped even than Hank Williams," says Cathal Coughlan. "It makes someone like John Lydon look fairly flowery."

Phillips regarded this brutal simplicity as intrinsic to Cash. He was magnetised by the ragged sound of him playing with The Tennessee Two and, like Rubin, felt this austerity was crucial, in order that "the fundamentals of his message would ring forth without being inundated with pretty music."[2]

Almost 40 years later, Cash immediately recognised the link between what he had done with Phillips in the very beginning and the way Rubin worked. "It gave me a profound sense of déjà vu," he said of making *American Recordings*. "It very much reminded me of the early days at Sun Records. Sam Phillips put me in front of that microphone at Sun Records in 1955 for the first time and said: let's hear what you've got. Sing your heart out. And I'd sing one or two and he'd say: sing another one, let's hear one more."[3]

"As producers, they both just let me do what I was feeling," he said on another occasion. "This album should have been called *Painfully Honest*, because that's what it is, just me and my guitar. ... The feeling was there, that was the important thing. That's the way it was with Sam, and that's the way it was with Rick Rubin. If it feels right, if you can stand to hear it, go for it."[4]

It sounds enticingly simple, but it was a methodology he was able to follow only sporadically throughout his career. Cash always chafed within the confines of any system. In the late 50s he battled with Phillips – and lost – over his desire to record a gospel album for Sun, a conflict which contributed to him leaving the label in July 1958. Under the auspices of Columbia's Nashville division and a producer, Don Law, who was over 30 years his senior and ruled with an iron hand, he had again often struggled to find his place. By 1963 he looked a little lost. Early on at Columbia he scored a couple of reasonably sized pop hits with 'The Ways Of A Woman In Love' and 'You're The Nearest Thing To Heaven', which charted toward the end of 1958, but he had produced nothing of real commercial note since 'Don't Take Your Guns To Town' in 1959, while Sun kept rehashing old material and putting out generally below-standard compilation albums.

Cash was more interested in ambitious concept albums about

American life and history, such as *Ride This Train, Blood, Sweat And Tears,* and *Ballads Of The True West,* which were commercial flops at the time and today are largely forgotten but which remain some of his most interesting work.

His contract with Columbia was due to expire at the end of 1963. He would most likely have been dropped had he not come up with a hit in the form of 'Ring Of Fire', written by his future wife June Carter and Merle Kilgore and released in April 1963. 'Ring Of Fire' as performed by Cash is not a piece of music anyone could routinely identify as a traditional country song. It is another prime example of him singing his soul, and is forever destined to be a comment on the inexorable progress of Carter and Cash's rather torturous love affair, which had already begun, when both were married to other people.

Despite the habitual production credit to Don Law, it's no surprise to learn that it was really produced by Jack Clement, another audio ally who knew that Cash needed to be treated differently from all the rest. It was Clement who brought Cash's vision on 'Ring Of Fire' to fruition after he called in desperation and said he needed something special.

"I was living in Beaumont, Texas, and I was at home taking a bath in the tub one night when John called me," says Clement. "I got out and went to talk to him and he said that June and Merle Kilgore had written this song and he'd had a dream where he heard these trumpets on it. He wanted me to come to Nashville and work it out. These two trumpeters were there with a blank music sheet, they didn't know what they were going to play, and I said: why don't you go: [sings] Da dadadada da da daaaaa – and they wrote that down – and then, Da dadadada da da daaaaa. I got my guitar out and we cut 'Ring Of Fire'. Three weeks later they were playing it all over the place. It's enduring. I love that lilt."

Whatever else 'Ring Of Fire' is, it's not a conventional record. It's a daring, voodoo mariachi, which Cash imbues with a terrible dark potency. Even as he exalts the transformative power of love he brings to the lyric the full, grim knowledge of the depths of despair hidden inside the act of devotion.

It dug him out of a hole, reaching Number One in the country charts and Number 17 in the *Billboard* Hot 100, and paved the way for a brief spurt of chart activity with his classic recordings, 'Understand Your Man' and 'It Ain't Me Babe'. His drug use and generally unfathomable behaviour had become so unmanageable by the mid 60s, however, that the record company all but gave up on him. *Everybody Loves A Nut*, an album of 'kooky' comedy songs and spoofs, was Columbia's rather blatant attempt at rebranding Cash as a harmless entertainer in the face of drug busts and personal mayhem.

The truth was that Cash never felt particularly understood or supported by the company suits. Recruited by Clive Davis in 1967, Dick Asher first arrived at Columbia as a private practice attorney. Prior to being despatched to Hendersonville to talk to Cash about new contract arrangements, he was struck by the fact that many of the executives at Columbia thought (with good reason, perhaps) that he was a loose cannon hillbilly hick who had outlasted his usefulness.

"I'd never met Johnny Cash, and my boss [Head of Business Affairs] Walter Dean had somewhat coloured my perspective on John at that point," says Asher. "He was saying all these things: this guy's going to kill himself before he's 40, and worse. I thought I was coming down to deal with some hillbilly, but I soon developed some perspective. As soon as I started waxing on any subject I realised I was talking to someone who probably knew more about that subject than I did. We did a deal and made a new seven-year contract. If I remember, it was for a guarantee of $50,000 a year, which was good money back then. There were some raised eyebrows at Columbia. Of course the next album that came out was *At Folsom Prison*. That paid for the whole seven years of the deal and I never heard another word about it, but before that they weren't really happy."

It was prison that saved him. Not just prison, but the fact that in 1967 Bob Johnston replaced Don Law as Cash's in-house producer at Columbia. Born in Hillsboro, Texas, in 1932, Johnston was Cash's exact contemporary in terms of age, and he was similarly idiosyncratic: a dope-smoking, highly opinionated, contrary, combative eccentric with sterling credentials in contemporary music circles. He had produced

Dylan's classic triptych *Highway 61 Revisited, Blonde On Blonde,* and *John Wesley Harding,* as well as Simon & Garfunkel's *Sounds Of Silence* and *Parsley, Sage, Rosemary And Thyme.* Like Sam Phillips and later Rubin, Johnston was a man who put the art and the artist first and to hell with all the rest.

His input brought immediate results. It was Johnston who helped Cash realise his ambition of recording a live album in a prison, an idea he had been nurturing for years. Having played prison concerts since near the very beginning of his career, Cash reasoned that no audience responded with more fervour than one that was incarcerated; he also understood that the concept chimed with some essential part of his image.

Columbia dismissed the idea as sheer madness. Given his relatively recent bust in El Paso, they preferred to keep any association between Cash and prison at arms' length. That was until Johnston swept in and as a priority made sure he got to do what he wanted. As with Rubin, the first and most important question was: "What can I do for you?"

"When I took over Cash he didn't hit the country charts," Johnston later said. "No one in eight years would let him go [to prison] to record live until he got to me and I said: let's do it. Everything I said and did was for the artist. I never gave a fuck what the company thought. ... The thing I wanted was the truth. And that's what Cash got."[5]

Recorded on January 13 1968 and released in May, the results were genuinely electrifying, and went further than any other record to secure Cash's status as an icon. The album has since been reissued two further times, has sold many millions of copies, and routinely features in lists of All Time Top 100 Albums; the tale of its making has become a legend in itself. *At Folsom Prison* not only utterly transformed Cash's career, but it recast Cash forever. In his contemporaneous review of the album in *Life,* journalist Al Aronowitz pointed out that Cash sang the songs like "someone who has grown up believing he is one of the people that these songs are about". Soon everyone else believed it as well. It was the version of Cash who walked out in front of Folsom's inmates as though he belonged among them that *American Recordings* used as its foundation stone; here was the same man 25 years down the line, with a wealth of hard-won experience to impart. A man condemned to a lifetime of imprisonment whether he was behind bars or not.

"*At Folsom Prison* was an amazing revelation, a huge-selling landmark record, and he had the guts to do it," says Bruce Lundvall, who was head of marketing at Columbia in the late 60s. "It made him the first outlaw artist in a way. That was very genuine with Cash. He was a man of principle and he was a man of extreme vision in terms of what he wanted to do artistically."

Johnston's approach was uncannily similar to Rubin's ethos: with an artist like Cash, you let him do what he wants and the truth of the performance will sing out. He repeated the trick with further Cash singles and albums during that period. *At San Quentin* revisited the Folsom theme to even greater commercial success, while *Hello, I'm Johnny Cash*, one of his very best albums, decanted the prowling menace of the prison albums into the studio, adding only slightly more frills around the edges.

As ever, Johnston kept the sound raw and gritty. There was still a whiff of pill poppin' menace and sexual urgency driving songs like 'Blistered', while the closing rendition of Chris Warren's 'Jesus Was A Carpenter' is a quietly extraordinary performance, just Cash and his (noticeably out-of-tune) acoustic guitar and a fistful of the kind of open-souled emotional honesty later found on *American Recordings*. Notably, the album also features his first recordings of Kris Kristofferson material with 'Devil To Pay' and 'To Beat The Devil', which firmly aligned him to the new country breed. Johnston remained at the controls for Cash's hugely successful version of Kristofferson's 'Sunday Morning Coming Down', another controversial and slyly countercultural performance.

It was no coincidence that after Cash stopped working with Johnston his recorded work began to fluctuate alarmingly. In 1971, the self-produced *Man In Black* album marked the end of his association with the mercurial Texan. Cash went on to work primarily with Larry Butler, Columbia's in-house producer, and then Billy Sherrill. Both were immensely talented men, but they were inextricably linked to the

Nashville studio system and adhered to a rather smoother country music sensibility. "Every artist has to have a producer to work with and the producers that he worked with were provided by the record companies," said his manager Lou Robin. "They and John didn't see eye to eye on philosophy and tunes so that was a problem."[6]

It's within the historical context of Cash finding tough, empathetic collaborators that Rubin and *American Recordings* start to make sense as the logical destination to his entire career, rather than a conceptual quirk or piece of good fortune that fell out of a clear blue sky. He had been talking about doing an acoustic album since the early 60s but somehow it never happened, whether through a lack of nerve on his part or because no one displayed much enthusiasm for the idea. Rick Rubin made it happen, just as Phillips and Johnston had previously brought other dearly held ideas to fruition.

Rubin saw this bigger picture long before he and Cash started recording. He saw it as soon as Cash appeared on stage at Madison Square Garden. Not only did he understand that the *American* albums would be an evolution of something extant rather than a clean slate, he also saw that filing Cash under country music always seemed in part to be a badge of convenience, a little like reducing Bob Dylan to a folk artist or defining Miles Davis as simply jazz.

It could be argued that Cash's entire career has been an exercise in mislabelling, as though he were some uniquely exotic creature captured in the wild and, for the want of any better available options, penned in with vaguely similar but less interesting animals. Calling Cash country has always seemed to present more problems than can comfortably be swatted away. "He was a genre unto himself," says Bruce Lundvall. "You couldn't really define him as a country artist, he was just a universally great storyteller." Steve Popovich says: "When you're Johnny Cash, there's no 'next' Johnny Cash. He's a once in a lifetime genre."

It's not just that his music frequently displayed very few of the standard tropes of the form: as a rule it foreswore pedal steel, fiddle, and honky-tonk piano for an awkward, bony mixture of rock'n'roll, rockabilly, gospel, folk, blues, and country. There's no ingratiating keen in his voice, no twang, just a cavernous boom which recognises no barriers. He connected with the up-close-and-personal sense of danger that courses through the blues, while his sweeping sense of empathy and compassion made him, perhaps more than anything else, a born folk singer.

It's more than that. It's that Cash is simply bigger than country music. He possessed a cultural hinterland and keen social awareness that lent his music a genuinely global reach, the kind that crossed borders and made sense all around the world. "He had that credibility with taxi drivers in Beijing, or Moscow, or Berlin, or London," says Steve Popovich. "I've seen it. This was prior to Twitter and *American Idol*; he did it the hard way."

It was always important to him to physically travel beyond his own back yard, but primarily his far-reaching impact was due to the all-too-obvious fact that he was never an insider. He made sense because he was an individual. This was made explicit to a new generation of fans on *American Recordings*, but it had been clear since the middle of the 60s. He smashed the footlights of the Grand Ole Opry in 1965, a gesture dripping with symbolism if ever there was one, and satirised Music City mores in 1984 on 'The Battle Of Nashville' even as he was being sucked up and spat out trying to conform to its machinations. "He was not one of the 'in' people in Nashville; he was a bit of a rebel," says Dick Asher. "He wasn't a redneck, and the rulers of country-music society were people like [comedienne] Minnie Pearl. He was a little bit of an outsider. He helped Bob Dylan, things like that."

Long before Kris Kristofferson was given deserved credit for filtering the challenging sound and sensibility of writers like Dylan and Leonard Cohen into the essentially conservative arena of country music, Cash was already doing it. The swaggering, dubiously thrilling machismo of his 1964 single 'Understand Your Man' is Cash at his most brilliantly primal. Lines like "lay in bed and keep your mouth shut till I'm gone" help explain why the likes of Ice-T and Tupac Shakur would later acknowledge an affinity, but more pertinent at the time was the fact that the song's musical structure was built on the bones on 'Don't Think

Twice, It's All Right', from Dylan's recently released second album, *The Freewheelin' Bob Dylan*.

As soon as he heard the album, Cash had sent Dylan a note of congratulation, beginning a correspondence and friendship that continued right up to his death. They first met at the 1964 Newport Folk Festival, where Cash played to the folk cognoscenti and Dylan gave him the recently written 'Mama, You Been On My Mind' and also 'It Ain't Me Babe', which Cash almost instantly recorded as a duet with June Carter. Having fallen hard for Dylan, he wasn't shy about advertising the fact. Immediately he started inching his music away from the smooth-cheeked countrypolitan sounds of Nashville and taking it somewhere closer to the college dorms, and on his 1965 album *Orange Blossom Special* he recorded three Dylan covers.

He felt he had a lot in common with what was happening in the coffee houses and basement clubs of Greenwich Village and Berkeley, and was regarded very much as part of the folk community by people like Judy Collins. It only seemed odd and anomalous in the context of country music; in Cash's eyes and ears it made perfect sense.

Ideologically, too, Cash started swinging through branches some way beyond the country zoo. Times were changing and he wanted to express a social conscience that didn't always conform to what Nashville wanted to hear. The folk movement of the 60s helped him embrace a more politically charged side of his innate outsiderdom, aligning himself with the Native American cause, even claiming he was a quarter Cherokee. It was a deeply felt, sincere and long lasting connection, fuelled by a sense of profound injustice but also something atavistic that had gnawed away at him as long as he could remember.

In 1964 he recorded 'The Ballad Of Ira Hayes', written by the left-wing New York folksinger Peter La Farge. It was a song of empathy and remembrance for an American Indian soldier who had fought for his country in WWII at Iwo Jima only to return to find his ancestral home in Arizona ravaged by neglect. Hayes rapidly descended through penury, prison, and poverty before dying in 1955 at the age of 32. The savage irony and striking symbolism wasn't lost on La Farge, nor on

Cash, who loved his country enough to feel compelled to speak out when it wasn't doing itself justice. In 1965 he set about making an entire album, *Bitter Tears*, about the trials of the Native American.

Despite rising to Number Three in the country charts, 'The Ballad Of Ira Hayes' received scant airplay on country radio, provoking Cash to take out a full-page ad in *Billboard* demanding: 'Where are your guts?' before eloquently refusing to be 'classified, categorized, stifled', and reminding Nashville that outside in the big, bad world lay 'Rochester–Harlem–Vietnam and Birmingham'.

The full-page *Billboard* ad that American Recordings ran to celebrate *Unchained* winning a Grammy in 1998, featuring Cash giving the finger to the Nashville establishment, was just another scuffle in a long-running skirmish against convention. It was another defiant 'fuck you' to the system and a timely reminder that, for all the talk of comebacks and reinventions, Cash really hadn't changed all that much at heart in the years between 'The Ballad Of Ira Hayes' and 'Rusty Cage'. His enduring identification with underdogs, convicts, and marginalised cultures was not merely philanthropic. It was personal, an expression of his own self-image and a clear attempt to find a home, both in his music and in his soul.

Indeed, his insistence on identifying with any section of society perceived as an oppressed minority sometimes took him to amusing extremes. As late as 1988 he wrote the woeful 'A Croft In Clachan' for *Water From The Wells Of Home*, on which he channelled his inner Scots patriot. "I really believe the people in Scotland are going to like this 17th century war ballad," he said at the time.[7] It's utter hokum, but it's sincere hokum. In the early 80s Cash discovered that his family had roots in the kingdom of Fife in Scotland that stretched back to 1160. He first visited the area in the 80s, when he recorded one of his televised Christmas specials there with Andy Williams, and returned several times prior to his death in 2003.

"It was a big thing in the family," says Rosanne Cash. "It was very important to him, he was incredibly proud of it. I guess it was the sense of place, it felt like home to him, but he also really revelled in it. He had a big enough ego to be seduced to the idea of being related to royalty back in the 12th century."

His engagement with the Native American cause was more creatively significant, as was his reaction to Vietnam, the driving socio-political issue of the 60s and 70s. Cash was conflicted. At first he supported the war, then he changed his mind and took a dignified opposing stance at a time when few other country artists dared to stick their necks out, other than with intentionally heightened, rabble-rousing Republican fare such as Merle Haggard's 'Okie From Muskogee'.

Recorded in 1971, 'Man In Black' and 'Singin' In Vietnam Talkin' Blues' are both extraordinary pieces of writing that engage directly with the human complexities of war. Written after Cash's visit with June to Saigon in 1969, 'Singin' In Vietnam Talkin' Blues' is a personalised commentary of that experience, which in his customary conversational manner brings the noise and continual fear of the battlefield to the front room; Cash lays bare his terror at being in a war zone, and in doing so humanises the conflict. There are no heroes here, least of all him. He sounds terrified. He stands side by side with the men putting their lives on the line, saluting their courage while making it clear that he believes America has no business sending them there in the first place.

'Man In Black' is a more far-reaching piece of protest-poetry, and simply an extraordinary song. It performs a similar trick to Dylan's 'Chimes Of Freedom', and shares a little of its language, creating a dramatic context wide enough to allow the singer to embrace the world's downtrodden and its misfits. For Dylan it was a lighting storm illuminating the earth and its sufferers; Cash, doing his Walt Whitman thing, is able to conduct the lightning through his own voice and frame, heaping the sorrow of the world onto his black-clad shoulders. When Cash is described as being mythic it's because of songs like this, in which he moves from the squarely self-referential ("You wonder why I always dress in black") to the plight of the poor, the old, the faithless; prisoners, young soldiers, drug casualties, the living and the dead. All fall within his reach with an easy, accessible grace.

It's one of the greatest examples of Cash singing from deep within himself and circling the cosmos; joining all the dots. He unveiled 'Man In Black' for the first time during a specially conceived 'On Campus' edition of *The Johnny Cash Show* in which he squeezed Neil Young and most of Vanderbilt University into the Ryman Auditorium in Nashville to ensure maximum impact for the premiere of one of his most culturally resonant songs. He had only finished the final draft that morning, inspired by meeting and talking to the student body in the days prior to the show. On the night, when he sang "each week we lose a hundred fine young men" the place erupted. Watching Cash's performance, even 40 years down the line, the hairs on the neck prickle at his extraordinarily generous, powerful act of cross-cultural, pan-generational communion during the height of a terribly divisive war.

These songs, and his 1970 single 'What Is Truth', an important and compassionate attempt by a man entering middle age to ford the generation gap, may have been Cash's last culturally relevant statements for 20 years; the last time until the 90s that he really *mattered* as an artist reflecting the changing times back at the world. Alongside the stark sound of his Sun records and the badass outlaw chic of *At Folsom Prison*, it's no coincidence that the albums *American Recordings* most resembles in terms of its level of engagement with the world around it are *Hello, I'm Johnny Cash*, *Man In Black*, and *Bitter Tears*. He was returning to reclaim a vital part of his armoury.

❧

The one aspect of the series of *American* albums that elicited most comment, discussion, and debate was Cash's willingness to tackle, alongside his own compositions and more traditional material, contemporary songs from outside of the country stable. It should not have come as any great surprise. Throughout his career Cash constantly sought to expand his means of expression by foraging well beyond the confines of his own notepad and the Nashville songwriting factories.

Aside from his early adoption of Dylan, there are countless examples in his career of Cash plucking material from across the musical spectrum. On *The Johnny Cash Show* he delighted in singing anything and everything with anyone. Although it was in many respects an old-fashioned television variety series, it was also a place where country culture met the counterculture, where pop and rock met folk, where tradition met resistance. Perhaps only Cash at that point in his career and at this time in popular music history could have brought it all together. He loomed over it all like some vast, sturdy redwood under which almost anyone could gather and exchange ideas.

Both Bono and Nick Cave, later staunch Cash allies, remember watching the show as pre-teens and finding it a vividly exciting experience. Bob Dylan was on the first taping, playing three songs with Cash from *Nashville Skyline*. On subsequent broadcasts you might have seen Roy Orbison next to Creedence Clearwater Revival, or Neil Young playing 'The Needle And The Damage Done'. Aretha Franklin showed up, The Who and Eric Clapton played, and backstage Kris Kristofferson ran through an early version of 'Me And Bobby McGee' for the benefit of Joni Mitchell. Although the corn-ball quotient could frequently flicker into the red zone, Cash certainly didn't water anything down. He sang Kristofferson's 'Sunday Morning Coming Down' complete with the dreaded word "stoned" left unexcised, and invited Pete Seeger on to sing when the veteran left-wing folk revivalist was regarded as something close to an anti-war pariah. Anyone who thought it was incongruous to hear Cash singing the songs of Beck or Depeche Mode in the 90s must have been unaware of the diversity of the material and artists he had invited on to his television show over two decades earlier.

It was not an isolated episode. His 1975 covers album *John R. Cash* is a sustained example of Cash performing quality, well-fitting contemporary material from outside of the country sphere with musicians who included Ry Cooder and Elvis's TCB Band. At this point he was gravitating toward songwriters such as Tim Hardin, Robbie Robertson, and Randy Newman; one could easily see parallels in 1993 on *American Recordings* with Leonard Cohen, Tom Waits, and Loudon Wainwright III. The two albums occupy similar conceptual territory, even if the finished results and the cultural impact ended up being very different.

Cash tackling 'My Old Kentucky Home', 'The Night They Drove

Old Dixie Down' and 'Reason To Believe' made perfect sense. He was always interested in good songs and interesting songwriters, and even in his doldrums recorded material by some fine composers. *Rockabilly Blues* alone has songs by John Prine, Billy Joe Shaver, Rodney Crowell, and Nick Lowe, whose 'Without Love' Cash recorded while a guest at Lowe and Carlene Carter's house during Christmas 1979, having communicated a sudden desire to record a session on Boxing Day. Lowe called up friends Elvis Costello, Pete Thomas, and Martin Belmont and the well-refreshed ensemble cut a few tracks in Lowe's basement studio, including 'Without Love' and a version of George Jones's 'We Ought To Be Ashamed' released in 2005 on *Johnny Cash: The Legend*.

As we've seen, mining Bruce Springsteen's *Nebraska* for inspiration on *Johnny 99* was another rewarding, meaningful dalliance with contemporary material. Even on 1978's largely inconsequential *Gone Girl*, Cash cut The Rolling Stones' 'No Expectations'. Imagine what he might have done with that song 15 years later, how much soul and lived-in weariness he could have breathed into it. On *Gone Girl*, sadly, it was cut as a break-neck country gallop and Cash sounds uninterested in what he's singing, although altering the lyric to "pour me on that plane" is a neat touch.

••

As we stand on the cusp, what do we learn from these history lessons? We learn that *American Recordings* is not remotely anomalous. We learn that even though it may have powerfully affirmed Cash's bigger-than-country, cooler-than-country status, it had antecedents in almost every respect: in the daring variety of its song choices, in aligning Cash with a maverick, independent-minded producer, in embracing a counter-cultural sensibility, and in stubbornly refusing to conform to any established genre other than Johnny Cash. *American Recordings* only really makes sense if we recognise the man who made it as a complicated, risk-taking, often deeply weird artist with a long and proud history of making unconventional records. And he was about to make one more.

8

American Recordings

The bulk of what became *American Recordings* was put down in Rick Rubin's living room between May 17 and May 20 1993. All that stood between Cash and his own reflection was a Martin dreadnought acoustic guitar. His voice and instrument were captured on one microphone, most often a Neumann U67 but sometimes a U87 or an AKG 414, and the results recorded on an ADAT (Alesis Digital Audio Tape) machine, at the time a relatively cutting-edge device on which eight tracks of digital audio could be recorded onto magnetic tape.

The bald facts barely hint at the scope, the colour, the sense of adventure and providence wrapped up in the recording process. Rubin's home in the Hollywood Hills was a three-storey Spanish villa built in 1923, which under his ownership had become a palace of eccentricity, a very American mix of the sacred and profane. Statues of Vishnu and Buddha mingled with cut-outs of The Beatles and framed portraits of Jim Morrison. Incense burned beneath chandeliers, wind chimes tinkled; a pair of pro-wrestling boots lay in the hall.

A stuffed polar bear, rearing up on its hind legs, dominated the huge library, which was a homely clutter of artfully worn furniture, CDs, and magazines. Doors opened out to the garden, while the walls were lined with literature on new age spirituality, esoteric philosophy, Sufi mysticism, health, fitness, and music; books on Kurt Cobain nestled next to copies of the Koran. Cash, an old-fashioned, close-text Bible-reading Christian, might have seemed an unlikely man to connect with this catch-all, very modern brand of Zen Gothic spirituality, in which the sum of the parts seems to add up to not much at all. But he and Rubin had developed an understanding which stripped away their surface differences and connected somewhere much deeper.

The downstairs living room where he recorded was large but suitably sparse, furnished with an elaborately carved Steinway grand piano, a huge Persian rug in the centre of the floor, and an enormous Buddha which loomed up to the ceiling and covered half the wall. A dozen feet away, a makeshift office space had been set up in Rubin's dining room. His Hungarian Puli, Monday, scampered in and out.

Over those four days in May, from two o'clock in the afternoon until sometimes late into the night, Cash picked up his guitar and sang for Rubin; it was a musical summation of his entire life, a climactic rendition of his one epic song distilled into spirituals, country standards, hymns, hillbilly numbers, old Cash songs and new Cash songs, vicious murder ballads, sincere country-gospel, train songs, dusty relics reclaimed from the ghosts of Americana, life-long favourites by Hank Williams, modern classics by Kris Kristofferson, cherished memories retrieved from Tin Pan Alley and Broadway.

It was almost like a process of wooing, an old fashioned courtship, two souls "just getting to know each other [by] him playing me songs," according to Rubin. "You know: this is a song that I remember, when I was picking cotton, that we used to sing. Or this is one that my mom used to sing to me. Or this is one that I used to hear on the radio. Or this is one that I recorded in 1957 and no one really ever heard it, but it always meant a lot to me."[1]

They were not, at this point, consciously making an album. "We recorded songs first for the *idea* of which ones should be on the album and then we recorded other songs, maybe not even thinking about the album," said Rubin. "[Cash] would say: do you know this song? and he would play it to me, so I got to learn his taste. And then I would suggest songs that I liked that I thought would fit the same world."[2]

They were looking for "trigger songs" that would bring the very best out of Cash, who estimated that in the end he recorded 110 songs for *American Recordings*, all of them captured on tape by Rubin.[3] This process may have seemed scattershot and unfocused, but in reality it couldn't have been further from the rather random and undignified scrabble for material that had often defined the record-making process in the recent past.

Rubin instinctively understood that the whole point about Cash, whether he was making great albums or not so great ones, was that the meaning of the song had to connect with his persona. The alchemy had nothing to do with finding a hit song, or a hip song, or a hot song. It was about finding a track and a performance that would reveal something about the singer; something which, even if he hadn't written the song, "sounded like they could have been his words," said Rubin. "With some of the lesser-known songs, people still often assume that he wrote them."[4] In this way, every landmark recording would become simultaneously a confession, an act of self discovery, and a comment on Cash's iconic status. Rubin wanted to present him the way people wanted to see him: mythic, troubled, defiant, conflicted, honest, alone.

"The work of the best ... producers, is to 'give voice' to a performer," says Will Oldham, who later sang with Cash on 'I See A Darkness'. "This can best be done by knowing who and what a performer is to himself or herself as well as who that performer is to an audience. This perspective is very difficult for a performer to have on him- or herself. Cash worked so much and so well with his image, with the perception others have of him. ... Well, we all need help in our work and our life."

In Rubin's living room Cash returned to songs that he had recorded before but which he felt he'd never quite got right ('Delia's Gone', 'Oh, Bury Me Not', 'I'm Going To Memphis', 'Casey's Last Ride'); some of his favourites from his own catalogue ('Understand Your Man', 'Flesh And Blood', 'No Earthly Good', 'The Caretaker'); and songs he'd always wanted to sing ('Tennessee Stud', 'Just The Other Side Of Nowhere') but had never quite got around to.

He recorded staples of the traditional canon ('Long Black Veil', 'The Banks Of The Ohio'), well-thumbed pages from the singer-songwriter songbook ('Bird On A Wire', 'Why Me Lord') and bespoke material written specifically with him in mind ('The Beast In Me', 'Thirteen'). He recorded a whole swathe of gospel songs, spirituals, and hymns, much of them later released on the *My Mother's Hymn Book* album. He recorded pop songs ('The Wonder Of You'), Vietnam songs, and several of his beloved train songs: one by Cash, one by Jimmie Rodgers, and one by Tom Waits. With unfamiliar material Cash would often learn the song one day and record it the next. The occasional house caller would drop by: ZZ Top's Billy Gibbons played a fuzzed-up approximation of Cash's chicka-boom guitar sound on the excellent 'I Witnessed A

Crime'; Glenn Danzig popped around with a gift in song. But mostly it was a solitary affair.

In trying to give his producer an impression of the kind of songs he wanted to record, and in responding to Rubin's reactions, Cash made a game-changing album without even realising he was doing so. There was a lesson in there somewhere. In the months following those exploratory living-room sessions, Rubin tried creating all kinds of other musical contexts for him. They made extensive recordings at Ocean Way Studios in Hollywood with some of Rubin's favourite musicians: Flea and Chad Smith from the Red Hot Chili Peppers, Mick Campbell from Tom Petty's Heartbreakers, all of whom would work with Cash again in the near future, as well as The Red Devils, the LA blues-rock band who had recently recorded with Mick Jagger. Nothing they cooked up matched the impact of that initial outpouring.

"They recorded stuff with various bands and wound up going back to those original demos," says engineer David Ferguson. "That whole first record was done in Rick's living room, they're work tapes, they just wanted him to sing a bunch of songs, but we finally came back to that. It's a mono recording, you know, but it's a good recording."

They may have stumbled upon it, but both Cash and Rubin immediately recognised simplicity as a virtue. Nothing was allowed to get in the way of the voice and the truth it told. "Rick is an absolute purist," says Adam Clayton, who with U2 later worked with Rubin. "He wants the voice and that's it, and that worked so well for what Johnny did."

There were already clear signs that Cash had been heading toward this kind of stripped-back austerity under his own steam. He had always longed to make an album featuring just his voice and his guitar, which he imagined would be something akin to an intimate, late-night conversation between him and his audience. He claimed both Columbia and Mercury had vetoed the idea in the past, which seems unlikely given the freedom he had enjoyed at both companies at various times; perhaps their lack of enthusiasm simply dissuaded him.

In the early 90s, the notion was frequently at the forefront of his mind. While playing at Bognor Regis in early 1993, before he had even met Rubin, he talked about making a pared down album with the working title *Johnny Cash: Songwriter*. "It will be the first album of songs I've written entirely myself," he said.[5] Around the same time he told *Country Music* magazine that he wanted "to do an album of real 'heart' folk songs, or country songs, or love songs, mainly with just me and my guitar, and I want to call it *Johnny Cash Alone And Late*." He said a similar thing to *Rolling Stone*.

The details changed somewhat, but in talking about singing his own songs, unobstructed by modish production gloss, the kernel of the idea was clearly already there. Cash was coming back to himself. After his bruising dealings with the country establishment, and his growing contact in the years immediately preceding with acts like U2 in the field of contemporary music, he had already reached the same conclusions as Rubin. "Really, what I discovered, I guess, is myself," he said of making *American Recordings*. "I discovered my own self and what makes me tick musically and what I really like. It was a great inward journey."[6]

He reconnected with something fundamental after a period of several years when he seemed utterly lost. "He was a peripatetic kind of guy," says Rosanne Cash. "He'd look a million places for his centre before realising it was right there. What's most obvious is sometimes the hardest to find."

He realised that no major record company was going to magically restore him as a major player in Nashville. He needed to jettison any notions of what was expected of him, or what might sell, and simply follow his instincts. Perhaps what he needed more than anything was somebody to tell him that it was all right to do just that. Rubin, like Bob Johnston before him, offered Cash the freedom to cut loose and walk down any path he wanted. "It was a master stroke," says Bruce Lundvall. "Rick Rubin was obviously an intelligent guy and a visionary producer. He let the artist sound like himself, and it takes real guts to do that."

Martyn Atkins, American Recordings' former creative director, says: "Rick is like an Olympic trainer almost. He got involved with Cash in all aspects of his life and put him mentally in a completely different space. He gave him the space to look inward and really come up with what he wanted to do. There was never any consideration from Rick or anybody: oh, we're going to make a hit record here. Over all the years I've worked with [Rick], the Cash thing was really special and precious to him. It also gave him huge credibility, which he hadn't had until that point, as someone who believes in people and believes in music."

On the surface, the 13 songs finally chosen for *American Recordings* from the vast reservoir of recorded material seem a rag bag. Look deeper and they encompass every major aspect of Cash's life and art: religion, death, personal struggle, America, comedy, love, sex, salvation.

'Oh, Bury Me Not' was the latest in a seemingly endless line of cowboy songs, the grizzled gunslinger nearing his own personal sunset, ticking off his manly virtues; it was on the album partly because this kind of campfire meditation was hardwired into the way Cash was perceived.

If that particular track veers toward caricature, the songs written specifically for Cash are more indicative of the kind of emotional landscape Rubin wanted him to inhabit. A richly decorated reimagining of 'This Train Is Bound For Glory', Tom Waits's 'Down There By The Train' depicts an endless line of clanking carriages peopled by sinners, killers, whores, gamblers, Judas Iscariot, and even the soldiers who killed Christ, all hopping aboard for their last shot at redemption. Waits was unutterably cool at the time, and indeed has remained so. His endorsement did no harm. Rubin sought him out quite consciously. "Somebody said: you got any songs for Johnny Cash?" Waits later recalled. "I just about fell off my chair. I had a song I hadn't recorded, so I said: hey, it's got all the stuff that Johnny likes – trains and death, John Wilkes Booth, the cross ..."[7]

Beneath his ragged ringmaster's holler and exaggerated eccentricities, Waits had much in common with Cash: both seemed to carry all of America's crooked, dusty, elliptical history on their back. At heart, Cash was a mystical artist. He believed in visions and portents, the old, strange ways. As a child, walking home at night from his friend's house in the thick blackness of the Arkansas delta, he would sing gospel songs to keep the circling panthers at bay. He had waking dreams where he thought he was an Indian flying through the woods. When he was wired on pills he would frequently head off on solo expeditions into the unmapped American wastelands, where he could compress time and travel back to some atavistic age where everything would somehow be simplified.

Paul Kennerley recalls one day receiving a present from Cash. "We swapped books, and he sent me *The Assassination Of Jesse James By The Coward Robert Ford*. On his stationery he'd written this letter, and he sent a little carved wooden box full of old Civil War bullets and belt buckles. He said he and Hank [Williams] Jr had found this stuff in a cave in Kentucky and he'd like me to have it."

Cash is part of that old, weird America of phantoms and demons, angels and devils, strange handed-down fables, darkness gathering in the trees, a sadness that can't be named, a beauty too fragile to hold too tight. His songs have that touch of mania and magic that only great artists can summon up with a following wind. Like Dylan, he pulls a black poetry from the world, teasing from it some enduring truths. You can hear it in 'I Still Miss Someone', which begins: "At my door the leaves are falling / A cold wild wind will come." It's still there decades later in songs like 'The Man Comes Around': "The terror in each sip and in each sup / For you partake of that last offered cup / Or disappear into the potter's ground." Much of the power of the *American* albums derives from Cash returning to this mercurial, twilit, half-forgotten place.

'Thirteen' belonged there. It was specifically written for him by Glenn Danzig, the ex-Misfits singer and now leader of Danzig, exponents of horror-punk, metal, and industrial music. The song he wrote for Cash was a brooding minor-chord howl about a man "born to bring trouble", branded with a cursed number rather than a name.

"I was asked to write a song for him, and I said: of course I'd write a song for Johnny Cash," Danzig later recalled. "There's always been something in what Johnny Cash has done that I was really drawn to. He did things his way. You have to be true to yourself; whether you go through good or bad times, you have to be true to yourself. This is why when I was asked to do the song for him, I was honoured and it ended up taking me all of 20 minutes to write it. That was basically my perception of Johnny Cash, that song. I think it's probably one of the best songs that I've ever written, and I taught it to him and he loved it."[8]

Cash arrived at Rubin's one day to find Danzig already there, song at the ready. "He sang it over four of five times, then I started singing it with him, then I sat down and recorded it," Cash said. "It was only after I got through that I knew who he was."[9]

Nick Lowe's 'The Beast In Me' was another darkly appropriate song, another made-to-measure character study that helped explain Cash to himself. "Nick saw that in me when he wrote that," Cash would tell people. The track had a rather painstaking genesis that's worth recounting, if only to show the lengths Cash would go in the pursuit of something he knew was right for him.

'The Beast In Me' dated back to April 1981, when Cash and June travelled to London to play Wembley Arena. They had promised to stop by to visit Lowe and his then wife Carlene Carter, and Lowe had stayed up the night before working on a song idea he'd had for Cash.

"I thought it was really a great title for him, so I started messing around with it with the aid of a few bottles of wine and whatever else was going on," says Lowe. "Carlene went off to bed and I stayed up to finish it. By the time I went to bed I was convinced I *was* Johnny Cash. I was singing in his voice and everything. The first verse was great and I finished the rest as well – but with a view to him hearing it the next day, I rushed it through.

"When I opened my eyes next morning the first thing I heard was Carlene on the phone to John, going: oh yeah, Nick stayed up all night writing a song for you, he can't wait to play it for you – he was saying how pleased he is with it. And I'm thinking: oh my God, oh no! Don't tell him that!"

In the clutches of a hangover from hell, Lowe was no longer quite so effusive about the merits of the song. "I looked at these scrawled words, and I couldn't quite remember how it went. I wasn't inhabiting it the way I was the night before. I certainly didn't feel like Johnny Cash any more, but there was no way out of it. They were on their way to Wembley for the soundcheck and they were going to call in on the way."

Lowe went out into the garden to clear his head and "do some digging". When he next looked up there was a huge shadow looming over him. It was Cash.

"How ya doing? I understand you have a song?"

"Well, I have and I haven't."

"Carlene says it's real good and you're real excited about it."

"Well, I am and I'm not."

"Well, I'd really like to hear it."

Lowe went inside to find his living room packed with the entire entourage from the Johnny Cash stage show: band, road crew, tour managers, children, cooks, wardrobe people, all crammed into his front room and waiting expectantly to hear this amazing new song.

"John sat front and centre on the sofa, and a guitar was placed in my hands," says Lowe. "By this point I was so hung-over. Shaking. Sweating. I opened my mouth and, whereas the night before I'd *been* Johnny Cash and this sonorous baritone was rolling round the house in the early hours of the morning, now I opened my mouth and out came this little squeaky, wobbly little voice. I struggled through it and when I finished there was this excruciating silence in the room and the odd forced grunt of approval. I can still recall how awful it was. John said: sing it again. The second time was even worse, and I wanted to run into the street. He said: 'It's not quite there, is it? But it's a really good idea. Give it a bit more thought and let me know.' I never wanted to even hear it again."

On every subsequent occasion that the two men met, Cash would ask Lowe about his song about the beast.

"It was one of the first things he'd do, with a kind of twinkle in his eye, because he knew what a hash I'd made of it," says Lowe. "I would have forgotten about it, but I'd always mentally get it out of the box and have a look at it. The first verse was really, really good, but I couldn't think of anywhere else to take it. One time he was playing at the Albert Hall [in 1989], and he asked me again about 'The Beast In Me', and he was quite earnest about it. The thing about John was that he saw something in me that I never saw. He was always telling me that I was good. This was about ten years later, and that night I went home and I just finished it. It was really peculiar, it was like somebody had turned a tap. It just came out and it all sounded as if it had all been written at the same time.

"I waited a few days to make sure it was right, demoed it, and I sent it off to John. I didn't hear anything else about it until I was talking to my stepdaughter Tiffany, who had just come back from staying with him in Jamaica, and she said: 'Grandpa loves your thing about the beast. He plays it to everyone who comes to the house.' He hadn't told me that he'd got it, but I sort of knew it was good and I knew he'd be pleased to get it. And the next thing I know, out it comes on *American Recordings*. He sent me a copy of the record and then he called me up. It was marvellous of him, and a real tonic to me."

Cash's reading of the song is beautifully measured, weary yet unashamed, without a trace of self-pity or melodrama. He understood it perfectly and pulled it on like a familiar old coat. His keenly felt version of Leonard Cohen's classic 'Bird On A Wire' covers much of the same waterfront, sung from the point of view of a man who is both terribly fragile and yet also bestial, who has "torn everyone who reached out for me".

As a result of tackling such defined and high quality material from so many diverse sources – Waits Danzig & Lowe, after all, was nobody's idea of the next Crosby Stills & Nash – something very interesting happened to Cash's own songwriting. It rose to the occasion, meeting the challenge of successfully living up to the standard that the songs around him set, as well as the best of his own past work. It was a fascinating process, almost as though he were conducting a kind of subliminal dialogue between the external perceptions held by other artists about him and the realities of his own internal nature. On *American Recordings* they meet half way, and the Cash that emerges is somewhere between self-made myth and naked humanity.

He had first recorded 'Delia's Gone' in 1962 on *The Sound Of Johnny Cash*, but this time he substantially changed the lyrics to include sub-machine guns and the hint of S&M: "I tied her to her chair." His amendments and additions amount to a major rewrite of the original song, and the stripped-down setting – the original has a slightly incongruous female vocal chorus chirping in the background – lends this version added menace; the overall tone is much more vicious. In this recording the killer's penance comes not merely from the judge and in the jailhouse, but in the fact that he's haunted in his cell by the sound of his dead wife's feet pacing around his bed. It is, quite simply, classic Cash. He said he had "sent [himself] to the same mental place where I found 'Folsom Prison Blues' and, being older and wiser to human depravity, picked up on some darker secrets than I'd seen in 1956."[10]

He hadn't visited that place for some time, at least not in his writing. 'Folsom Prison Blues' was written because Cash "sat with my pen in my hand, trying to think up the worst reason a person could have for killing another person, and that's what came to mind".[11] At the time he was 22, newly married and with a daughter only months old. Now, with so much hard, fast water passed under the bridge, he was once again regularly revisiting that uncomfortable psychic terrain.

Not including the major rewrite to 'Delia's Gone', he had another four new songs on the album, all of them written either shortly before or during recording. "I haven't been writing all that much, but I'm beginning to," he said at the time, with obvious satisfaction.[12] Many of them are quite astonishing: dense, dark, unflinching poetry, packed with hugely arresting imagery.

'Drive On' was the kind of song Cash had rarely sunk his teeth into over the past 20 years, a piece of bareback poetry based on the memory of his experiences visiting Vietnam in 1969, and also from reading extensively on the subject, notably John Del Vecchio's heavily researched war novel, *The Thirteenth Valley*. 'Drive On' picked up the thread where 'Singin' In Vietnam Talkin' Blues' had left it hanging. The narrator sounds like one of the boys encountered by Cash in his earlier song, back home and still haunted by the experience 25 years down the line. Written soon after Cash had sent a note to President George Bush protesting at the war in Iraq, its anti-war message is not overplayed but remains clear.

Cash captures the almost lysergic horror of combat with brutally economic poetry: he has "heard the men and monkeys in the jungle scream", faced "the tiger smile", and spat in the "the bamboo viper's face". Panning away from the war zone, he then homes in the immeasurable personal price paid by each man who lived through it, doing so with an unsparing eye. A line originally written as "My children love me and they understand" was later changed to "My children love me but they don't understand", an incremental shift on the page but a powerful emotional gear change when sung. Cash loved the vernacular language used by soldiers, and the title phrase – "Drive on, it don't mean nothin'" – became a kind of mantra for the whole series of *American* albums: whatever the cost, keep on keeping on until the end. And as he knew only too well, you didn't need to be a Vietnam vet to have a "tremolo" when you talked and a "little limp" when you walked.

'Like A Soldier' was a song of bruised valediction – "I survived the battles" – which resonated powerfully with Cash in his current situation as a man who somehow believed he had profited from his many mistakes. A deeply touching song of love to June, it sees him facing up all his past misdemeanours while making no attempt at excising or excusing all the trouble and terrors. Instead he deploys them as a springboard to affirmation. It's a great tune, too, one of his best. 'Let The Train Blow The Whistle', meanwhile, acts as a bookend to Tom Waits's song. There can never be too many trains in Cash's music. It is perhaps his central metaphor, signifying freedom, flight, adventure, smoke, and steam; it can take him between women or between whole worlds. 'Let The Train Blow The Whistle' is a carefree farewell song, unrepentant to the last.

Perhaps the most powerful example of Cash's rejuvenation is

'Redemption', where the imagery makes Nick Cave sound like Ricky Martin. It's not the most celebrated track on *American Recordings*, nor of those that Cash has written, but it is one of the most revealing, and like nothing he'd ever attempted before. It is perhaps the best song he ever wrote about his relationship with God; so simple, so hard-won, so all-encompassing, so unsparing, it all but erases the necessity for the rest. It even makes his stentorian, heartfelt reading of Kris Kristofferson's 'Why Me Lord' on the same album seem somehow frivolous by comparison.

Everywhere in his writing there was evidence of regained power and clarity. Cash had absorbed the depths of songs such as 'The Beast In Me' and 'Thirteen', as well as that other recent bespoke portrait on *Zooropa*, 'The Wanderer'. He had heard what they were saying and recognised the voice they were channelling. It was his own. And he reclaimed it.

In the end, ten of the 13 tracks on *American Recordings* are taken from the initial four days of woodshedding in Rubin's Hollywood home. Of the remaining three songs, one, 'Drive On', was recorded at Cash's cabin studio in Hendersonville during a test run for the new gear he had had installed there. "Rick asked me to set up some recording equipment up at Johnny's cabin, and the first time I met him neither he or Rick could work out how to turn it on," says David Ferguson. "I rushed up there to get it started, then I left. That was 'Drive On'."

The two live cuts – 'Tennessee Stud' and 'The Man Who Couldn't Cry' – were recorded at the much vaunted showcase gig at the Viper Room in December 1993. They jar a little, for different reasons. 'The Man Who Couldn't Cry' is simply the wrong song for Cash. He had a sense of humour to match his size but this version of Loudon Wainwright III's wordy satire – from his 1973 *Attempted Moustache* album – sounds like a misguided attempt at ending the album on a jaunty, upbeat note. Cash's delivery is stiff and uncomfortable, and he absolutely tramples all over the melody.

'Tennessee Stud', on the other hand, is a fine performance, but the general good sense in including live tracks on the album remains open to question. The ostentatious hipster whoops and hollers make the audience seem like intruders on what is otherwise a very personal and self-contained piece of work. This isn't a record where it feels natural for anyone else to register on the radar. It's about Cash and Cash alone.

It took a lot of guts to release the album that way. He needed some persuading that the best thing they could do was, in Rubin's words, "follow the magic" and present this rough-and-ready potion unsweetened.[13] Rubin pointed out that there was no sacred text that insists expensive studio recordings have to be better than ones made in your producer's living room on an old guitar: whatever felt best, whatever spoke to the listener, had to *be* best. But Cash, already at a low ebb and lacking confidence in his recording career, was aware that these unadorned cuts left him more exposed than he had ever been before. "I know there was a part of him that was excited about it, and that always wanted to do it," said Rubin. "But there was another part of him that was insecure about it, and felt, 'Well, if they don't like this, I'm really in trouble, because this is really me.'"[14]

On the completion of *American Recordings*, Cash said: "I think they'll know the real me, whatever that's worth."[15] He later added: "There was nothing to hide behind and that was scary."[16]

Strip it all down, after all, and there's nothing much to it: 13 songs, one voice and Cash's very rudimentary acoustic guitar accompaniment. It was recorded in mono in a living room in California, in a makeshift cabin in Tennessee and on stage at a Hollywood night club. No echo, no reverb, no splicing of multiple takes, no mixing, no overdubs. Even a guitar pick was deemed unnecessarily extravagant; every note is played with thumb and fingers, skin, bone, and nail drumming the strings. Cash's guitar on 'Drive On' is noticeably out-of-tune and his voice sounds as creased, weathered, and worn as an old boot. He wasn't the only one who had doubts. "We heard the record and it was really surprising," says David Ferguson. "There's no echo, no other instruments, it's just raw. I found I liked it after I'd listened to it a few times, but everybody was kind of surprised."

But it wasn't simply the spare concept – voice and guitar – that made *American Recordings* such a success. It was the intelligence of most of the song choices, and above all the sense of truth being conveyed. On paper it seems like a rag-bag recorded almost as an afterthought, but both the diversity of the material and the sheer simplicity of the methodology was misleading. When the time came to compile the album he and Rubin didn't just release the first songs that came into their heads; the 13 tracks finally selected run deeper and wider than might at first be apparent. With *American Recordings* Cash not only sang himself, but sang his legacy, his legend, looked over all the parts of his being and pulled them together, song by song and line by line. His ego was big enough to recognise his own mythology, just as he was sufficiently aware of his own failings to address his own fractured humanity. *American Recordings* very cleverly addresses both the man and the icon at the same time.

It is a multi-layered, tentacular piece of work, the songs reaching out to all corners of Cash's being until, cumulatively, it becomes not just a late-flowering blossom of his artistry, but the first instalment of a final reckoning of all that had gone before: there is a song for every hurt, a word for every triumph. It was nothing as contrived as a 'new direction', rather it was an elevation of Cash's work to a new stage, a point where he is no longer inventing anything but instead honing, absorbing, boiling things down to their essence, disgorging all he has learned up to this point.

This was a new level of artistry for Cash, more focused, and he maintained it until his death despite bewildering odds. Rosanne Cash regarded it as a transition to "that stage where you're in mastery of who you are. I think he had to get through that difficult middle-aged period when he was second guessing himself so much, then all these things came along – Bono, but most of all Rick Rubin – to help remind him of who he was, and to help him toward a graceful transition to the last years of his life. Part of the genius and chemistry of that collaboration was finding things that were absolutely resonant with the truth of him".

All Cash needed was someone to point him in the right direction, to sit him down in front of a mirror and show him who he was. Rubin, very wisely, did not attempt to turn him into something he was not or make him hip. "I thought they'd just modernise him, I didn't know it would be so cool, with all this authority and wisdom," says Nick Lowe. "It was a wonderful thing to happen to a man like that right at the end of his career."

American Recordings was no nearer to the sound of Nick Cave than it was to Charlie Rich; it was quintessential Cash. He sang as a man who knew exactly who he was and had resolved to present it to the world, however dark and conflicted it might seem. It appeared so simple, but really it was all about timing. The right time in Cash's life, the right time in the industry, the right time to meet the right man.

"He was *completely* re-energised by this relationship," says Rosanne Cash. "Completely. It was so beautiful, it was as if two long lost brothers had found each other. They really loved each other and connected in a really deep way. It developed very quickly; they fitted together. I was tremendously relieved, I have to tell you. It was like: somebody is going to take care of dad, somebody who really gets him. I stopped worrying about him so much after he met Rick. I was just so relieved and happy."

"I know how much Rick brought the inspiration back to John," says Rodney Crowell. "I *saw* it happen, and Rubin helped translate it so that that audience that was there for him found him. It was good. It was a good thing to see. It was a good job of curation."

It's no exaggeration to say that the hours Cash spent alone with his guitar in Rubin's living room saved him. In their own way those recordings are as astonishing and surprising and resonant to the culture as the ones Cash made in Sun studios in Memphis back in 1955 and 1956. Listen to *The Outtakes (Sun Studio Recordings)*, released in 2007 and covering all the unreleased material from Cash's early days at Sun, and you can plainly hear a sonic and emotional sibling to *American Recordings*.

From this point forward the *American* albums became an evolving idea based on the central premise that Cash was the concept. His reckoning with his past, his facing of an ever-shortening future, his way of dealing with the here and now, became the frame into which every song had to fit. He embraced the idea with such commitment and fearlessness that many listeners had to turn away and several of his most devoted long-term fans backed off. Many more found immense solace there.

"That kind of comforting thing is rare," says Cash's granddaughter Chelsea Crowell. "Not everyone can do this. It's raw and exposed without being inappropriate or tacky – with this total lack of pretence. On a bad day I feel very protective of it, and I want it to belong just to me. On a good day I think: thank God it belongs to the world, because it is so important just to have something that simple and universal and raw and complex and straightforward, perfect in its imperfection. It's a diagram of a human being, which is all those different things."

It remains a deep and powerful document of an extraordinary burst of creativity. Over the previous decades it had seemed as though Cash's work and his most private, complex feelings had been two trains running side by side along parallel tracks; or as though the two dogs on the cover of the album had lost sight of each other, fleeing to the corners of two separate frames. Both sides met at last and fused together on *American Recordings* and the albums that followed. They were Cash's final destination.

9

**Selling A Man,
Selling A Myth**

here was no great epiphany. Cash had encountered fresh starts before. He enjoyed the freedom Rubin had given him, loved the music they made, and felt a close affiliation with the producer, but his expectations for the record weren't especially high. He had all but given up on albums as an art-form and had become used to seeing work he felt was strong being released into a vacuum. He was wary of allowing himself to fall into that trap again.

"I think the idea of doing something new appealed to him, but I don't think it was that big of a deal," said Rubin. "Until we started having some success, I don't know that he cared that much about his recording career again, only because of the way he had been treated. It was almost beaten out of him in some way."[1]

What Cash didn't immediately recognise was how completely his partnership with Rubin would reshape the way he was perceived, and how crucial that was to prove to his success. It is the music that endures, but every bit as important at the time was the way in which Cash's new label mapped out an entire context for him to inhabit leading up to the release of the album.

It's easy to forget what an impressive process of image retrieval *American Recordings* was. When the album hit its mark there was a tendency to shrug dismissively, as if to say 'well of course, Johnny Cash has been cool all along', but by the early 90s Cash's aura was far removed from its ideal. When Rubin came knocking, his cred was in need of substantial renovation. While Cash may have mentally gunned down anyone who dared mention 'demographics' within his earshot, American Recordings knew exactly who they were selling him to and how to do it. If the music was beautifully curated, the quest to get him back on the contemporary cultural radar was orchestrated with similar precision. The marketing campaign was calculated, meticulous, and inspired.

"When John said yes to us initially, Rick called me up and we talked about it," says Martyn Atkins. "I said what we had to do was kind of reinvent him as we imagined the legend of Johnny Cash. I suggested we call him 'Cash' rather than 'Johnny Cash', almost rebrand him. We wanted to completely make people forget all the shit he'd done in the late 70s and through the 80s. We wanted to erase that from people's memories and almost make it seem like what he was doing at American led straight on from the success he'd had in the 60s. In some ways it was an easy job: what is great about Johnny Cash? What is special about him, what makes him stand out in our minds? That's also the approach Rick took with his music: what do *you* want to do? not what can we tell you to create?"

A huge part of the success of *American Recordings* lay in reaffirming these connections between the Cash of 1994 and the one forever burned in people's minds. It was about resurrecting the image of him snarling "San Quentin, I hate every inch of you" to a gang of lifers, at the same time erasing memories of the man who recorded 'Chicken In Black', made so-so TV films, and appeared as a regular on *Dr Quinn, Medicine Woman*. The version of Cash who endorsed the Johnny Cash Card and the Johnny Cash Machine in a deal with Canada Trust bank would, if all went to plan, be quietly expunged from the history books. And in many ways he has been.

Cash's cool was a complex, multi-layered thing. He was always in possession of a residual magnetism that emanated from his voice and his stature and centred around the easily accessible iconography of prison, pills, death, and darkness. Many of us will remember first hearing him sing that he had "shot a man in Reno just to watch him die" and instinctively feeling that here was someone who had, at some point, probably done something terrible; if not *that*, exactly, then some similarly grave misdeed. We may remember, too, that we rather liked that idea.

Cash owes more of his success than anyone would probably care to acknowledge to precisely that premise, even if it is, by and large, a false one. He had been reckless in his life but he was never a genuine outlaw: he did not shoot a man just to watch him die; rather, he spent a night in the cells for picking flowers. The scar on the right hand side of his jaw was not a bullet hole or a knife wound, but the legacy of nothing more savage than the removal of a cyst.

"The major misconception about Cash was that he'd done hard time," says Martyn Atkins. "The distinction between him as a person and his songs was totally blurred by that point. Rick's always drawn to that stuff, he had more of a handle on what the kids want." And what the kids wanted was a cartoon, the mythic cool of the man in black, which in human terms was a reductive, less interesting version of the wider cool that Cash actually possessed; that of man unafraid to be himself.

"He seemed like he had all the answers, but he was flawed," says Nick Lowe. "He could be very uncool. He'd get excited, do things that cool people aren't supposed to do, tell rather bad jokes and laugh uproariously. In a way, another thing starts to happen when you're not trying [to be cool]. You see someone who is absolutely natural and not guarded, and then it becomes very cool indeed."

"He was not a big old, dark, weird dude," says David Ferguson. "The dark thing is marketing, and that's fine. He had a darkness in him, we all do, but he wasn't that way 24/7. He was very human, very concerned about people's feelings, he'd worry about stuff. He was a clown; he'd play tricks on you. He was a very light-hearted man, he loved pretty things, he loved people, and he loved God."

This kind of unstudied, complex, contradictory portrait is less easy to put on a poster. It doesn't translate to a mass audience, particularly a younger one, which had been part of the problem in the late 70s and 80s. With *American Recordings* the idea was to connect Cash back to his most iconic persona. If in doubt, go with the myth. Rubin, after all, had turned himself into a myth too: the beard-stroking guru-producer, meditating on songs, eyes closed, as though each line was being handed down from Mount Sinai, was in itself a carefully cultivated construct. He knew all about the art of smoke and mirrors and how to massage reality into something vast and symbolic.

"I guess I thought of the legendary image of the man in black, and thought that we could find material, or write material, and kind of use that imagery as a framework ... for what we were going to do," he said. "Make sure that whatever he sang suited the mythic character that was really maybe a caricature of himself. There was probably some of him in it."[2]

Cash, of course, also understood this. "I think Cash was comfortable with caricature," says Will Oldham. "He was a showman. Music makes mythology. We are showmen who know that songs are dreams and skeletons on which we all can hang our fears and feelings about ourselves, fears and feelings that have no earthly home. The writer/performer has to have a relationship with myth, but that relationship will always be particular to the individual. I do feel like Rubin began to present Rubin's [version of] Cash to us, but Johnny Cash [was] strong enough to withstand this. He's one of the few people strong and complex enough to use caricature as a Trojan Horse. He wrote his own caricature song in 'Man In Black', which stirs and invites ... then once you are *in* there, you are in there with musical history and Jesus Christ and social justice and silliness and anger, all dished out with seductive and satisfying conviction."

While Cash was once again singing the kind of songs in which he could unite all of his various stances and feelings, the label was very consciously selling the man who once said: "I came as close to death as anyone can come and still remain alive." As Atkins points out: "The songs were always honest, so you could go the extra mile with the image." With the help of Cash's stored-up gravitas and American Recordings' considerable credentials in the current marketplace, the idea was to entirely bypass anything to do with country music and catapult Cash straight back into the vibrant heartlands of college dorms, high schools, and pool bars, making a beeline for alternative radio and TV video shows. He had always enjoyed considerable crossover appeal, both musically – he connected with early rock'n'roll, rockabilly, folk – and culturally, where he had reached places most country artists didn't even know existed. Now it was time to exploit it.

It was no accident that the first single from *American Recordings* was a plain-speaking blues about a man murdering his woman and paying the price. 'Delia's Gone' transported Cash straight back to the days of 'Folsom Prison Blues', '15 Minutes To Go', and the lusty ferocity of his version of 'Cocaine Blues', which at Folsom prison had brought testosterone-fuelled whoops of delight from the inmates. It also connected him to what was happening in the wider musical culture at the time, whether it was Tupac's '16 On Death Row' ("Today's my final day / I'm counting every breath") or Nirvana covering Leadbelly's 'Where Did You Sleep Last Night?' It was somehow both contrived and perfectly apt. "Rick Rubin brought Cash's attention to a greater pool of musicians, but one that was a direct descendant of the community Cash came up in," says Oldham.

The news that Cash had signed with American Recordings generated an instant buzz of interest throughout the industry. One of Rubin's most recent signings, the Scottish band The Jesus & Mary Chain, famed for their riotous early gigs, abrasive feedback, and the wholesale adoption of Lower East Side nihilist chic, returned to the UK after playing some festivals in the States fizzing with news of the Cash/Rubin project.

"They came back with a tape of some of the songs he'd recorded, and I remember them playing it to me," says Mick Houghton, the band's press agent at that time. "It was a really bizarre mixture of stuff, a lot of which wasn't on the first album. I guess that's where Rick Rubin really came into play, sorting out the wheat from the chaff. Jim and William [Reid] were huge fans, and I think they were hoping to get him to record a Mary Chain song, something like 'Darklands'."

The subtext was clear. Cash was once again making music that was big enough to carry both him and his mythology. It was soul searching, confrontational and anti-authoritarian. It was *now* music.

✦

Persuading a slightly sceptical 62-year-old to recognise that it was necessary to present himself in a manner that would complement and enhance the powerful austerity of the music he was making did not always make for an easy ride. There were several areas where Cash's rather old-school sensibilities conflicted with Rubin's image-conscious contemporary approach. A man who placed great store in his sense of self and his sense of dignity, who was still mindful of what a disaster the 'Chicken In Black' video had been, he was extremely wary about being awkwardly recast as something he wasn't, dressed up in a suit of clothes that didn't belong to him in order to appeal to a younger crowd. That struck him as rather desperate. "I have no illusions about who I am, how old I am, and what a stretch it might be to relate to these young people," he said.[3] Yet American Recordings understood what Cash couldn't quite see. That simply by being himself, presented in a carefully controlled light, he already fitted into the contemporary music scene. All the label had to do was accentuate certain key characteristics.

The gig at the Viper Room was a vital first step in this process. It was the opening night of this new stage in Cash's career, recasting him as 'The Singer' in Nick Cave's brooding cover version, the lone gunslinger in the spotlight dispensing hard-won wisdom to a select group of eager young acolytes anxious to bathe in his brilliant blackness. It took place on December 7 1993, more than four months before the album's slated release. The driving initiative behind the gig was to build a word-of-mouth buzz. The idea was to get the right kind of people talking about Cash, to create an almost mythical one-off event witnessed in the flesh by only a select few but which would go on to enjoy an extended and expanded afterlife, talked about for years to come by thousands of people who weren't even in the same State or country at the time but fervently wished they had been privileged enough to be allowed access.

In this respect it worked brilliantly. The Viper Room was located on Sunset Strip on West Hollywood, right in the belly of the beast, and at the time was owned by Johnny Depp. It was the favoured hang-out for young actors, alternative rock'n'roll groups, and well-connected patriarchal figures like Tom Petty, who had played with The Heartbreakers on its opening night. Sean Penn, Quentin Tarantino, and Jennifer Aniston were frequent visitors. Only a few weeks before Cash played, the young actor River Phoenix had died of a drug overdose on the premises. The club had only recently reopened. It would have been hard to find a venue more replete with a somewhat seedy yet high-end glamour.

It was a tiny place with old-fashioned booths and a dark, slightly decadent atmosphere. On the night of the performance the audience included various Red Hot Chili Peppers, Juliette Lewis, Henry Rollins, Jeff Lynne, Penn, and Petty. Cash was introduced on stage by Depp, who was a bag of nerves at the prospect. Cash was extremely nervous, too. Not because of the nature of the crowd – he'd played to more important people, although admittedly he was in a somewhat alien environment – but because he was performing an entire concert alone for the first time. Backstage he was a huge, black blur of nervous tics, fidgeting and jerking, rubbing his face, blinking, sweating heavily.

"Dad said he was very nervous," says Rosanne Cash. "I don't even think in the old days he did stuff just by himself. Maybe in the middle of the set he might do one or two songs, but not the whole set. Do you know how much harder it is to sit alone before a small crowd than it is to be on stage with your band in a stadium? But he was always nervous before he went on stage. It means you still care about what you do."

He opened with 'Drive On' and played many more songs from *American Recordings*, as well as classics like 'Folsom Prison Blues'. "It was an incredible night," said Rick Rubin. "Dead silent. You could hear a pin drop. People couldn't believe that it was Johnny Cash there in the Viper Room. He started playing, and I could see how nervous he was, but by the middle of the first song or the beginning of the second song, all of the fear was gone. He was in the music and it was beautiful. People who were there that night still talk about it as one of the greatest things they've ever seen."[4]

Into this hushed, charged reverie stumbled two of the more chemically enhanced members of the audience: Gibby Haynes of Texan psychedelic provocateurs Butthole Surfers and his partner in crime for the evening, 73-year-old counter-cultural figurehead and renowned tripper Dr Timothy Leary. Both were in the throes of a prolonged bender in which they seemed hell bent on re-enacting some of the more unhinged passages from Hunter S. Thompson's *Fear And Loathing In Las Vegas*.

"About three songs in, Tim starts heckling Johnny, shouting 'You're a fraud, you're a fraud!'" says Haynes. "Mr Cash took it really well. He didn't really respond, he just smiled. Tim just wouldn't let it go, he kept on with this 'fraud' business. Half the eyes were on us, and eventually club management came over and kicked us out. It was really embarrassing, and it says a lot when I'm embarrassed. We walked out and I was, like: what's the deal with the fraud thing? Tim was a bit blurry, but he said: he didn't shoot a man in Reno! This was a man who was great friends with William Burroughs, who shot his wife in the head. His point was, Cash was a man who *said* he'd shot a man in Reno, and he really didn't. He was upset that Cash was a storyteller and not a murderer. In Tim's book, if you're going to say you're a murderer you'd better be one."

There's probably a deeper point to be gleaned from this bizarre vignette, something to do with the relationship between truth, identity, and artistic expression, but the upshot on the night was that after four songs Haynes left – "eight-balled" – with Leary. He was, however, at the show long enough to take its temperature. With the Hollywood brats at play, there could so easily have been a kind of ironic, mock-reverential tone to the whole evening; indeed, some of the inane, ill-timed whooping heard on the two live tracks on *American Recordings* suggest there may have been a touch of that, but Cash – rather solemn, serious, playing without any hint of pretence or ingratiation – succeeded in winning over the audience entirely on his own terms.

"Johnny Cash, in a small club, playing by himself? It was fucking awesome," says Haynes. "Everyone was just focused, that quiet and respectful vibe. It was really cool. He didn't have that Willie Nelson hipster vibe, it was when Rick's record came out that he really crossed over to this new crowd, but it was a big night, probably the best night at the Viper Room. I don't think it was ironic that he was there at all; it seemed appropriate. He was the man in black and he'd had a well documented drug problem. It was a real easy fit."

And an entirely deliberate one. Bringing Cash into the orbit of the Viper Room lent him a whiff of the underground again. Never mind that he was still playing 120 shows a year with his sprawling cornball jamboree, or that anybody who wanted to watch him perform could have seen him anywhere in America at virtually any time. The Viper Room created the illusion of exclusivity, a staple in rock'n'roll, where it was always at a premium, but not something country music has much time for.

Though not playing, Earl Poole Ball, the piano player in Cash's touring band, turned up at the Viper Room performance, watching the entire concert squeezed in next to the toilets. He remembers the starry, respectful atmosphere. "Johnny did a great job," he says. "After the show, and after exchanging pleasantries with Randy Quaid, Johnny Depp came up and invited me into the kitchen to chat. We talked at length about the life of a travelling musician and travelling the world with the man in black. He was very much a gentleman and a bona fide fan, and I will always remember the night."

The show had the desired effect, not only in handing Cash back a large chunk of his kudos, but in building momentum. The gig was written up in the news section of the following issue of *Rolling Stone*, and word quickly started to spread that Johnny Cash was up to something. "It really started to make young people interested," says Martyn Atkins, who had filmed the show and subsequently released 'Drive On' and 'The Man Who Couldn't Cry', bundled up with 'Delia's Gone' from an Austin club show, as part of a 13-minute electronic press kit distributed to TV stations and media outlets before the album's release. Artfully shot in grainy black and white, it was an electrifying little film that mixed the musical performance with jump-cut backstage footage and a snatch of Cash talking about his love of his new album after "years of frustrations".

"We put it out, let it be seen, and got people talking," says Atkins. "It was like: oh man, I would have loved to have been there. How could you get in?"

The Viper Room gig was a highly astute piece of old-school industry business, letting demand appear to outstrip supply. The next considerations were purely aesthetic. The album title itself was inspired, encapsulating as it did Cash's longstanding and instantly identifiable reputation as a chronicler of all aspects of his country, but also – in its direct, almost artless simplicity – making clear that this was a fresh start, a stripping away of all the gloss and distractions that had conspired to foul up the lines of communication between Cash, his audience, and himself.

To match the music, everything on *American Recordings* had to be starker on the outside, too, the symbolism sharper and more menacing. The most important element in this respect was the cover image. Country records are not necessarily renowned for their artistic merits, and Cash had a particularly unhappy history in this regard. In recent years, each new album had generally shown him striking some stiff pose, often dressed up to the nines in his country finery, chest puffed out, legs astride, standing resolute against a falling crimson sunset or rugged clump of nature. The effect was to make him look like a piece of the past preserved in aspic and Kodachrome. *Rainbow* had been a particularly poor example.

His new label had experience working with alternative acts to whom image was hugely important in predetermining the way their music was perceived and received, while Martyn Atkins had designed sleeves for some of the most visually conscious bands of the 80s, including Joy Division, Depeche Mode, and Echo & The Bunnymen.

"If you put Johnny Cash on a cover and it's shot right you have something that people just gravitate toward," he says. "The thing I thought might be difficult was John. It was so alien to him to go back to doing things this way, to almost kind of reinvent him and him just to accept that. He'd done so much stuff that was 'professional' – stylists, make-up artists, loads of people hanging around on sessions – and I said we wanted to do something really simple, that contained the essence of him, just like the music. That just says 'I'm Johnny Cash, and I'm still here'. And of course he had to look American, a real man of people."

American or not, because of the compressions of time and the fact that Cash was still pursuing a relentless pace on the road, the cover shoot was arranged to take place in Australia, where he was on tour with Kris Kristofferson. Atkins and photographer Andy Earl met up with him in Melbourne on February 22 1994. Earl, a veteran of rock photography at the top end of the scale, at first didn't understand what he was doing there.

"I was completely confused as to what this was all about," he says. "I couldn't quite see why the guy who had done Def Jam had an interest in what Johnny Cash was up to. Martyn brought the tapes and I heard a couple of bits but the significance didn't really register. We saw him playing that night at Melbourne with The Carter Family and Kris Kristofferson, and it was just this country & western jamboree. I was scratching my head. I felt his star had lost his shine a little bit."

With the album title settled as *American Recordings*, they wanted the image to be similarly archetypal: the distilled essence of man-on-the-road in the middle of nowhere. Atkins and Earl spent a day scouting locations around Melbourne, and found an old railway line and some station buildings near Geelong, about 50 miles south-west of the city. The idea was to shoot him walking alone along the tracks with his guitar in his hand. Frankly, Cash couldn't really see why something so elaborate was required.

"We met him backstage," says Earl. "Martyn had met him before. We told him about the session the next day and he looked completely perplexed. He said: look, I normally just get shot on stage or backstage. What do you guys wanna do? We picked him up the next day, put him in a car, and he was a bit grumpy: why are we sitting in a car for an hour in the middle of nowhere?"

"I had some kind of rapport with him but it was still a little bit prickly, he wasn't used to doing stuff on the fly," says Martyn Atkins. "It took an hour to get there and we wanted him for a few hours, and after about half an hour in the car he started to moan a bit. We shot him for about 15 minutes and he said he needed a rest: 'Once we do one more shot I'm done. I usually spend 15 minutes on my photographs.'"

For Cash this was all mere frippery, a trifling adjunct to the important business of making records and, above all, playing shows. Atkins knew how vital it was to get the right photograph if they wanted to present him in a way that would both acknowledge his rebellious past image and also portray him in a modern, relevant context. And having spent 22 hours getting to Australia from London and Los Angeles respectively, and then a further day driving around looking for locations, both he and Earl were keen to get what they came for.

"We talked him into doing more shots for another 45 minutes," says Atkins. "Then he said: I'm about done. We knew by then the album would be called *American Recordings*, so I got him over to the cornfield. It looked so American. It reminded me of a Depeche Mode cover I'd done years ago; it felt right. The dogs belonged to the station master. John made a big fuss of them and they just wanted to stand by his side. It was almost biblical. That was the last five minutes of that session. It was one of those magic moments when we got exactly what we wanted. When we took it knew we'd got it."

Andy Earl: "I liked the fact that there he was, all in black, looking like a preacher man, and there was this field of wheat, and storm clouds. It all came together, and for two or three frames those dogs sat by his side, and that ended up being the cover. It really captured the moment. It was all about cajoling him along, then he started messing around quite a bit, which was lovely. He did those ones where he is throwing up the guitar. The menacing, naughty bit: he was up for that. He'd play up to the camera. It turned out that he was a receiver of ideas, not at all set in his ways."

None of this detail was incidental to the eventual success of *American Recordings*. With that huge CASH banner along the top, the album cover was highly significant in securing the attention of the critics and the public. The instantly iconic sepia-tinted portrait of the singer as a looming old testament prophet, or perhaps a mercenary bounty hunter, or maybe even the angel of death himself, flanked by his two hell-hounds, ensured interested parties approached the album from the right angle even before they'd heard a note. If it had merely featured a gaudy colour picture of Cash in a big hat and a bootlace tie grinning through gritted teeth, the way the album was received could have been very different.

"I think it was [quite important]," says Earl. "Before it was that whole country and western feel, this was to put him more into popular culture. Rick Rubin and American Recordings liked it because it just looked quite cool and had a contemporary feel. I'm not sure visually he'd ever done something in a conceptual way ... it was a completely new way of him being seen."

It set a stylistic context (the sepia tones, the bold CASH strapline) and thematic template (unvarnished, raw, honest) that the label followed for the rest of the album series. The idea of emphasising Cash's age and his lived-in quality was one that developed as the *American* series evolved and his health declined, but Cash possessed enough vanity and ego to ensure he never quite got used to the idea that what was required of him visually was to look as rough and as weathered as possible. "The early images Rick and I would work out and we'd show him the finished cover," says Atkins. "Sometimes I'd show him stuff and he might say something like 'I don't like that, I look old', and Rick would explain: 'Yeah, but that's what people want. They don't want you to look young.'"

"His face had so much character, it was like a geography map," says Andy Earl. "It was lovely to have something like that to work with, though he hated those close-ups. He thought they were horrible."

As important as the cover was the video for the first single, 'Delia's Gone'. Much of the marketing momentum for *American Recordings* derived from reviving the idea of Cash as a menace to both himself and the public at large, resurrecting the implied threat behind America's great outlaw artist. Just as radio had played its part in his exile in the 80s, so it was that MTV went some way to restoring his presence in the 90s.

The video to 'Delia's Gone' was shot by Anton Corbijn, the Dutch photographer, designer, and director renowned for creating effortlessly cool, monochrome portraits of Cash-friendly acts like U2 and Nick Cave. Corbijn was a widely respected craftsman in the aesthetics of alienation and loneliness. Instructed to find a location within 15 minutes of Cash's house – "he went home for lunch!" – Corbijn shot an artfully simmering clip on Super 8 of Cash looking haggard and cool and a little dangerous, as he tied his woman to the chair and then later dumped her in the back of his car. The clincher was the appearance as the doomed Delia of supermodel Kate Moss, who was at the time dating Johnny Depp.

"Kate Moss was in the video before I was," said Cash. "They said: Kate Moss is doing it for you. I said: fine. Great."[5]

"Rick really wanted to get him into a younger audience and MTV," says Anton Corbijn. "I knew Kate Moss so I asked her to be in the video, which was not so difficult. We filmed it like a documentary, watching the events in flashback with him also being the singer telling the story by the graveside. I loved it. It's one of the few videos he acted in, and it's beautiful piece of work."

"I wasn't sure about the Kate Moss thing," says Martyn Atkins. "I almost felt: keep him pure, don't let anybody else get involved. Rick will always go with the lower common denominator, but it worked. That video got played a lot. At that time American were functioning like a proper record label, they had a video plugger, and by that point Heidi [Robinson-Fitzgerald, American Recordings' publicist] had done a good job of getting everybody excited about Cash, so it was inevitable [with Corbijn directing] and Kate Moss in the video that it was going to get played."

In a deliciously symbolic twist, Country Music Television banned the video for its portrayal of violence toward women, which only served to strengthen its credentials and its impact. It was also banned in Canada. "It was crazy, a great example of how people mix up what they hear and what they see," says Corbijn. "The video is about the aftermath of [someone] killing a woman and it basically ends his life. That was the message; it was anti-violence."

Of course, the controversy did Cash's image no harm whatsoever.

The video appeared on heavy rotation on MTV and even popped up on *Beavis And Butthead*. Watching from his Nashville eyrie, Rick Blackburn was not unaware of the significance of it all.

"John wasn't rebellious when I worked with him at all," says Blackburn. "Later on, in the 90s, he gave the finger to the industry. Rubin picked him up. Whoever had the guts to put that video on MTV deserves an award. That wasn't about country music or the industry, that was about Johnny Cash – a legend. Then Nashville said: oh my God – he got away from us! He changed the platform, and that didn't happen for Willie, or Merle, or George Jones. It only happened for Johnny."

10 You
Remembered
Me

rom the moment of its US release, on April 26 1994, *American Recordings* was acknowledged as being culturally resonant. Primed, the music press fell on it with glee. The *LA Times* wrote: "Cash has collected 13 songs that peer into the dark corners of the American soul. A milestone work for this legendary singer." *Rolling Stone* wrote: "His voice is the best it has sounded in more than 30 years. Cash has made what is unquestionably one of his best albums." In *Mojo*, Mark Cooper called it a "breathtaking blend of the confessional and the self-mythologising".

The widespread critical acclaim was consolidated in 1995 when *American Recordings* won Cash yet another Grammy in the 'Best Contemporary Folk Album' category.

Some of the reviews, in the rush to embrace his return to greatness, were perhaps too eager to dismiss all he had done before. *Billboard* even declared: "Never has the man in black produced a work of such brilliance as this one." Robert Christgau in *The Village Voice* provided some balance, bemoaning the lack of rhythm on the record and disputing the received wisdom that Rubin "had rescued a Nashville legend from Nashville".

He was right about one thing: Cash's version of 'The Man Who Couldn't Cry' isn't very good at all. But after 30 years chugging along to the old boom-chicka-boom sound, it was a relief to hear him freed from those rhythmic shackles and able to tackle songs like 'The Beast In Me', with their slightly unusual structures and fresh shapes. The assumption that Cash could still have prospered creatively within the Nashville system is highly dubious. It's no coincidence that *American Recordings* has echoes of the stripped-down feel of the *Man In Black* album, recorded more than 20 years earlier and one of the last times Cash had sounded really powerful and in creative control in the studio.

It was no coincidence either that there was a renewed affinity with Bob Dylan, who in 1992 and 1993 had released *Good As I Been To You* and *World Gone Wrong*, his twinned voice-and-acoustic-guitar albums of traditional folk and blues songs. The latter release in particular had gone a long way to restoring Dylan's critical credibility, and had featured 'Delia', a more reflective, blues-based account of the murder of Delia Green in Savannah, Georgia, in 1900, the same story that had inspired 'Delia's Gone'. In turn, Dylan's *Time Out Of Mind* album, released in 1997, stalks much of the same sonic and thematic territory as *American Recordings*.

If this process of mutual inspiration between two old friends was long established, placing Cash in the teen heartlands at the height of the popularity of rap and grunge was something entirely new, and a stroke of genius. It made him instantly relevant and ensured that *American Recordings'* direct, unsparing message made absolute sense. The album was released just three weeks after Kurt Cobain's suicide; here was the Nirvana singer's battered, embattled forebear, the man who had lived through what Cobain could not and was here to tell the tale without shame, apology, or melodrama.

An entire generation of kids and young adults, from pre-teen to college age, began to hear about Cash for the first time. One of his grand-daughters, Chelsea Crowell, was just entering the demographic that he was reaching out to: kids in their early teens, already well versed in hip-hop and alternative rock. Aged 12 when she heard *American Recordings*, she recalls: "Anyone my age that I was close to was suddenly very aware of him, I definitely noticed. When the first *American Recordings* came out he kind of hit it on the pulse of what was going on musically around then. It was right for that time. I remember having a conversation with him; he talked a bit about Rick Rubin and I played him The Beastie Boys' *Paul's Boutique* and [*Check Your Head*], and gave him some insight into that early Brooklyn hip-hop scene. I played him The Dead Kennedys' version of 'I Fought The Law', and we had a really funny conversation about it. Looking back I feel like it was just dropped into his lap. He had his badass image from earlier working for him, but there was no jump between the songs and the person. The *American Recordings* record was so much like the person that I knew, it felt very normal. I felt very proud that the person I knew had made this record without compromising any of himself."

As part of this major shift in perceptions, Cash ticked off some landmark destinations on the concert calendar. In March 1994 he went down to Austin, Texas, to play South By Southwest (SXSW), one of the biggest and most significant music festivals in the States, and one with a clear alternative agenda. He gave a keynote address that involved strumming a couple of songs and charming everyone with a short speech. Later, he played Emo's on Sixth Street, opening solo and then bringing on the band halfway through. Afterward he quipped about "learning a new chord" as a crowd of hip Gen X-ers swarmed around him. "Part of the thing that clicked him over again besides Rick Rubin was that he did a stripped-down raw show at the Viper Room and a show at SXSW," says Rodney Crowell. "There it was again. That raw thing revitalised him again for a new audience."

When he played at Fez, in New York, on April 13, there were enough supermodels to grace a Milanese catwalk, including Kate Moss. This was all Rubin's doing: he had ensured that Cash had become a hip name to drop and that his shows were a fashionable backdrop for some high end schmoozing. In June he played a concert at the Manhattan Center that was edited and broadcast on VH1. A few days later he was booked to play Glastonbury, the annual three-day British festival which had morphed from laidback hippie idyll to cutting-edge cool without losing its unique flavour or its place as the most eagerly anticipated event on the musical calendar.

Organiser Michael Eavis had to battle to get Cash on the bill. The album's release was delayed by five months in the UK due to a legal dispute between Rubin's American label and Polygram, its European licensee at the time, which meant that it was not available in Britain until September, long after his appearance at the festival on June 26 1994. Not everyone appreciated that he was entering a new phase.

"I decided I wanted him to come, and our really trendy booking boys said: oh no, that's out of date, that's not really our thing," says Eavis. "And of course they were wrong and I was right. I couldn't think of anything better than Johnny Cash on the Pyramid Stage, so I worked at it, because they were boycotting his phone numbers and saying 'I don't know who his agent is' and all that rot. I had to fight my own corner. They were terrified of falling into a Radio Two, Womad context. It had to be The Smiths and Radiohead, which is fair enough, they're absolutely brilliant, but just for a break, nothing better than Johnny Cash."

Cash was booked to play on the Sunday afternoon, which was a somewhat backhanded compliment. Tom Jones, Rolf Harris, and Tony Bennett had played the same slot in the recent past: all fine exponents in their own field, and in Bennett's case an absolute master, but the suspicion remained that they were nostalgia acts there to be lightly patronised. It was not quite a novelty booking, but neither was it quite viewed with the same seriousness as the rest of the bill.

Backstage, Cash was unusually nervous. He asked how many people were out there. About 50,000, he was told. All kids? Not *all* kids, was the response. Sweat. Blink. Fidget. Pace. Scratch. He needn't have worried. He was given an ovation even before he played a note, so overwhelming in its intensity and affection that he wept as it rolled over him. "He was well up to the job," says Eavis. "And the band were so excited. I was standing right by the side of him. I watched him from the stage, and he just couldn't fail. Everyone knows his songs."

Televised by the BBC in Britain, Cash's Glastonbury performance featured several songs from *American Recordings* played solo and made a perceptible impact. After his set Cash was collared by the local Bishop of Bath and Wells, who traditionally addressed the Glastonbury crowd in his God Slot. He invited Cash, June, and the band to his residence, The Palace, in Wells, for lunch the next day. "He had the full treatment," says Eavis. "Johnny went straight for the purple tunic."

He knew his limitations. There was talk around the same time, instigated by American Recordings, of him joining the annual Lollapalooza festival, a showcase for alternative rock, industrial, heavy metal, and hip-hop. It would have been a stretch.

"He was going to go out on Lollapalooza," says Rosanne Cash, "and I said: dad, don't do it. Don't go out and play to a bunch of snot-nosed 14-year-olds who don't know who you are. They'll put you on a smaller stage. Just don't do it. Thank God he didn't; he didn't have the platform at that time to pull it off."

There were more triumphs, other significant landmarks. He did a concert in early 1995, at the Pantages Theater in Los Angeles with Beck as supporting act, when everybody seemed to turn up, among them Joe Strummer, Sheryl Crow, and the Red Hot Chili Peppers, all of whom figured in Cash's life later on. In July 1995 he played two gigs in Seattle and Portland with Mark Lanegan from abrasive grunge forefathers The Screaming Trees as his support act. "I was really proud of him, then, to see those young people respond," says Rosanne Cash. "I kept thinking it was like Matisse. He started out being representational, then he did the impressionist stuff, and then this explosion at the end of his life. Just when he expected the guy to fade out quietly he just explodes with this incredible creative burst."

American Recordings penetrated the culture, even if it did not penetrate the charts. One of the major misconceptions about the album, and the two that followed, is that it launched Cash back into the commercial big league. "You know what's really funny?" says Martyn Atkins. "None of those records sold more than 65,000 copies until he had that hit [in 2003] with 'Hurt'." *American Recordings* reached Number 110 in the *Billboard* charts, his best placing for a new album since *Man In Black*, but hardly a smash, and not significantly better than his sales in the 80s. There were no real hits. Out of the ten singles taken from the *American* series of albums, including posthumous releases, only 'Hurt' charted, getting to Number 65 in the US country charts and to Number 39 in the UK charts. And it all meant precisely nothing to the country community. It was like something that existed in a parallel dimension. Country radio studiously avoided it.

But Cash's sheer presence, with very few exceptions, had always outstripped his sales. The success of *American Recordings* wasn't about totting up units, scrutinising chart positions, analysing radio rotation, or counting the end-of-night takings in the cash box, just as the failures of his 80s albums hadn't been all about commercial stagnation. He was an artist, and his work had to be judged first and foremost on artistic merit. The triumph of *American Recordings* spoke of a different kind of success, and one that didn't always translate to Cash's management. When Rick Rubin suggested that Cash capitalise on the buzz created by the Viper Room show by playing a short tour of similarly exclusive club dates at Ronnie Scott's in London and comparable hip, bijou venues in New York, Paris, Rome, and other major cities, the idea was swiftly kiboshed.

"Rick really wanted to put together a small tour where John would go and play a bunch of tastemaker shows for maximum impact and media exposure," says Martyn Atkins. "Do it in small spaces so that nobody really got to see the show, but the press fallout would be great and it would pique everybody's interest. But his manager didn't want to do that. He was like: John earns X amount of dollars per show. Why would he want to go to London and play Ronnie Scott's for a few thousand pounds and we can only get 250 people in there?

"He couldn't see the logic. I'm sure John might have seen the logic, but it's a tough re-evaluation of your financial value, isn't it? 'I played all my life to work my way up to playing 200-seat clubs in London?' I think that's the way they saw it."

There was more to it than that. The notion of exclusivity didn't sit well with Cash. The idea of selling below demand and deliberately booking somewhere that ensured his fans would miss out was an alien one. The result was that suddenly it felt like he was conducting two careers at the same time, living a kind of parallel professional life. He was appearing at Glastonbury, the Fillmore, and sharing bills with Beck and Mark Lanegan. He was covering Danzig and Tom Waits. Yet in 1994 he still showed up on Billy Graham's Crusades, and also played almost 50 dates at the Shenandoah South Theatre in Branson to fulfil his commitments after the Cash Country project fell through. If it was a little schizophrenic, it was also appropriate, a fitting representation of his twin loyalties, his dual nature, and somehow entirely honest.

He kept up a relentless touring pace through 1994 and into 1995, 1996, and 1997, until his health finally gave in and he was forced to stop. He regularly played not just in America and Europe, but also in

Australia, New Zealand, Thailand, and Hong Kong. When *Unchained* came out in late 1996 he could still be found spinning through America in a converted Greyhound bus, performing in fields and beneath the anonymous, generic neon blare of shopping malls and cattle sheds to the diehard country fraternity, a sea of conservatism in their baseball caps, Stetsons, and mullets. He was still trading those corny lines with June on 'Jackson' and 'If I Were A Carpenter', and yet he was also throwing his mighty version of Soundgarden's 'Rusty Cage' into the mix, often to a less than enthusiastic response.

After a couple of decades when his live act was to all intents and purposes his livelihood, Cash wasn't going to pin his entire career at this stage on the fortunes of a record that had attracted a bunch of rave reviews but had generated hardly any commercial heat. He still measured success in the old way: by the number of faces looking in his direction when he sang.

A more insistent factor in his continued desire to keep touring was the role of provider. The passing fancies of the cognoscenti were one thing; the pressing concerns of loyalty and family quite another.

"At one point he was on the road and I dropped in to see him and he didn't look real well," says Dick Asher. "I said: John, why are you beating yourself up like this? You don't need the money any more, I know that. And he said: Well The Tennessee Three and The Carter Family have been travelling with me for many years, and they need the money. That says something right there."

"Sometimes he'd go out on his own to his farm in Bon Aqua, just to cool off," says Rodney Crowell. "I went there to see him a few times and he'd make these little passive aggressive remarks about everybody he was dragging around on the road. Our conversations would invariably go back to: God, it sounds so good when it's just voice, bass and guitar. Stop taking these 40 people on the road, make some money! He'd say yeah, but there were a lot of people who were counting on him to cover their rent. Even after *American Recordings* he was still covering everybody's bills."

Not everybody's. Cash kept the core of the Tennessee Three together, but he did finally make a few hard calls. "During this time I was informed that my services were not required as he planned to tour much of the time with only the three pieces: bass, drums, guitar," says the band's piano player, Earl Poole Ball. "Which he did, then gradually adding a piece at a time back into the show. I was the last one back. It was anticipated I would bide my time with other income during this time off. Instead I fell into dire financial straits and emotional turmoil as a result of this situation and other personal problems. The camel was already loaded pretty heavily before this was added to the mix."

Cash could no longer continue being responsible for everyone in his court. Nevertheless, as a result of the decision to try and be all things to all people, at least musically, after *American Recordings* his stage show became a strange, hydra-headed beast. This frustrated many people at his new record label and often confused his core audience, who had come to hear 'Folsom Prison Blues' and hadn't really bargained for Danzig.

"Because of John's loyalty he didn't want to blow off his band, so he'd do a bunch of old stuff and then he'd do a little acoustic set in the middle, for 20 minutes, and he'd still do a little bit where he'd bring June out and did 'Jackson'," says Martyn Atkins. "Rick hated that. It pissed me off a bit as well. We have this great show that's super-legendary, and then there's this cabaret section. It's like saying: we're doing this, but we have to do *this* as well. At the Manhattan Center show for VH1, we only broadcast a few of the classic songs and the solo stuff. We cut all the cabaret out."

"I saw that show that he did in London [at Shepherd's Bush Empire]," says Nick Cave. "It was at the time the first of those *American Recordings* came out, I guess. It was in three parts. He did early stuff with a small band, and then in the middle he sat and played this new stuff on the guitar by himself, and then at the end June came out, and it was a big kind of knees-up end to the whole thing. And it really showed these three sides of him in quite an unconscious kind of way. When he did this stuff in the middle it was spine-chilling ... so beautiful, and so wracked at the same time. And such a contrast to that early stuff. Then he went on and did the thing with June Carter, doing 'Jackson' and all that kind of stuff, slapping their knees. I could be reading things into it, but he looked on stage as if he was quite uncomfortable doing that: that he was now somewhere else. It was when he was doing that stuff on his own that it was just so beautiful."[1]

There was, indeed, a degree of sufferance in keeping elements of his old show going. "I'll do ['A Boy Named Sue'] but I hate to have to," he said in 1993. "It's not funny to me any more."[2] But he was aware that he had a loyal audience to satisfy, who had stuck by him through thick and thin, and he wasn't about to alienate them simply for the sake of appearances, or indeed to completely indulge his own artistic cravings.

He was always very proud of having June by his side and letting her participate in this resurgence, but the abrupt gear change in Cash's music and image meant some of his family were a little worried about how it would affect his home life. June had invested an enormous amount of love, effort, energy, and devotion into protecting and supporting Cash, helping him rebuild his reputation and being instrumental in perpetuating the image – however hokey and fundamentally one-dimensional – that this was an archetypal country music family. Now her husband was once again making dark, damaged music, and lurching around in videos killing young girls and sticking them in the trunk of his car. As an artist herself she understood his need to be energised and to keep moving forward, but the transition didn't necessarily sit easily. It may have reminded her of less happy, less secure times. Theirs was not the fairytale marriage it is so often portrayed as being. They were both strong-willed and argued often.

"It was a tricky thing to navigate for June," says Rosanne Cash. "He'd had this kind of family country thing, and now here he is stripped down to nothing, just him and a guitar playing at the House Of Blues, for God's sake. I was a little worried, like: I hope they know how to navigate this properly. But they did."

There was another narrative strand to Cash's re-emergence with *American Recordings*, something much bigger and wider that would reshape the industry in the years to come. The rise of CDs in the late 80s and beyond meant that catalogues were now being treated with more respect; instead of simply being ransacked every so often for cheap compilations, usually with a lack of quality control, they were being curated. It gave an impetus to the careers of many artists, not least Bob Dylan, whose *Biograph* anthology was one of the first of its kind to appear in 1985, and whose first three volumes of his continuing *Bootleg Series*, released in 1991, set the benchmark for re-evaluating the work of musicians who were seen to be a little past their prime.

The idea of the 'legacy artist' was emerging, centred around re-examining and recontextualising an artist's past work. Instead of trying to reinvent and escape the past, it became more rewarding for musicians to embrace it, acknowledge it, and wrestle with its meaning. There was an acceptance that, after unsuccessful travails in the 80s spent trying to figure out where they fitted in to the musical landscape, many of these artists might be better served going back to basics. 'Just do what you used to do' became a mantra, and there was a new audience emerging who were young enough not to have their perceptions tainted by what had occurred in the 70s and 80s. They could connect the dots between the 50s and 60s and the 90s without worrying about what came in between.

Cash undoubtedly benefited from this sea-change. In 1992 Columbia had compiled the excellent three-disc overview of his CBS years, entitled *Essential Johnny Cash 1955–1983*. It hadn't sold especially well but it was warmly received critically and it helped put his old work into a new light. His whole span was here, and it was plain to anyone with a working set of ears that this was remarkable stuff, even if the quality tailed off toward the middle of disc three. There's no question it alerted critics to Cash's enduring prowess as an artist just at the time when he was engineering *American Recordings*. Meanwhile, the record itself, when it arrived, was partially about the almost impossible task of a mere man matching up to his legendary status and his vast, dark iconography, the love/hate wrestling match he fought with his past. Everything seemed to be pulling in the same direction all of a sudden.

With *American Recordings,* Cash once again became the country artist of choice for people who didn't like country music. Perhaps it was because he wasn't really country music at all. Once again he belonged to punks, college kids, preachers, folkies, convicts, alt-rockers, patriots, liberals, junkies, rebels, rednecks, progressives, hippies, and hillbillies. He was timeless, again. He had a platform all laid out for him to do whatever he wanted, and an audience primed to listen. Best of all, according to Rubin, he became "obsessed with wanting to do great work. It was about everything being great and whatever it took".[3]

11

I Won't
Back Down

fter the success of *American Recordings* all Cash wanted to do was keep going. Although he was still only 62, keeping going wasn't as easy as it sounds. To put his age in context: Bob Dylan is still rolling around the USA and the world in his late sixties, while Paul McCartney and countless other musicians are doing the same, looking lithe of limb and showing few signs of major wear and tear. Cash's dear friends Kris Kristofferson and Willie Nelson are both well into their seventies and yet show few signs of stopping.

Cash was not an old man in years, but the cover of *Unchained* tells its own story. Released a little over two years after the first, his second album with Rubin featured on its front a man who seemed to have aged a decade in the intervening period. His hair had greyed and thinned, his face had softened and lost much of its definition. Still only in his early sixties, he looked shockingly old.

"The next time I went out to Nashville to his house to do the shoot," says Andy Earl, who once again took the cover photograph, "it was only a couple of years later, but he had aged enormously. His face had changed slightly and he was [physically] much slower. He took us round the farm in his old Land Rover, which had flowers painted all over it. We came out to a corner of the field, desolate, an old barn there, and he said: I know, I know, this is the kind of stuff you're looking for! He was very fragile, he had to sit down all the time, and I initially felt quite uncomfortable photographing him. Before, he had such gravitas and strength and power to the way he looked; going into this period he was more frail. One of the [pictures] we did was for *My Mother's Hymn Book*. I photographed him holding the hymn book and I cropped his face out. To me, that kind of summed it up in a slightly more abstract and delicate way."

Cash was once again enduring a torrid time with his health. His swollen jaw continued to give him constant pain and had now been operated on 34 times, but to no gain. More significantly, he had begun suffering the effects of what was initially diagnosed as Parkinson's disease: he had shaking spells, he lost his balance, and sometimes struggled to sing.

Cash and his producer kept in close contact throughout the period between the first and second records. While Rubin was working on a plethora of other projects and Cash was away touring with his band, or making the final Highwaymen album and going on the road with them, they would send each other cassettes and CDs. Sometimes they contained up to 30 songs, sometimes just one; later they would discuss their preferences on the phone, debating why they thought a song might work, worrying away "to find the core of what was possible", as Rodney Crowell puts it. Cash recalled they eventually recorded around 50 songs; 14 were used on the album.

They had developed a shared language, but even Cash was shocked when Rubin suggested Soundgarden's 'Rusty Cage' as a potential song choice. The missing link between blues, grunge, and metal, it was a full-tilt hard-rock song from their album *Badmotorfinger*. Chris Cornell's high-octane vocals screamed at the top end of the register, scaling the kind of snow-tipped peaks that Cash could only gaze up at from his imperious base at the foot of the mountain. "I just couldn't see me doing it," he later admitted, "didn't think it would work at all."[1]

Rubin was trenchant, however, and recorded an acoustic demo of the song with him singing and Dave Navarro on guitar before Cash could begin to see the possibilities. Even then, the pair chiselled out a more definable melody and added a twanging guitar figure not unlike the one from '(Ghost) Riders In The Sky' to hold the whole thing together. When Cornell, its composer, heard the song he said approvingly: "He just made it sound like he wrote the song. That's what you're supposed to do with a cover and that's what he did."[2]

There was a important lesson in the deconstruction of 'Rusty Cage' that served Cash and Rubin well right up until the end of the collaboration: the musical structure of any song could always be demolished and rebuilt to fit Cash's voice and sensibilities. What was important, what was *always* absolutely crucial, was the emotional resonance of the words Cash sang. "'I'm going to break this rusty cage' is as powerful as 'I Walk The Line'," says Rodney Crowell, and he's absolutely right. Scattered with references to broken nails, boiling blood, dinosaur bones, it is a song about intense suffering, entrapment, but also about liberation. Once Cash got the measure of 'Rusty Cage' it proved easy to record; they ran through it once and it was done.

Cash was remarkably open to suggestion and experimentation, even when he was being given a bum steer. At one session Rubin suggested they try a version of Robert Palmer's 'Addicted To Love'. "We recorded a basic track of it, and it was hard to stop from laughing," said Heartbreakers' guitarist Mick Campbell. "But the thing is, Johnny wasn't laughing. He was totally caught up in it, trying to learn it and find a way into it: 'Might as well face it, you're addicted to love ...'"[3]

For all Cash's poor health, *Unchained* is certainly the most sparky and vibrant of all the Rubin collaborations. The series of *American* albums is often characterised – dismissed, sometimes – as being all shadow and no sun, but there's an abundance of joy and a wonderful snap and snarl to some of the more upbeat performances on *Unchained*.

Recorded over a period of six months, primarily in Ocean Way's Studio 2 in Hollywood, with overdubs added and mixing completed at Rubin's home studio (which he had dubbed the Akademie Mathematique of Philosophical Sound Research), *Unchained* quite deliberately has a very different feel to *American Recordings*.

"We wanted to give the disc a vintage character," said the album's engineer, Sylvia Massey. "I relied on the help of classic broadcast compressors to achieve the album's unique sound. I would drag my racks of vintage gear to the sessions, loaded with old radio compressors and oddities that no other studios had. Out of those racks, we found the signature sound for Johnny's voice for the record: the Gates Sta-Level tube-limiting amplifier. It was the only special item I brought to vocal sessions. Rick ... wanted simplicity in the way it was recorded and mixed."[4]

Realising that another album of purely acoustic material would have seemed like mere repetition, and mindful of the quality of some of the unused group recordings they had made in 1994, Rubin paired up Cash with Tom Petty & The Heartbreakers as his core band, augmented by appearances from Mick Fleetwood and Lindsey Buckingham from

Fleetwood Mac on 'Sea Of Heartbreak', with Flea from Red Hot Chili Peppers contributing some bass.

For half of the record they cooked up a joyous, rough-and-ready mix of alt.country and old school rock'n'roll, like The Tennessee Three with 200 volts fired through them. Perhaps *Unchained*'s greatest legacy, and one that now seems to be overlooked, is that it is the last sighting of Cash as a swaggering force of nature, cutting loose and singing about "long-legged girls" and wayward women leaving on the eastbound train. It's the last time his voice was able to carry that kind of wallop and really cut through; from hereon until his death, the power burned at a lower heat and came from a very different source.

'Never Picked Cotton', 'I've Been Everywhere', and especially 'Mean Eyed Cat' and the transcendentally wired 'Country Boy', a fizzing reworking of the song from his debut album *With His Hot And Blue Guitar*, are just terrific, the quintessence of window-rattling, tree-shaking good-rocking. An entire album of this kind of glorious racket would have made for a truly fantastic rock'n'roll album of a kind Cash hadn't made since the early 70s, and which would have given his early Sun records a run for their money in terms of raw power.

But in the end *Unchained* is an album of two distinct moods, embracing his abrasive earthly struggle and the more contemplative, eternal, and quietly agonising search for heavenly peace. He would record the more energetic material during the day and then, as night fell and his stamina waned, his thoughts would turn to slower, softer songs.

Of these, Josh Haden's 'Spiritual' is the standout track, a performance as deeply felt as anything he had ever sung, wrenched from the depths of his soul. Pitched somewhere between a hymn and a southern soul ballad, it's beautifully produced, a lone mandolin twinkling into life half way through, the power of the music slowing building with Cash's deeply moving vocal. It's wonderful to really hear him pushing himself as a vocalist, singing in an octave span.

With it's central refrain of "Oh Jesus, I don't want to die alone", 'Spiritual' sketched out the emotional territory Cash would map more assiduously with his final two albums. There is nothing exclusive and pious about it; it's a simple testament of faith and fear that reaches out to everyone. "I remember listening to that song with my dad's mother and she just wept like a baby," says Chelsea Crowell. "She was old Southern Pentecostal from Texas, she was 72 at the time and she had a very emotional and religious experience hearing it. And so did I, and I was only 13 or 14. Talk about reaching everybody. That was a first hand experience of his ability to do that."

The title track is cut from similar cloth. Written by the relatively unknown songwriter Jude Johnstone, a friend of Cash's daughter Kathy, it's replete with that stiff, dignified, hymn-like quality that Cash devours, but it's more ponderous than uplifting. Petty's 'Southern Accent' is similarly noble but also a little dull. It's a beautifully pitched performance, Cash wading in as deep as his memories, but there's something sluggish about it.

"If I can't make these songs my own, they don't belong," said Cash in the liner notes. He doesn't quite succeed on parts of *Unchained*. There's no doubt that he claims 'Sea Of Heartbreak', a great climbing country standard that he'd been singing almost since it was written, so much so that he felt it was "my song now".[5]

Here, his performance brooks no argument, and he certainly captures the essence of 'Rusty Cage' and 'Spiritual'. Some of the rest, however, seems a little more in love with the *idea* of Cash singing Beck's 'Rowboat' and Dean Martin's 'Memories Are Made Of This' than the reality.

Unchained is the weakest of the *American* albums because it doesn't seem quite sure of what it's supposed to be saying. Perhaps based on the mistaken belief that *American Recordings* had shown only one side of his personality, when it had in fact revealed almost everything, *Unchained* strives to cover more ground. It didn't help that after the explosion of new writing that held all the threads of *American Recordings* in place, 'Meet Me In Heaven' was the only new Cash song recorded this time. It's a good song, but it wasn't powerful enough to pull the album together. Despite the rich, black imagery – houses falling from the sky, blackbirds circling a castle keep – it is a song of eternal love that reaches from the transience of this passing world and travels "beyond the stars".

Cash was never a contrived artist but there is a hint of calculation about the composition of this record, a sense of trying to ensure that alternative radio and TV in the USA remained on board. Soundgarden's version of 'Rusty Cage' had been an MTV hit on its release as a single in 1992; its inclusion on the Cash album and its release as a single was a talking point that kept the hipsters interested, as was the Beck cover.

Someone was paying attention, of course, to the dreaded demographics. American Recordings' UK managing director Joe O'Neill said at the time of its release that "this album will appeal to a broader audience [than *American Recordings*]".[6] In the end the numbers, the 'business of the business', didn't back this statement up. *Unchained* was released in November 1996 to yet more ecstatic reviews, yet another Grammy (this time for Best Country Album), but to a *Billboard* chart peak of only Number 170. What it did become, importantly, was a bridge between the austerity of the previous album and the more painterly, finely realised band performances that would characterise the next. *Unchained* proved again that Cash could pull off contemporary material, but for maximum impact the song choices would have to be a little more astute.

Listening again to the hot-wired rumble of 'Country Boy' it's hard not to imagine the kind of kicks Cash could have had if he had taken this energy and this group onto the road with him. He loyally stuck with his own regular touring band, however, and in any case that side of his career was swiftly drawing to a close.

Cash had set out on his regular run of dates at the beginning of 1997, but by the autumn he was beginning to feel the pace. In September he called everyone involved in the tour to a meeting and said that he would be scaling things down gradually, with the aim of retiring from the road in 2000. In the event, the end came much quicker than that.

On October 25 1997, while playing a concert at the Whiting

Auditorium in Flint, Michigan, Cash became ill on stage and almost fell over. God knows it wasn't the first time he had faltered during a performance, but it would prove to be the last. Flint was the final full concert he ever played. There would be a brief appearance at the Hammerstein Ballroom in New York in 1999, during an all-star tribute concert held in his honour, featuring U2, Bruce Springsteen, and Bob Dylan, when he came on at the end to sing two songs. He also supported June at her own show at the Bottom Line, and he made a regular summer appearance in 2001 and 2002 at the Carter Family Fold in Hiltons, Virginia, a date he kept even after June's death, playing there in June and July of 2003. By then he could barely see and couldn't feel his fingers on the strings of the guitar, but he was desperately trying to find some way to connect with and honour the woman he had just lost.

He had announced to the audience at Flint that he was suffering from Parkinson's Disease, but this was a misdiagnosis. Four days later, on October 29 1997, Cash was hospitalised with pneumonia, diabetes and nerve damage. He was put into a medically induced coma, during which his family thought his time was finally up. "He had pneumonia, and his lungs were so weakened that they had to put him on a ventilator," said Rosanne. "And because they put him on a ventilator, he couldn't be conscious the whole time. So they put him under with medication, to keep him sedated and give his lungs a chance to heal. And they tried to bring him out, but he wouldn't come out."[7]

June publicly pleaded for all his fans to pray for him; Rubin hired a woman who apparently had special powers; the family kept a bedside vigil. And after 12 days, he woke up. Cash survived, but when he resumed consciousness he was told he had what was then called Shy-Drager Syndrome, named after the doctors who identified it in the 60s, but which was later known as Multiple System Atrophy. A complex degenerative neurological condition that affects nerve cells in the brain and leads to a multitude of symptoms affecting movement, balance, bodily functions and temperature, it has no cure. Life expectancy averages nine years, though it varies wildly, and disability often occurs much sooner.

Later, Cash's diagnosis would change again, to autonomic

neuropathy, a catch-all term for a similar group of degenerative symptoms. In his final years there was such a multitude of things wrong with him that, whatever name one wanted to attach to it, the spectre of debilitation and death rarely left his side. He was battling a bewildering array of foes. He had diabetes, asthma, respiratory dysfunction, glaucoma and partial deafness, and suffered from ultra sensitive nerve endings and abscesses, while his jaw remained ravaged by continuous pain that he likened to the bone being held against a fire.

And yet he still wanted to work. "I remember seeing him when he was really sick, when he had his ventilator on in hospital, and I got all my daughters together to say goodbye," says Rodney Crowell. "I said: he's not going to make it. I'd seen my father in that state and I thought he was done. A month later he was talking about songs he wanted to record, getting a song for me for an upcoming thing. He did 'I'm Never Going To Roam Again' [which appeared posthumously on *The Legend*]. I was like: man, I thought you were dead! In the midst of all that physical pain he created so much good stuff."

After the setbacks of the previous year, by April 1999 Cash was enjoying sufficiently better health to start recording again. The pre-production setup was much the same as before, a series of conversations flying back and forth between Rubin and Cash. Cash had an archivist's brain. From as far back as his concept albums of the 60s he took an obsessive approach to collecting material; for *Ballads Of The True West* in 1965 he interviewed songwriter Tex Ritter for many hours, in the process unearthing nearly 300 potential song choices. He loved disinterring old songs almost as much as he loved singing them; his mind was a vast reservoir of music and for *Solitary Man* he dived deep, retrieving old treasures such as 'That Lucky Old Sun', and finally claiming 'Mary Of The Wild Moor', a traditional song he had always wanted to record.

The song-gathering process may have run along familiar lines, but there was a significant shift in both mood and recording practices. From this point on, aged 67, Cash was living with hard evidence of his mortality and set about addressing it in his work in a much more direct manner. His world narrowed. No more touring, far less travel – writing and recording became his sole means of musical expression. The temptations of the dark side became less of a pressing issue, and in his work he began to think less about sin and redemption and more about the great sweep of his life and the advancing spectre of death. There was a realisation that now he could make music that truly reflected all his contradictions.

There was an ineffable sorrow in Cash, an inability to find true peace that troubled him his whole life and never ceased snapping at his heels. "He would come to the session every day dressed as if he were going to a funeral," says Sylvia Massey. "He had a sadness about him."[8]

Sometimes he ran toward it and at other times he tried to run as far away as he could. He had driven into the endless American plains to try to lose its scent, bombarded his mind and body with drink and drugs to shake free, crawled into caves and into the arms of a very conservative God to try and make it stop. But this restless soul was his centre, and his centre was where he was born to sing from. And so the conflict raged on. Only when some of his physical energy finally deserted him, and he no longer had the means to get himself into real trouble, could he really reflect on everything he had done.

The *American* albums were his songs of experience. *American Recordings* is about Cash wrestling with his past and his vast, dark mythology. It is an album about the historical weight of being Johnny Cash as much as anything else. *Unchained* is a lighter ride, Cash consolidating his success by showing a fuller musical range even if the cumulative punch is less hard-hitting.

With *Solitary Man*, he started singing from two ends of the human spectrum, dredging up old, familiar tunes from long ago that captured something profound and moving about life's fleeting joys and its more entrenched sadnesses; and also singing contemporary songs from deep within the here and now, trying to debrief himself of what he had learned throughout his extraordinary life, his hands tracing the line of every scar life had inflicted on him without shame or pity. He would tell his granddaughter Chelsea: "'Never trust anybody who doesn't have scars.' That was a direct quote," she says. "That's incredibly generous. I'm a total tom boy and I have them all over my body, and I think about that line several times a week sometimes. Those *American* albums are his scars, and much more beautiful because of it."

Solitary Man is the album that sealed the now popular if erroneous perception of the *American* albums as being almost exclusively concerned with mortality. Cash had never regarded death as a stranger. He was always aware it was only ever a hair's breath away, and now he faced it full on. "The songs just kept coming round about pain and death so I keep singing about it," he said.[9]

It was not just his own health that was failing. June's sisters Helen and Anita died in 1998 and 1999 respectively, and many more friends and family were passing on, but it is his own tread toward journey's end that brings something powerful to these performances and song choices. It sent the *American* series down a very different path – it solidified it as a concept: Cash on Cash. Because of his increasing frailty and breathlessness, his voice comes with a new rasp of humility, a quality always apparent in Cash as a man, but something his vast, cavernous baritone seemed almost genetically disinclined to convey.

Because of his health, the final two albums and the majority of the material on the two posthumous albums, *A Hundred Highways* and *Ain't No Grave*, were recorded almost entirely at Cash's cabin studio at Hendersonville, and even occasionally at Cinnamon Hill in Jamaica. He now preferred to be at home, visiting California only infrequently to see Rubin and occasionally to record a vocal with other people. Rubin would come down to Tennessee to discuss projects and talk things through with Cash, but he was not on hand in Hendersonville as a day-to-day figure; from here on he took on an executive role, although he still oversaw every part of the process and worked meticulously on the final tracks to get them absolutely right.

At the cabin, recording was overseen by engineer David Ferguson, with Cash's son John Carter Cash as associate producer and his son-in-law Jimmy Tittle, husband to his daughter Kathy, also lending a hand.

"*Solitary Man* is where I took the reins," says Ferguson. "All those records took a long time to make – record a lot of songs, pick a few. What would happen is Johnny and Rick would talk about what songs to record. He would send Rick songs, and they would swap back and forth ideas. Johnny being so open-minded about songs is really a big part of the success of the American Recordings records. Then we'd go over to the cabin, set up a bunch of equipment and record. He would get musicians to play with him. If someone was a great musician he loved them, didn't matter who they were. We'd record and then go through the stuff later. Then we'd take it out to Rick's place in California and finish it, overdub some more people out there. Especially for that third record that was the process."

On *Solitary Man* there was a sparser band sound, an almost exact balance between albums one and two. There was no bass or drums, but some songs were fleshed out with piano, organ, accordion and fiddle, backing vocals and additional guitars; others were just voice and guitar, which once again was the binding combination. Who played guitar depended initially on who was around in Hendersonville: Cash picked along, of course, and at other times Marty Stuart, Larry Perkins, Randy Scruggs, Norman Blake, and Mike Campbell provided the backing, sometimes playing along with Cash in Hendersonville, sometimes overdubbing their contributions later in California.

The result is a kind of stately, Gothic folk music. Severely weakened by age and illness, Cash no longer had the punch required to cut through a rock band. As his voice started to sound more ravaged, so the music became more stately and the shadows began to thicken and lengthen.

If the suitability of the contemporary choices on *Unchained* was moot, the ones on *Solitary Man* were exceptional. The outstanding performance is his reading of Nick Cave & The Bad Seeds' 1988 single, 'The Mercy Seat'. As deep and dark as the caverns of the sea, Cave sings the original as a death-row prisoner in the throes of being executed, preparing to meet his maker and putting what's left of his faith in divine rather than earthly judgement. "And anyway I told the truth / And I'm not afraid to die," he sings, over a block of churning noise that almost disguises the epiphanic punch-line: "But I'm afraid I told a lie." Has he been lying about his innocence all this time? If so, he's about to get found out. Or is he simply lying about his courage in the face of death? If so, again he's been found out. Guilt, sin, faith, redemption, and the measuring of truth in the face of imminent death. How could Cash have resisted?

"I got a call from Rick Rubin that Johnny Cash wanted to record it and was that all right," said Cave later. "That was pretty exciting. The version is so good. He just claims that song as he does with so many. There's no one who can touch him. I wrote and recorded that when I was fairly young, but he has a wealth of experience which he can bring. He can sing a line and give that line both heaven and hell."[10]

Cave didn't sing with Cash on the song, but the two finally got to sing together early in 2002, on Hank Williams's 'I'm So Lonesome I Could Cry', released on *The Man Comes Around*, and the traditional 'Cindy', released on *Unearthed*. Finally their paths crossed, a symbolic handshake.

Cash loved 'The Mercy Seat' but it was not an easy song to get to grips with. "Johnny had a hard time with 'The Mercy Seat'," says David Ferguson. "He came out to finish that record in California and he wasn't in the best health at that time. I remember picking him up at the Four Seasons and he said: 'Man, I've got this "Mercy Seat" hanging over my head, I don't know if I can do it. I like it, but I don't know if it's for me, I don't know if I can feel it.'

"It's a complex song, and it's a different beat than he was used to singing on," Ferguson continues. "A lot of songs he would find it difficult to put it where Rick wanted it, but Rick's very patient."

The music resets Cash's voice in a rich, fantastic new musical context, a rolling, Gothic rumble, hugely dramatic and affecting. And the humbling of that once-mighty baritone had become an asset; now there's a crack to let the light in. Nonetheless, Rubin recalls that Cash would get terribly frustrated by his physical frailties. Some days his voice would be fine and he could sing well; other days he could barely catch his breath and he would become exhausted very easily. No matter what happened in the past, he had always been able to work; now, some days he couldn't, and even when he could, he was not always happy with what he produced.

"I know there were times when he wished his voice was better," said Rubin. "Sometimes he felt embarrassed, and it really took the people around him to say: this is beautiful, and we love it. And again, he trusted the people who were saying that because we really did feel that way."[11]

It certainly added a whole new level of poignancy and urgency to the songs, a factor that Rubin exploited. Filled with compassion for Cash as a man, he also still believed in him as an evolving artist, and was determined to pick songs that would continue to resonate with the circumstances of the man singing them. Often, Cash's obvious weakness completely upturned the meaning of familiar material. His cover of U2's 'One', already a deeply moving, bittersweet song, comes packed tight with the extra weight a man of his age and experience could bring to it. "All of a sudden the words took on a whole new seriousness," said Rubin. "[U2] said that when Johnny sang it, the words rang true in a way that was different from what they had heard before."[12]

"Sometimes there's a line of truth and purity in songs, and maybe it's always based on looking back rather than looking forward," says Adam Clayton. "I can understand people wanting music with a bit more lushness, but that's not what those recordings are about. They step into Leonard Cohen territory, in a sense, where it's all about the voice and the tone and making that connection. He was willing to admit his humanity was very frail; that's really what made him such a powerful icon of that era. It wasn't sugar-coated, it was real and it was nasty."

'I Won't Back Down' ("you can stand me up at the gates of Hell") and Neil Diamond's 'Solitary Man' both – perhaps a little too obviously – were chosen to embody some of Cash's core traits: his resilience, his stubborn tenacity, his essential aloneness in the face of some terrible impending battle. His wry, amused reading of the old vaudeville song 'Nobody' covers the same territory with a lighter touch.

There was new Cash. 'Before My Time' is a lovely, sun-dappled moment of quiet nostalgia that touchingly notes Cash's general inconsequence in the great scheme of things, how all his words of love and devotion have been expressed countless times by countless others over hundreds of years, and yet here he is saying it again to his beloved as best he can.

There was also old Cash. He revisited 'Country Trash', a self-deprecating obscurity from his 1973 album, *Any Old Wind That Blows*, strummed idly as though he were killing time beneath an old tree between shifts working in the field. He had some laughs with his old friend Merle Haggard on 'I'm Leavin' Now', originally recorded for Columbia just over a decade earlier. It seemed like another world from this one. He even managed a whooping 'Adios!'

The most obvious new development on *Solitary Man* was the addition of several guest vocalists, almost certainly invited to appear not just to bolster Cash's cool credentials (and top up their own), but also to colour in some of the gaps left by his vocal decline. Haggard came down to Hendersonvile to sing on 'I'm Leavin' Now'. Tom Petty, less involved this time around, flew down to sing on his own 'I Won't Back Down' and 'Solitary Man'. In Los Angeles, Sheryl Crow came in to play accordion on 'Wayfaring Stranger' and 'Mary Of The Wild Moor' and duet on the lilting, yearning 'Fields Of Diamonds'.

Will Oldham sang with him on 'I See A Darkness', the other contemporary composition on *Solitary Man* that succeeds in stretching all the way around Cash, the man and the myth. A song of awkward fraternity, according to Oldham, it was "an attempt to explore a particular kind of friendship and view of the world. There was an attempt to take Springsteen's use of 'darkness', as in 'Darkness On The Edge Of Town', and take it somewhere else, somewhere closer. Probably the biggest and most unexpected thing was how and what he brought to the session in terms of openness, humility, humanity, and energy. My expectation was that I would be meeting a man understandably crippled by his image and ego, not to mention his advanced age and health issues. All of these expectations were obliterated. He was good. He sang [it] in a way that is unique and powerful. He brought maturity to it and, mostly, fame".

Everything had to fit around the ebb and flow of Cash's health and mobility. "The thing about having guest stars is you just get them while you can," says David Ferguson. "If Johnny was in town of course he'd be there but he wasn't always there. When he was in LA we did as much as we could. He had a great work ethic. He'd show up about 11am and work until he was really tired and then go back to the hotel." When Cash was in Los Angeles he usually booked into the Four Seasons Hotel but sometimes stayed at Rubin's house, given a guest bedroom on the third floor with views looking out over the city. There was an elevator which took him down to the studio situated in the basement.

In October 1999 he caught pneumonia again and progress on the record stopped. "It kept me out of work for about six months each time," he said. "It's terrible. Pneumonia is just devastating. At my age it is anyway."[13]

"That was hard on him," says Martyn Atkins. "His appearance changed really quickly over that three, four year period. You hate to see him sick and feeble, but he really wanted to work and you'd put up a front and act like everything was normal, and got on with it."

When it was finally released on October 17 2000, *Solitary Man* featured on its cover a photo taken from back in the days when Cash was still touring. "I went down to Hendersonville to his house to take photos for the cover of the third album," says Atkins. "He'd had pneumonia, then got over it, and I went down there a few weeks after and he'd got really sick again. I tried to take a few photographs but it really wasn't nice because I felt I was shooting a guy who was really on his last legs. Rubin said that integrity and honesty were what Cash was all about, and maybe we should see photographs of him where he doesn't look good, but it was weird. You felt you were stealing somebody's soul. The photo we eventually used was backstage, I think from the Manhattan Center [in 1994]."

This kind of ambivalence about documenting Cash's decline both visually and aurally would grow into a distinct uneasiness amongst many critics, observers, and friends in the last couple of years of his life. But he was at the gates, and he was not for turning.

12

Drive On

In 2010, the British poet laureate Carol Ann Duffy described reading Ted Hughes's final poem 'Last Letter', written about the night his wife Sylvia Plath killed herself. It was, she said, "a bit like looking into the sun as it's dying. It seems to touch a deeper, darker place than any poem he's ever written". The same could be said of Cash's series of *American* records as they advanced toward their conclusion. They mined the darkness at the centre of the light, revealing the blackest black and the whitest white, his eternal conflict that needed to be sung out until the very end.

Cash recalled in his 1997 autobiography that when he had almost died in 1988 he felt himself fading into "the *essence* of light, a safe, warm, joyous brilliance".[1] His music in these last years became a kind of evolving reckoning, advancing toward that point of dazzling finality. There was an unmistakeable relish in his confrontation with his own demise; these were the stakes he's been playing for his entire life, and he raised his game accordingly

In the period following the release of *Solitary Man* in October 2000, Cash worked whenever he could. As his eyesight worsened through glaucoma, as the feeling left his fingers, as asthma gripped his lungs and his mobility decreased, he spent more and more time revisiting beloved stories, past moments, the enduring narratives of his life. The age of mastery. Weighing and measuring.

"I moved back to Nashville in 2001, and he was really getting sick around that time," says Chelsea Crowell. "I was at school at Belmont [university], where you had to take Bible Studies class. It was a couple of blocks from [Baptist] hospital, where he was at on and off. He couldn't read anymore, his eyes were so bad, so I'd bring over my Bible Studies book and sit with him in his room. His favourite book in the Bible was Ecclesiastes, and I'd sit and read to him and he'd pass on these stories. Simple stories. Not like: when I was with Bob Dylan ... More like: your grandmother and I were on the bus and it broke down in Mississippi one time ... He'd get tired quickly, but I have a ton of memories of very simple stories."

Solitary Man had featured just one new Cash original. The renewed vigour of his writing had been sapped immediately after he got sick in 1997, but with time and determination the strength in that muscle returned. A substantial portion of the last reserves of his energy were poured into his songwriting. By now, it was a matter of quality, not quantity. "He was still writing great songs right up to the end," says David Ferguson. "He wasn't writing as much as he had, if he had felt better he would have written more. Songs were working models. He'd do pieces of them, bits at a time, come in and say: I have the verse to that one now. '1 Corinthians' is great; '309' was another one."

'On The 309' is his last train song, Cash slinging his suitcase on board for the final time, the burner stoked with the fires of his defiant humour: "The whistle blows an' I'm gone again / It will take me higher than a Georgia Pine," he wheezes, sounding like an old engine himself as he bemoans the "asthma coming down". Now he couldn't focus on anything else other than the end of the line. There was no time to waste his shallow breath on frivolities.

Most frequently in his new songs he proclaimed his faith and mined the Bible. '1 Corinthians 15:55' is named from the lines it borrows – "O death, where is thy sting? O grave, where is thy victory?" – from that Biblical verse, which he used to begin a song about coming home to his Maker. The words are set to a peaceful, almost mocking sing-song nursery rhyme melody that suggests this last part of his journey was occurring in calm waters. There may have been a degree of wishful thinking involved. 'I Came To Believe' is about surrendering to the will of God, having the humility to admit he "needed help to get by". Like 'Redemption', it returns to the pain and loneliness he felt during his many shameful periods in the past, when he lost himself to pills, infidelity, and self-destruction, and recounts the point where he reached out to Jesus in "child-like faith".

The centrepiece of these final compositional flurries, and the only one that in the end made the album, was 'The Man Comes Around'. It rifled through Job, Matthew, and the Book of Revelation, referencing Judas, God, Alpha and Omega, Jacob's Ladder, the Four Horsemen of the Apocalypse, the Apostle Paul, and the Potter's Ground, a biblical term for a burial place for strangers. It was a song Cash worked on for months. Years, in fact. The catalyst had been a dream he'd had in Nottingham while touring Britain in the early 90s. In it he had met the Queen, who described him as being "like a thorn tree in a whirlwind". Cash had liked this phrase and written it down. Now he toiled as hard as his health would allow: honing, reshaping, getting it right. He worked on it like he had never worked on a song before, reducing it slowly from a thick sheaf of papers with endless stanzas and alternate lines to its final six verses, each one as powerful as a hammer blow.

Cash in all his past incarnations had never turned in a song quite as richly foreboding as 'The Man Comes Around'. It's a brilliant piece of writing, opaque and impressionistic in its language, yet forthright and clear-eyed in intent. Cash is contemplating the End Times. This is a premonition of judgement day, and "the man" – Jesus – is taking the final score. He is not doing the bidding of a benevolent God, but rather a God who treats everyone the way they deserve to be treated. Even now, when he could be forgiven for doing so, Cash did not take refuge in easy comfort. After 50 years of walking hither and thither, often losing his way, sometimes getting back on course, this is the sound of Cash at the gates, arms open, undaunted and unaffected, saying 'Here I am.' But the bar for salvation is raised high indeed. There's no guarantee he will make the cut. He knows his failings all too well.

It's a brooding gem of a song, studded with apocalyptic menace but with a wry sense of fun skimming through its tick-tock melody. Cash was obviously and justifiably proud of it, spending the lion's share of his liner note of the album discussing its provenance and its meaning. It is his final masterpiece, and one suspects he knew it.

In these final years and months Cash was not doing anything quite so straightforward as simply making another album. A series of focused bursts of intense writing and recording intended both to belie and document his frailties, his efforts spoke of a calling far beyond a concern with units and release schedules. His work had become a matter of life and death. "Clarity seems to come to you whereby you don't necessarily have to work any more, but you choose to because it's the only thing you know," says Adam Clayton. "And that keeps you alive, in a way. I think that gives you a reason to get up in the morning, and becomes very valuable. That seemed to be where Johnny was."

"I worked ... in spite of everything," Cash said. "I found strength to work just to spite this disease. Sometimes I came to the studio and I couldn't sing – I came in with no voice when I could have stayed at home and pouted in my room and cried in my beer or my milk, but I didn't let that happen. I came in and opened up my mouth and tried to let something come out. There are tracks I recorded when that was the last thing in the world I thought I could do, and those are the ones that have the feeling and the fire and the fervour and the passion. A great deal of strength came out of that weakness."[2]

More than ever this time, the material selected had to fit. "They were wide open to suggestion," said Cash's manager, Lou Robin. "John and Rick would often exchange cassettes of songs that they'd heard someone else sing that they liked, or a new song that John had written, like 'The Man Comes Around'."[3] There was a high rate of attrition. On one tape compilation that Rubin sent to Cash, he included two songs by The Cure: 'Never Enough' and 'Lovesong'. Cash listened and never mentioned them again.

On the same tape was another track he also felt wasn't right for him: 'Hurt' by Nine Inch Nails, six minutes of despair and self-loathing from Trent Reznor's suicide concept album *The Downward Spiral*. Rubin felt it was another one of those all-important trigger songs. Cash wasn't convinced. "We were looking for a song that we felt had an impact," said Cash. "[Rick] found this one and he asked me what I thought of it. I said: I think it's probably the best anti-drug song I ever heard, but I don't think it's for me. It's not my style, it's not the way I do it."[4]

They were back in 'Rusty Cage' territory, although in fact 'Hurt', even in its original form, is not quite the slavering Gothic monster it's sometimes depicted as being. It's a relatively approachable piece of music: it has a clear melody, has very little of the pneumatic industrial clatter often found on NiN's records, and for the most part Reznor's voice barely rises above a whisper.

Still, it came at Cash from left field and he was caught off guard. Rubin eventually persuaded him to try it, asking him to look beyond the abrasive surface and explore the personal resonance in the words. 'Hurt' is a song about the terrible damage we inflict on ourselves, the urge to self-harm in order simply to feel. It was a subject that Cash understood all too well, and he turns it from a song explicitly about addiction into a song about his own pain and loneliness. When he sings "I remember everything" it seems to carry the weight of all he had seen and done and lost and won and written and sung up to that point. His version, almost inevitably, also acknowledges the process of ageing, tracking his transformation from the monolithic, unbreachable specimen he had once seemed to be into the gnarly, damaged man now confronting him when he looked in the mirror. He sings "What have I become?" with devastating self-awareness.

"I probably sang the song 100 times before I went and recorded it, because I had to make it mine," he said. "It's a song I wish I had written. Back in the 60s I think I could have written something like this."¹ Perhaps. But it is a song heavy with experience and regret and wisdom; the long shadows cast by age and time make it truly unforgettable. Aside from the layers of meaning he brought to the lyric, Cash's version is also a superbly dramatic piece of music. Particularly effective is the staccato piano hammering away at a single note, building in power and increasing the tension as the song forges to its climax.

'Hurt' was a match for 'The Man Comes Around' in its resonance and impact. Combined, these two songs gave Cash an immensely powerful platform from which to contemplate the rest of the album. Rubin, as ever, nosed out songs he felt Cash could inhabit from all over the range. He encouraged him to see the words in fresh contexts, to frame them in a way that would make sense at this stage in his life. This approach worked not only for 'Hurt', but also for his interpretation of Ewan MacColl's classic folk composition 'The First Time Ever I Saw Your Face'.

"It's a love song, but I asked him to not sing it as a love song to a person, but as a love song to God," said Rubin. "That idea really excited him, and it gave him a point of view. Sometimes, before starting a song, I would just say: think about this – whatever that might be. The idea was to give something a new point of view, or give it a touchstone."[6]

His version of Depeche Mode's pounding electro-blues 'Personal Jesus' was another example of Cash twisting the meaning. The original was a song about giving yourself over completely to a lover, idolising them to obsessive, disturbing lengths until they became God-like; in Depeche Mode's version, the religious framework was all metaphor. Cash demolished this dual meaning and simply turned it into a evangelical hymn to his own, very idiosyncratic faith; in his hands it really *was* personal, a message to a God who he felt finally understood him and whom he understood in return.

Rubin held doggedly on to the founding ethos of the American records. Cash – or at least the enhanced version of him, the one characterised by Kris Kristofferson in his song 'The Pilgrim: Chapter 33' as "partly truth and partly fiction" – was the crucible in which these songs made sense. The material he was now singing went "in so many different directions but they all come together in a one-ness with me: that I could make these songs my own. They come together in being my songs. The theme is spirit, the human spirit more than the spiritual or godly spirit, the human spirit fighting for survival. It probably reflects a little of the maturity that I've experienced with the pain that I've suffered with the illnesses that brought me so close to death."[7]

Mostly this theme was referenced with originality, grace, and power; occasionally it felt a little heavy-handed. Rubin rarely deployed the subtlest of strokes when it came to publicly presenting Cash as an artist. He liked painting on a big canvas, and sometimes the choice of material explicitly referring to Cash's failing health felt overplayed.

The hymn-like ballads fail to spark into life – they can seem obvious and even crass, toppling under the weight of all the heavily signified portentousness. Cash's take on The Beatles' 'In My Life' veers toward the limp and maudlin; 'Bridge Over Troubled Water' is dull and ponderous. 'Danny Boy' was recorded at the St James Episcopal church in Los Angeles, with Benmont Tech playing the church's beautiful pipe organ. Not everyone fell for its austere, cracked emotion, but Cash loved it. "The session lasted about two hours and it was over," he said. "Just exactly the way we had hoped and planned and prayed it would be. It really adds an element that I've never had on record before. Never had anything like that."[8]

Which is true. But Cash seems looser and more vibrant when freed from the shackles of material laden with so much telegraphed 'significance'. 'Sam Hall' really scoots along, an outlaw song with bawdy saloon bar piano and Cash dredging up a holler of defiance: "Damn your eyes!"

'Tear Stained Letter', an old Cash original from *A Thing Called Love* in 1972, recalls the swashbuckling tyrant of old. He also plays some interesting games with his past cowboy outlaw image. The traditional 'Streets Of Laredo' is one last gunslinger song, played dark and true, but 'I Hung My Head' is more layered. Written by Sting as a pastiche/tribute to the kind of cowboy morality tale that Cash had practically patented throughout his career, sung by Cash it acknowledged the long shadow of his own greatness. After all, without Johnny Cash, 'I Hung My Head', a pale echo of songs like 'Folsom Prison Blues', as well as the traditional 'Long Black Veil', couldn't have been written. "This is really one of *my* songs," he seems to say, and made it so, despite its second hand provenance.

The brilliant, lazy stroll through 'We'll Meet Again' is an inspired payoff – a jaunty salute, a raised hat, lacking any twinge of self-pity. All that's left is a bareback ride through the classic stranger song 'Big Iron' – and he's off. Who was that masked man?

The Man Comes Around sessions were punctuated by the appearances of several guest stars, some of whom ended up on the album, some of whom later featured on posthumous releases, and some of whom are on both. During 2002 there were times when Rubin's home in Los Angeles seemed like the central meeting place for all Cash-related communal gatherings: Joe Strummer stopped by, Tom Petty & The Heartbreakers were always around; Nick Cave dropped in. Don Henley, Billy Preston, Sheryl Crow ...

"You never knew who might turn up," said Lou Robin. "I was there the afternoon Joe Strummer showed up. I walked into the studio at Rick's house, and there were a lot of people there in the control room, and here was a guy sitting in the corner of the room on the floor. And finally I said to someone: who is he? This was Joe Strummer. So I met him, and he said: I'm so thrilled to be here, I just don't want to be in anyone's way. He cut a couple of songs with John, he gave John a couple of other songs that he wanted him to have. That's the way it was: people would just come and go."[9]

"Joe Strummer was hanging around there, he was a really lovely guy," says David Ferguson. "He loved it. He laid on the floor watching through the baffle at Johnny singing, just amazed. Fiona Apple was really nice and friendly. Tom Petty just loved Johnny Cash, he worked and worked on it. Don Henley came in. I'm not going to go into too much detail about Don Henley ... Nick Cave was good. He might have been a little strange, I can't tell."

Cave came to LA in March 2002, finally meeting one of his most significant and enduring influences. They sang 'I'm So Lonesome I Could Cry', a standout performance on the record, and 'Cindy', which later showed up on *Unearthed*. He knew Cash was ailing but he wasn't quite prepared to witness the state of his health first hand.

"If he went from light into dark he couldn't see; he was basically blind for ten minutes, so when he came into the studio he looked real ill, and was helped down the stairs by two people," Cave said. "He had his arms out in front of him going: are you there Nick? Are you there? And I'm like, fucking hell, how's this guy going to be able to sing anything? Let alone get down the stairs. So it was quite a shock. He sat down and his eyes adjusted to the light, so he could see, and we sat around and talked about things for a while. In some ways when I was sitting there talking to him I was kind of wondering how this man was going to be able to sing anything at all, [but] when he started singing all his illness just seemed to fall away. He became energised by that. There was just this real strength – this force of nature that came out of him. It was two hours, and I walked out thinking: fuck, what happened then? That was the extraordinary thing. I felt I had really seen something that for me was hugely comforting, and inspirational, and truly incredible."[10]

It was a rare sighting of Cash at work in Rubin's Akademie Mathematique of Philosophical Sound Research. He now recorded almost exclusively within a few hundred yards of home: at his cabin studio, or in his late mother's house across the street, or even in his house, in the round room overlooking the lake. He recorded directly to Pro-Tools through a Universal Audio 6176 610 Valve Mic-Amp. If he was in Jamaica, where he spent increasing amounts of time to escape the winter weather, he could record onto a Roland VS-2480 desktop audio workstation.

"Rick didn't come to Nashville [much] any more and Johnny didn't really go there [to Rubin's house]," says Ferguson, who was once again chief engineer. "I'd work on the tracks in both places. In Nashville there was quite an array of people to play with John: Cowboy Jack Clement, Mark Howard, Randy Scruggs, Pat McLaughlin. Johnny would be in different moods for different folks. Of course John Carter was always there as associate producer."

Cash's health problems meant that, even as his voice and his themes were being boiled down to their most elemental characteristics, the process of capturing it all on tape became much more complex. The lyrics were printed out in 18 point bold print – you can see the sheets with their huge lettering in the photographs included with the album – while just capturing his voice on tape was increasingly tricky. Everyone had to play quietly and everything had to be close-miked. There had to be enough separation between Cash's vocal and the musicians he played with so they could later isolate his voice when it was taken to Los Angeles for overdubs to be added. Most of all these Nashville sessions were all about ensuring that there was any kind of vocal to work with at all.

"Recording the vocal could be really tough," says Ferguson. "It was hard to muster up the energy and get his voice working. He was singing very soft and he'd give you a few passes and he'd say: that's it, that's the best I can do on that, and move on. Some things we would only sing once and that was it. I don't think any of those have ever come out."

Since the first *American* album was recorded in 1993 the process of recording Cash had become significantly more hi-tech, complicated and sophisticated. *American Recordings* is audio vérité at its most stripped down – everything on that record occurred exactly as the listener hears it, accidents and all. There is, however, nothing accidental about the construction of the music on *The Man Comes Around*, nor spontaneous. Despite appearing to offer the stark, unvarnished truth, both emotionally and aurally, Cash's final recordings are wholly artificial constructs, laboriously pieced together.

If writing and singing had become a heroic act of will on his part, crafting his original vocal into a piece of music that remained true to his vision and yet was also suitably defined for general release required feats of often dazzling technical skill from Rubin and his team of engineers.

"It was very complex, and it was tough music to make," says Ferguson. "The whole point of anybody playing with Johnny [in Nashville] was to get the vocal. I'd do stuff at the Cabin and then we'd go to LA and replace the band. If anything still worked we would use it, of course, but for the most part we replaced everything. We'd put his voice to a click and then the [new] band would play along just like Johnny was singing it in the headphones. They'd overdub to a click and Johnny's voice, and they would do it as a [live] band for the most part."

Almost like the process of restoring a fragile work of art, making *The Man Comes Around* – and the posthumous albums *A Hundred Highways* and *Ain't No Grave* – was about preserving the moment of original inspiration, then going to often painstaking lengths to construct an appropriately authentic structure around it. They even added tape hiss.

These recordings are acts of emotional preservation, taking the core truth of Cash's vocal and then building a setting in which that truth is not only protected, but in which it can bloom and reverberate. The first, last, and ongoing consideration was honouring the meaning resonant in Cash's voice. Everything started and ended with that historic yawp placed front and centre, the totem around which all the other colours and textures were added. Often that was the only thing that was kept from the original Nashville tapes, but everything that was later added was done so in order to complement, strengthen, amplify and pay fealty to it. "It was all about mood with Rick, especially with John," says Ferguson.

This piecemeal process might appear to contradict the entire premise of the *American* albums – Cash: alone, late, ungroomed – but conceptually it was a perfectly fitting way for him to pull together the last climactic notes in his epic song. Now he was literally conducting the music and the mood – the entire truth of each performance – through his voice. For a man who strived always to sing himself, there was something rather wonderful about the way in which finally that inimitable voice – now stripped of its surface power yet somehow even more powerful for it – was writing the music.

The Man Comes Around was released on November 5 2002. It opens with the title track and follows with 'Hurt'. Bang! Bang! Have we got your attention? "Johnny would leave it up to Rick what went on the record, unless there was something he really wanted to be on there," says David Ferguson. "I remember *The Man Comes Around*, Rick and I had all the mixes, and Rick said: what kind of sequence will we do? I said: well, if we put one of Johnny's songs up front he's going to like it! So we put that on first, and then it doesn't matter."

'The Man Comes Around' had gone through several incarnations since Cash had had that strange dream in the East Midlands of England, and not only lyrically. Like the rest of the album, the final version was a mongrel mix of bottled lightning and lab-coated heavy lifting: it had an odd time signature; bars were chopped out, edited, shifted around. "There were several working versions of 'The Man Comes Around'," says Ferguson. "We did the final version with Rick, moved the tracks around a bit."

Cash's last album of his lifetime, *The Man Comes Around* divided reviewers, even those who had, certainly since *American Recordings*, traditionally greeted each new record with joy unconfined. *Mojo*, *LA Times*, *The Village Voice*, and *Uncut* loved it; but *Rolling Stone*, *Q*, and *Austin Chronicle* shivered with embarrassment at the croaky vocals and creaky phrasing, and felt that somehow this was an album too far. Some of his old friends and colleagues were also ambivalent about its musical merits. "I prefer to hear him sing 'Ring Of Fire' or something like that," says Jack Clement. "I wasn't knocked out personally by those records."

The Man Comes Around certainly raised some legitimate questions: Was the airing of all these fleshy frailties and failings a bold, fearless form of expression, a new kind of confrontational old man's music which turned pop's culture of youth on its head? Or was it undignified, slightly cringeworthy, distasteful even? There was some discomfort about the way in which a man's physical disintegration was so graphically documented. "We should turn and switch off the tape when our listening energy would be better spent *helping* a living songwriter/performer than marvelling at his or her mental or physical decrepitude," says Will Oldham, somewhat obliquely. Which begs the question: how much suffering do we really need to hear?

There is no definitive answer. In many ways the line drawn depends on the extent to which a listener has previously been paying attention. The *American* albums are very much part of a story, and *The Man Comes Around* makes perfect, deeply satisfying sense within that wider narrative. A knowledge and understanding of Cash's trials and travails, his journey, his myth, would help initially to orientate. From that point on, it is down to taste and human connection whether Cash's voice speaks to you or not. Context is important, too. Put on *The Man Comes Around* untrailed at a dinner party and it will struggle; it may even repulse, or invite ridicule. Listen to it alone in a time of need and it is more likely to be embraced, and embrace in return.

But it is not easy music. All powerful art is divisive, and this was far from the music of consensus. The *American* albums force us to ask awkward questions of ourselves and about the purpose of art in general, and not everyone – quite acceptably – wants that from their evening's entertainment. Even today, there's a suspicion that these recordings are more widely discussed, referenced, and contemplated in theory than regularly listened to; that's fine, too. They are valuable not simply for their content, but for the fact that they reflect a blinding spotlight back upon the artist: they tie together Cash's many incarnations; they show that his fires were still burning, that great work was still being made. And they prove beyond question that Cash was an outsider artist to the very end; he was not in the business of churning out mass-market product.

In an interview at the time of the album's release, Cash spoke proudly of *The Man Comes Around* and defiantly looked forward: "I firmly believe that it's the best record we've done. It reaches out even farther than the others, it goes in so many different directions. We take no prisoners, we do it the way we want to. And we look forward to the work to be done."[11]

This was Cash debriefing himself of what he had learned over his life, trying to make sense of it all and give the shadows some shape. And if you couldn't handle it? "Damn your eyes!" Lurking behind some of the more critical reviews was the suggestion – rarely stated, often implied – that Cash in his fading years was being manipulated, in a creative sense, by Rubin, steered in certain directions by the producer and too frail to resist. Or even that he was in no fit state to be recording at all.

"I've heard criticisms from certain people that Rick was kind of bleeding him dry by getting him back into the studio," says Nick Cave. "But I've gotta say, it was the other way around. He was energising this man and giving him something that he hadn't had for a while. Now there were certain songs that he got Johnny Cash to sing that were stepping into really risky areas, 'Personal Jesus' and stuff like that. It's risky, to haul this legend right up to the cliff face of contemporary music and expect him to do something with it. But I love the way he did those songs: the U2 song ['One'], they were great. And I think there were enough older songs to make those records really work."[12]

Cash was wholly aware of what he was doing and why. "I don't think you could say that my dad was unaware of the significance of *anything*!" says Rosanne Cash. "He got it. Rick truly loved Dad, and it was mutual. They were like brothers, and it seemed to be a kind of mystical connection. The music was just a natural expression that came from that deep connection."

Like them or not, the artistic choices Cash made were his own until the very end. He was much more passive in the 80s than he was now, ill and in his seventies. Playing up to his own iconography and his cracked grandeur – sometimes overstating the case, perhaps – was part of the deal, and he had to follow it through to the end. His faith afforded him the strength not to skirt around the issue. There are other examples of 'mortality albums' – Dylan's *Time Out Of Mind*, Warren Zevon's *The Wind*, Lou Reed's *Magic And Loss* – that have a similar kind of dark, elegiac resonance, but none of them is quite as direct and unflinching as *The Man Comes Around*. "That fearlessness at looking at your own mortality is the sign of a great artist," says Rosanne Cash. "It sent waves through the entire culture."

Mark Romanek's film for 'Hurt', which was released as a single in March 2003, was the final strand that pulled it all together, somehow encapsulating in four minutes not only everything the *American* series had been striving toward for the past decade, but the proud and painful path Cash had walked his entire life.

As originally conceived, the video was to be a somewhat theatrical piece shot on a soundstage in Los Angeles, featuring Johnny Depp and Beck. But in the autumn of 2002 Cash was too ill to make that idea work, and there was a little time to come up with another. Again, the mountain had to come to Mohammed, and Romanek was forced to find inspiration on the hoof at Hendersonville. It was Rubin who suggested using the House Of Cash museum, which had been closed for many years and was now in a semi-derelict state after suffering flood damage.

Thrumming with symbolism, it was a building Cash was very sensitive about. In 1996, when Andy Earl had visited Hendersonville to shoot the cover of *Unchained*, the House Of Cash was regarded as off-limits.

"It was all boarded up and locked, and he wouldn't let me take any pictures there," says Earl. "There were old gold discs, all smashed, a Cadillac in bits – it was stunning, but he was very much: 'This was what it was', and at that point he wasn't ready to expose that again."

Now, it seemed, he was prepared to be candid. When Romanek saw the museum he immediately recognised the obvious parallels between its decrepit state and Cash's ravaged health, and married the two together in a stunning piece of film-making which fused man and myth in an extraordinarily moving fashion. He mixed archive footage of Cash in his impossibly potent pomp, a swaggering approximation of immortality, with new shots of him in the present day, his skin mottled, lumpy and eerily waxy, his hair all but gone. He sits like Lear in a darkened room in the museum, surveying his broken "empire of dirt" while June looks on, a mixture of emotions which would take an eternity to fathom flitting across her strong, beautiful face. "This incredibly complex look," said Romanek. "Filled with love and earnestness and pride, and a certain amount of sadness."[13]

While the video for 'Delia's Gone' in 1994 had done much to re-establish Cash as a brooding, dangerous presence, the promo for 'Hurt' looked right over the edge of his darkness, into the abyss. 'Delia's Gone' may have been banned for its 'violent' imagery, but it was 'Hurt' that was truly, violently shocking. It's hard to believe there is less than a decade between the two.

"It's my favourite video ever by anybody, the only one where I've felt a real emotion," says 'Delia's Gone' director Anton Corbijn. "It's almost impossible in music videos to get that emotion, but this has an incredible weight of history. I always thought mine was the best Johnny Cash video until that point! Well, at least it was the best he made until 'Hurt'."

"When the video for 'Hurt' was done they sent each of his children a copy, and I didn't watch it," says Rosanne Cash. "My sister called me and said: have you seen the video yet?, and I said that I was a little nervous about it. And all she said was: be careful. So I didn't watch it. Then I was going to Nashville and I saw my dad and he asked me If I'd seen the video yet, and when I said no, he said: come in here and we'll watch it together. So of course I was just wrecked watching it, but he was completely clear-eyed, watching it from an artistic point of view: does it work, is it real, is it truthful? Completely detaching [himself] from his own physical disintegration. It was really amazing, and a real lesson to me. If he hadn't done that, it would have reeked of self-pity and sentimentality and it wouldn't have worked at all. But he didn't have an ounce of that in his body – ever, ever, ever in his life. It was not an emotion he ever traded in."

Indeed, Cash *played* his part in 'Hurt'. He wasn't just being passively filmed in the latter stages of disrepair. That would have been pathetic. He was acting: sweeping his arms dramatically in the air, pouring wine over the lavish feast set on the table in front of him, its riches mocking him, brooding dramatically at the piano. This was an artist very calmly and consciously capturing his own decline, because he knew how powerful it was as art, not just human history. For those who felt that Rubin was pulling his strings, it proved he was still more than capable of standing back and seeing himself objectively.

It was the 'Hurt' video that really catapulted Cash and his *American* records into commercial territory after a decade of acclaim but relatively modest sales. *The Man Comes Around* rose to Number 22 on the *Billboard* chart and was certified Platinum in the USA, denoting over one million sales, figures he hadn't enjoyed since *At Folsom Prison* and *At San Quentin*. He also forced his way back into the country pantheon on his own terms: the album went to Number Two in the country charts, 'Hurt' was given the Country Music Award for 'Single of the Year' in 2003 and was ranked as CMT's top video for that year. It also reached Number 33 on the Modern Rock Charts (unheard of for a 71-year-old) and was a Top 40 single in the UK, his first for almost 30 years. 'Hurt' won Cash a posthumous Grammy in 2004 for Best Short Form Music Video, and when Justin Timberlake won the Best

Male Video at the 2003 MTV Awards he called it "a travesty" that 'Hurt' didn't win. Few disagreed.

●●

'Hurt' was not just a final triumph both artistically and commercially. It was also designed to serve as an epitaph. Everyone was waiting for Cash to die. His imminent mortality was now hardwired into his music and his image. No one expected his wife to go first. Footage of June Carter Cash from 2002 fooling around singing 'Temptation' on stage with her husband reveals a shameless ham who loved her spot in the limelight and still seemed vibrant, joyful, and healthy. In the 'Hurt' video she was cast as the protector, gazing proprietarily over her husband.

She wasn't one to make a fuss. At the end of April 2003 June was admitted to hospital for what was expected to be fairly routine surgery on her gallbladder. While in hospital, doctors discovered problems with her heart, and her condition rapidly worsened. She died on May 15 2003, aged 73.

Cash was broken. Bereft. They had been together, after a fashion, for more than four decades, and married for 35 years. In the coming weeks he would pick up the phone and talk to her down the line; he would chat to her photograph. It was the kind of grief that made all his other physical ailments seem inconsequential.

In order not to have to dwell on his utter desolation any more than he was compelled to, he quickly expressed an almost obsessional desire to keep recording. "He was in the studio two days after June died," says Lou Robin. "That was one of her wishes, that he continue with his music."[14]

"It actually got more intense after June died," Rick Rubin said. "Before, we always worked kind of casually, either whenever we had a song or whenever he felt like recording. Now he said to me: 'I want to work every day, and I need you to have something for me to do every day. Because if I don't have something to focus on, I'm gonna die.'"[15]

"When my wife died I booked myself into the studio just to work, to occupy myself," Cash said. "I started recording all these things that

I found, songs that people had sent me. I've got a potful of them. That's what I'm gonna be doing for a while."[16]

Friends and family might drive over to the Cabin to see how he was getting on, check the fridge for a coke, grab a snack, say hello and hang out for a while, but it was clear he was there to work. There was an intensity to his determination, and everyone tried to facilitate it with a missionary zeal. Cash had a team around him who were ready to work any time he felt able, at a moment's notice. "I was on call all the time," says David Ferguson. "I had made an agreement with him, any time he wanted me – even if I had something else booked, I would change it or cancel it to come work for him. He knew that and appreciated it."

These final sessions created the bulk of the material released posthumously on *A Hundred Highways* and *Ain't No Grave*, and many more pieces that have yet to be released, and likely never will be. Many of the songs were ones already stored in his memory bank. This was a time for gathering up stray ends, not creating new ones. He finally finished '1 Corinthians 15:55' and 'On The 309', and recorded a new song called 'Engine 143'. Many more were old favourites, plucked from the ether.

"Johnny recorded around 60 songs," says David Ferguson. "Later, it got really hard for him to see, so he would lean more on songs that he knew. When you're in the kind of pain and bad health he was in, it's hard enough to learn a new song anyway. The older you get the harder it is to learn a new song, unless you write it. He'd try anything if he thought that it would fit his voice. Even if it didn't, he would try to make it work."

"June passed away, and he was determined just to stay busy making records," says Jack Clement. "He was fading, but he still wanted to record. I played rhythm [guitar] and dobro on a whole lot of that stuff. You'd be amazed at how many songs he did that he never recorded: Ink Spots songs, 'The Whiffenpoof Song', he just learned a lot of songs you'd never imagine he'd be singing. If he liked it, he liked it. I played dobro, Hawaiian style, on 'Aloha Oe', which he sings in Hawaiian. That was real close to his last session."

In the height of summer Cash was still defiant, talking about spending a month is Los Angeles to work with Rubin on a new album, but his health prevented it. Instead, the producer flew down to Nashville for a few days of recording and extended his stay because they "were on a roll".[17] However, during Rubin's visit Cash was hospitalised again. In the final few months he was wheelchair-bound and in and out of Baptist Hospital ICU Unit. He was aware that his time was short. "Occasionally I'd push him around the hallways in his wheelchair," says Chelsea Crowell. "He was very peaceful. It was very human – you're born, you live, you die."

Not everyone around him was so sanguine. "I still have some anger about his medical care," says Rosanne Cash. "I was talking to a doctor friend of mine about this and he said that famous people get the worst care, because the doctors just want to give them anything they want. They're in awe and they want to be their doctor, and they don't treat them with the same kind of care they would a normal person. My dad was on 30 different medications at the time of his death. He probably needed three of them. How about the contra-indications of all of them together? Of course it was raised at the time. My brother and I were so concerned about this and brought it up many, many times. He was so sick it was beyond addiction stuff, it was really hard to pull apart what was going on and what he needed, and it was also like: what's the point? Let him be comfortable."

Rubin also played an active role in trying to keep Cash both mentally and physically well. "Rick was trying to get him to refocus on his health," says Martyn Atkins. "He was on all these different prescription drugs, and Rick managed to get him to see a couple of good, modern specialists who didn't believe in giving you as many pills as possible. He tried to get him on a healthy food regime. He was trying hard to get him to do better things to enable his health to last. Which it did to some extent."

"In the last few months of Dad's life Rick was so concerned about his health," Rosanne Cash says. "We had several conversations about our mutual anxiety and concern, and Rick sent his own nutritionist/

physical therapist [Phil Maffetone] to Nashville to work with Dad, but by then of course it was too late. He was in a spiral."

There is a bright, brilliant heroism bound up in those last months of Cash's life. Everyone who talks about them does so with a kind of baffled awe, as though they still can't quite believe what he did and how he did it. As well as recording whenever he could, he also somehow found the strength to play at the Carter Family Fold on July 5. This was the historic seat of The Carter Family in Hiltons, Virginia, and the footage capturing Cash's performance is quite extraordinary. He is visibly shaking, near-blind, desperately weak, hoarse, heartbroken. And yet still he performs. His fingers can't feel the strings on his guitar. And yet still he plays. He can't sing. And yet still he sings. He rumbles through 'I Walk The Line' for his departed wife, an affirmation of faith and fidelity sent from one world to the next in the knowledge that they will soon be reunited. He sings 'Ring Of Fire' and there's a familiar look in his eye, a clear and strong sense of purpose which belies his broken voice and body.

It's uncomfortable viewing. This is not really music but something else. Brave and thrilling and affirming, yes, but also desperate and enormously sad. It would be remiss not to pause and note the pain, the huge cloud of sorrow hanging over it all. "I remember those months so vividly, and how excruciating they were," says Rosanne Cash, who still struggles to listen to the music Cash made in this last weeks, because "I don't want to be reminded of it in a more visceral way than I already am".

A much loved, truly irreplaceable man was going through his own private torture, and his family and friends were, in effect, watching him do so while at the same time watching him die.

The end wasn't a shock but it came relatively suddenly. Acting on medical advice after a bout of peritonitis, Cash had been unable to travel to New York to attend the MTV Video Music Awards in late August, for which 'Hurt' won Best Cinematography but should, in a just world, have won all seven categories for which it was nominated. Within days he had been hospitalised yet again, and although he was in and out of his ICU unit, and even made further plans to record with Rubin in LA, within two weeks he was gone. His death on September 12 2003 was attributed to pancreatitis. Really, his body had only found the strength to keep going for so long because his heart willed it to; and with June gone, his heart had finally caved in.

In the mid 90s he had expressed his wish to "die with my boots on – really!"[18] He wasn't able to go out on stage, as perhaps he might have desired, but he did not waste those last years, months, weeks, and days. He had fulfilled his promise. He had kept working almost right until the end. "They were just recording so much," says Rodney Crowell. "I remember going over to the Cabin, and they'd just sit and play songs all day, almost like he was stockpiling all this stuff. This was right toward the end."

"Right up until a week before he died he was still re-recording songs that he wasn't happy with, that he had put down maybe a month earlier," says Lou Robin. "He did the best he could."

"A lot of people were worried by it, but it worked out," says Chelsea Crowell. "He had to get that last drop out of his system. He felt he had things to complete."

In the end, not even music could sustain his life force after June's death, but his late burst ensured his songs would outlive his corporeal form. Not just his old music, but new music, music that reached out from beyond the grave. Even now he was gone, his song was not yet sung out.

13

**Oh, Bury
Me Not**

ohnny Cash's death was semaphored so explicitly in his music that when it finally arrived it felt almost like his last great career move. Like a gangsta rapper who dies an early, violent death, there was something artistically satisfying buried within all the pain and sadness of his passing; it sounded a powerful, perfect note at the end of a sad yet affirming song.

Death fascinates and death sells. Death has a strange momentum all of its own. Cash, of course, knew this better than most. Death certainly hasn't halted his progress; the resurgence he experienced with his *American* records has carried on even in his absence. There have been three further releases under that banner, two of which became *Billboard* Top Three albums, including his first Number One since *At San Quentin*; there have been three Grammies; an Oscar-winning film; numerous compilations and expanded reissues; documentaries, even posthumous collaborations. He remains a thriving industry. In death, the commercial success that largely eluded the *American* albums in his lifetime duly arrived.

The most significant musical activities have been instigated and endorsed by the Cash Estate, headed by John Carter Cash and Cash's former manager Lou Robin, and their completion overseen by Rick Rubin. *Unearthed*, a five-disc boxed set spanning 1993–2003, was released in late November 2003, barely two months after his funeral. The timing was coincidental, but suitably auspicious: here was a towering last will and testament comprised entirely of recent glories rather than past ones. *Unearthed* was already being compiled while Cash was alive, intended as a celebration of his extraordinary decade with American Recordings. The first three discs feature out-takes and alternate versions of songs recorded for *American Recordings*, *Unchained*, *Solitary Man*, and *The Man Comes Around*. The fourth disc, *My Mother's Hymn Book*, consists entirely of voice and guitar renditions of the country-gospel songs Cash first learned from his mother as a child; it is stark, foreboding, and impressive, without ever being somewhere you'd want to spend a lot of time regularly visiting. The final disc is a 'Best Of' distillation of the first four *American* albums. Combined, *Unearthed* is a monolithic achievement, and clear evidence of how utterly rejuvenated Cash had been in those final ten years.

Since then there have been two more posthumous albums in the series: *A Hundred Highways* and the final instalment, *Ain't No Grave*, were released almost four years apart, but were both compiled at the same time. The idea of releasing two further, final *American* albums was settled upon in the year after Cash's death.

"We knew we were doing that as we were doing it," says David Ferguson. "Those two were finished at the same time. Rick didn't want to have his hands tied by having to pick cuts for a particular record [beforehand], so we wound up doing it all to the point where [later] he could pick what he wanted [for] the two records."

Both albums were built almost completely from scratch. Late in 2005, Rubin assembled a team at the Akademie Mathematique of Philosophical Sound Research and pored over what was left in the Cash vaults. He assembled a core band of musicians: Mike Campbell, Smokey Hormel, Matt Sweeney, Benmont Tench, and Jonny Polonsky. All had played on previous *American* albums and were therefore aware of what was required. Equally important was the team of technicians, consisting of Ferguson as lead engineer and his assistants, including Dan Leffler, Greg Fidelman, Phillip Broussard, and Paul Fig.

Collectively they were charged with the task of capturing Cash's ghost music and adding flesh and bone. They trawled through all the songs Cash had recorded in his final years, many of them during those intense few last months between June's death and his own. A few songs – such as 'Satisfied Mind' and 'Redemption Day' – dated back to the *Solitary Man* sessions, when Cash could still accompany himself satisfactorily on guitar, but most of the material from that period had been mopped up on *Unearthed*.

What was left was in highly provisional shape; the challenge that lay ahead was a painstaking one, a process of mapping entirely new music onto Cash's original vocals. First, they would stitch together multiple takes of Cash's isolated vocal, tune it, and pump a barrage of effects into it to boost its volume and presence. Sometimes he hadn't sung to a click track, which meant the tempo might vary throughout the song, which caused some headaches. The musicians would add acoustic guitar before building up other textures, such as organ, bass, bells, chains. Where possible the band would try to play live to Cash's vocal: they'd sit in a circle, with Tench's B3 organ out in the hallway, and play along, Rubin guiding them like a conductor, instructing them in the mood he was after.

Every note of every take was scrutinised, and the best bits of each performance spliced together to make the final track, which was then edited, shifted around, manipulated. "There are guys who are really expert in doing that – a core of engineers," says Ferguson. "They were guys Rick trusted and I trusted. It was a team effort, absolutely."

This mind-bogglingly complex process took several months. After the initial band sessions had captured the music, Ferguson was in charge of the editing and mixing, finishing up the tracks to the required specification. Rubin insisted on hearing everything beforehand

"He was relentless, man!" says Ferguson. "He'd send constant notes. I remember this one note – I sent something to him and he sent a note back saying: that's the worst thing I ever heard. Or: that sounds like it's *broken*. It's not like he sits and explains to you what he wants, he doesn't do that. You do many takes with the band, you comp the takes and then you send that to him, and then he says let's start mixing on that. He's really wide open to your ideas. If there's something you want to add, do it – as long as you're working on the music, he's happy."

Barring a few minor tweaks and some late additions in 2009, the songs that comprised *A Hundred Highways* and *Ain't No Grave* were completed – that is recorded, edited, and mixed – all at the same time in the spring of 2006. *A Hundred Highways* was released shortly afterward, on July 4 2006, and became a Number One album, his first for 37 years. *Ain't No Grave* was held back until what would have been Cash's 78th birthday, on February 23 2010. "Rick just waited," says Ferguson. "He wanted everything else to get out of the way so it could draw more of a spotlight on its own. It was the sixth album, and a little after six years after his death. It made sense."

They are both fine albums. They lack the dramatic tension that had built up over the course of the first four records, based on the knowledge that we were listening to a man facing up to his impending death. For obvious reasons, some of that narrative momentum dissipated. Nonetheless, *A Hundred Highways* features some exemplary performances, notably Cash's version of Bruce Springsteen's 'Further On Up The Road' and his own compositions, 'On The 309' and 'I Came To Believe'.

There is a wry, self-deprecating glance back at his past achievements on Don Gibson's 'A Legend In My Time', and a tender love-hymn to June in 'Rose Of My Heart'. By and large the backing is restrained, and so are the song choices: nothing is laid on too thick. There is, however, a newly polished studio sheen to the album and a certain saccharine quality to some of the sounds and textures: Cash's standout vocal performance on 'Help Me' – with its heartbreaking *"pleeease"* – is partially undermined by less than subtle backing. There are other moments when Rubin's personality strays into the audio frame perhaps more than it might have.

"When Johnny first recorded 'God's Gonna Cut You Down' it sounded completely different," says David Ferguson. "It was a different groove and everything. We took his voice and put it to a click, and then the guys played the guitar parts, and Rick says to try some foot stomps. So we ran some microphones up to Rick's living room, which was above the studio, and we had some of the help in the house – a couple of errand boys – and some engineers and we recorded those foot stomps; then we did the claps."

The clanking percussive effects are impressive but rather swamp Cash. The title track of *Ain't No Grave* was similarly at the mercy of over-interpretative production. After piecing the song together in 2006, in late 2009 final overdubs were added to the mix. "They put on banjo, chains, and foot stomps way after the fact," says Ferguson. "They overdubbed that to my mix about a year before it came out."

It's still a great track. Cash rumbles "Ain't no grave gonna hold this body down" with the kind of ornery life-force that defies you to disbelieve him. Singing these words from beyond the grave does not seem distasteful, gratuitous or discordant; this was precisely the territory Cash had mapped out in his latter years.

He is a fading blood-and-thunder prophet, testifying over swirling minor chords, on Sheryl Crow's 'Redemption Day', and revisits the old country standard 'Cool Water' with brio. He finally thumbs his nose at death's sting on 'I Corinthians 15:55', which gains extra poignancy in this context, and takes his leave with 'Aloha Oe', a twinkling Hawaiian song of farewell, among the last songs he would ever sing.

It was an ending in more ways than one. *Ain't No Grave* will be the final instalment of Cash's unreleased work. "We knew for years that it was going to be the last album," says Rosanne Cash. "Even before [*A Hundred Highways*] we knew that this one was coming and would be the last. Other people can go ahead and scrape the bottom of the barrel and put together things that were never intended to be released, but this is the last thing that has the stamp of authenticity on it as far as his recorded work."

The question of authenticity is an interesting one. With *A Hundred Highways* and *Ain't No Grave*, whose record are we hearing? There are always delicate questions to be addressed about the presentation of posthumous work, but particularly so when so much of the music on *Ain't No Grave* and *A Hundred Highways* is essentially speculative, amounting to expertly informed guesswork. Clearly, a huge amount of care, forethought, and attention to detail went into the creation of both these records, from the song choices and quality of the mixes to the cover artwork. Yet this was not simply a case of tidying up some original Cash tracks. This was often an act of independent creation, a 'based on an original concept by ...' deal. Not everyone is comfortable with the idea of a franchise that lives on after the CEO has departed.

"I have, until recently, had a strong aversion to the recordings that Rubin has overseen of the Cash material undertaken since Cash's death," says Will Oldham. "They began with promise when Cash and Rubin were working *together*. With the last two releases, at one point I thought I hit on a real winning concept when I likened the recordings to something like necrophilia. Rubin's hubris in stating that the first posthumously constructed Cash record [*A Hundred Highways*] was possibly his favourite is truly disgusting. We all have skewed perspectives; Rubin has the added handicap of power.

"Still, where I once cringed at the idea that Cash 'would have wanted it' (the latter records to have been made at all, and in the way they were made), I have started to believe that that is probably not far at all from the truth. Rubin & Co have continued to give life to music and work to musicians, which were both obviously huge motivators for Cash. Possibly the releases could have been slightly more tastefully presented, but then maybe not. For myself, it will still be a while before I turn to those last two records and dig in; it may never happen. If it doesn't happen it's because there's enough power inherent in the previous decades' worth of recordings to last any listener a lifetime. I *want* to get into those last two records, though, because I have friends and colleagues that I love, personally and musically, who worked on them; because there are songs that Cash does on those records that already mean a lot to me when sung by others; and because I know there is power in there, hidden and ugly and strong. I'm not there yet, though."

It's worth picking through Oldham's frank and thoughtful comments, because they encapsulate many of the misgivings that arise around questions of artistic license and emotional – rather than aural – authenticity. We are instinctively uneasy about somebody signing off on another artist's work, but there is a need to consider whether these albums misrepresent Cash in any way.

It's not easy, but if we try to imagine *A Hundred Highways* and *Ain't No Grave* being released in Cash's lifetime, it's highly probable that they would not have sounded much different, given the limitations he was already working under, nor would the working practices have radically changed. *The Man Comes Around*, after all, was pieced together in a similar way; once Cash had played his part he was not one to haggle over final mixes or even the final song selection and running order. He trusted Rubin's final judgement implicitly.

Cash no longer has the power of final veto, but in light of what had been released prior to his death it's hard to hear anything on these albums he would have been uncomfortable with. "There is nothing that Rick has done to any of those songs that Johnny would not have loved," says David Ferguson. "I know that. He trusted me and he trusted Rick and he trusted John Carter, and it's part of our legacy too."

It's almost impossible not to agree, which isn't to suggest that certain aspects of *A Hundred Highways* and *Ain't No Grave* don't jar: matters of taste and artistic merit are occasionally questionable, but that is the case with all the *American* albums – not everything works, and when things misfire it tends to be because sentiments are overplayed and caricatures are stretched beyond their usefulness. These seem to me to be the result of honest creative misjudgements, rather than rampant ego.

On the issue of Rubins's motives, at least, there can be little room for confusion. "Johnny was his pet project, this was a labour of love for this guy," says Ferguson. "They had a really great relationship, you can hear that." Jack Clement, who doesn't particularly care for the *American* records, adds: "Rick Rubin had a definite sense for these things. I liked the guy, I liked his motives, he was a fan." Perhaps most importantly, none of the Cash family has ever had a bad word to say about him.

●●

As *A Hundred Highways* and *Ain't No Grave* have gone about their business, other versions of Cash have staked a claim from beyond the grave. *Walk The Line*, the Oscar-winning Hollywood biopic released in 2005, starred Joaquin Phoenix as Cash and Reese Witherspoon as June and focused on the love affair between the pair in the 60s, enacted against the backdrop of Cash's battles with drug addiction. Not a bad film by conventional standards, it followed the wearily traditional arc of the inspirational artist biography – passing from childhood trauma to self-destruction to salvation-through-love – without every giving any real hint of what made Cash such a unique and powerful figure.

"How could I be happy with *Walk The Line?*" says Rosanne Cash. "How could you be happy with the Hollywood version of your childhood? It was a cartoon. Just looking at it from my perspective, they take the two single most devastating events of my childhood – my father's drug addiction and my parent's divorce – and they make a Hollywood film about it and encapsulate it in two hours. How could that possibly reflect reality? In a more objective way, they completely missed the most important thing about my dad: which was what a transcendent artist he was. It was about loss and drugs and some kind of mundane redemption, but it missed the most potent part of the story."

There have been other endeavours which have seemed ill-formed and perhaps unworthy of Cash's legacy. The 'he would have wanted it' argument that Oldham mentions has again reared its head at times. In June 2010 a sample of the rhythm from Cash's version of 'God's Gonna Cut You Down' was used as background music for a series of television commercials for the 2011 Jeep Grand Cherokee; would Cash have approved? Very possibly. He had indulged in much gaudier commercial endorsements in his time.

Less easy to commend is anything which fundamentally plays around with the identity of his music, without Cash's consent. In June 2009 *Johnny Cash: Remixed* was released, executive-produced by John Carter Cash alongside Snoop Dogg and carrying "the blessing of the custodians of Johnny Cash's incredible legacy". On it, a selection of Cash's Sun Records classics – including 'Big River', 'Hey Porter', and 'Get Rhythm' – were remixed by, among others, Alabama 3, The Heavy, Buck 65, Sonny J, Count De Money, and Pete Rock. In the press release Carter Cash explained that "my father made his stead defying the expected and accepted way of things ... he would have loved this remix record". Perhaps that's true – there's a clear link, after all, between the swaggering braggadocio of lines like "I shot a man in Reno just to watch him die" and the pitiless gaze of many rap records – but the results still feel contrived. Worse, they're obvious and not very interesting. Worse even than that, they seem to be lazily perpetuating what Rosanne Cash calls "the bad, hip version" of Cash.

"I think that some things have been unnecessarily cheap, that the level of dignity I would like to have seen for my dad hasn't been maintained," she says. "If it's been something real, I've loved it. The fact that he was the 10 billionth download on iTunes was incredibly cool and real; nobody engineered that. But attempts to trade on his fame or reduce his image to a cartoon, I've just hated that. To turn his songs into hip-hop jokes … I can't stand any of that shit. It was embarrassing. If I had been making the decisions I would have made some of them differently."

The huge success of the *American* series, combined with the success of *Walk The Line*, which opened him up yet again to another generation of young people, has threatened to imprison Cash in his own legend. The video for his posthumous 2006 single 'God's Gonna Cut You Down' featured a parade of celebrities, among them Jay-Z, Justin Timberlake, Kate Moss, Kid Rock, Iggy Pop, Kanye West, and Mötley Crüe's Tommy Lee. It was at once a reminder of how far Cash's music had travelled, but also a final warning of how fame takes on a momentum of its own that is almost uncontrollable.

Some of the featured artists in the video – Bono, Sheryl Crow, Johnny Depp, Kris Kristofferson – had established links with Cash and his music; but at other times the video looked suspiciously like a visual inventory of Rubin's Rolodex, as though every look-at-me wannabe hipster – all surface, no feeling – was queuing up to catch a blast of the latest action. Cash has become a blank canvas upon which others rush to project their own studied, watery, Hollywoodised approximation of his all too real darkness. He always was, but since his death he can do little to change it. This is the downside of the myth he has helped create. It can be a struggle to cut through the dead wood of fashionable, one-dimensional iconography and get to the human being trying to sing his life, but it's far from impossible. Cash is hemmed in by preconception all the time, but he is powerful enough to transcend it, and his song is strong enough to cut through the wires.

●●

The *American* albums reshaped forever the way we see Johnny Cash: musically, the first record is timeless, an almost instant classic, but both individually and cumulatively they add significantly to his legacy as a writer and performer. It's almost unheard of for an artist in the latter stages of his career to make music that can compete, in terms of its cultural impact, its quality, vitality, clarity and staying power, with the songs that defined him in the first place. Cash succeeded. In the last ten years of his life he recorded several songs that would demand to be on any *Greatest Hits* record. "There are ten or 12 classic recordings in his early career, and then six-to-eight later on," says Rodney Crowell. "Which statistically is very high."

In terms of the way he was visually perceived, the *American* albums recast him once again. Post-1994, every cheap, re-released cash-in has stolen from the iconography of that first record: the bold strap line, the grave, grainy sepia tones, the sense of solitude and menace. "You notice now that all the compilations put CASH at the top of the cover, which is really irritating but it also shows how strong that branding was," says Martyn Atkins. "We'd set a bit of a house style for them. I always try to think: what are people going to think of this in 20 years time? You can't misrepresent an artist."

His resurgence had wider repercussions. Cash was at the vanguard of a whole swathe of artists who were looking for a way out of the corner they'd painted themselves into in the 80s. His elevation to a new kind of iconic status in the mid 90s not only changed forever the way in which he was regarded, it also quietly helped change the face of music. Pre-1990, there simply wasn't an artist over the age of 60 who commanded a wide-ranging mainstream audience that bridged generational and genre divides, who was a mainstay of MTV and a sought-after face in the biggest music magazines and style bibles. Artists like The Rolling Stones and Paul McCartney were only in their early forties but were already considered creaky veterans; their legacy was colossal but their contemporary relevance was negligible. Anyone beyond their age range was considered a fossil.

Cash changed all that. There has always been a James Dean angle to his appeal, but unlike James Dean he didn't live fast and die young: so what happens when James Dean grows up? *American Recordings* not only legitimised a new and more truthful emotional vocabulary for ageing artists, but it is a landmark record in terms of music's growing thirst for authenticity: where the 80s was all about acquisition and the search for sleek sonic perfection, the 90s would become about hearing the squeak of the strings, the ache in the bones, the weight of the world pressing down like snow on the roof. Its success in dealing honestly with age, illness, and experience helped the likes of Bob Dylan walk a little straighter and taller, while Leonard Cohen's recent triumphant return to live performance has a distinctly Cashian mix of charm, power, and wisdom about it.

Meanwhile, from Solomon Burke to Santana to Loretta Lynn, the often star-studded rehabilitation album has become a staple of the legacy artist. Cash was there first, and indisputably he did it best. It has become a mixed legacy. The 'Rubin Effect' has been diluted to the point of cliché: take a struggling oldie – Neil Diamond, perhaps Donovan – and lay them bare in the studio with a microphone and a guitar and a few tasteful extras, gaining critical kudos and emotional gravitas in the process. What began as a wonderful and original accident has become yet another template.

Yet Rubin did Cash an immense service in re-energising him, reminding him of himself and, yes, reinventing him. He has arguably done us all an equal service in ensuring that Cash's voice is still here, several years after he himself has gone, and that the songs he sang in his final decade, which taken as a whole amount to both a sweeping personal history and an American epic, capture the complexity of the man so thoroughly.

It's entirely fitting that the *American* series starts with a murder ballad and ends with a gentle Hawaiian song of farewell that speaks of the "birds of love". The inclusion of 'Aloha Oe' as a closing curtain call is not only a neat, unexpected touch, but it sums up the lifetime's worth of diversity in this extraordinary series of albums; they happily play up to Cash's mythic status, they document his decline, but they also recognise and acknowledge that he was never just a man in black. Much more than the sum of his many parts, he *could* also wear a rainbow when the mood took him; and sing it and every other colour in his heart and soul besides.

Endnotes

All quotations in this book are taken from interviews conducted by the author, unless otherwise stated in the text or listed here. Entries with just an author's name refer to books listed in the bibliography.

Chapter 1

1 Sylvia Massey, mixonline.com
2 Nathan Rabin, avclub.com
3 Sirona Knight and Michael Starwyn, dcsi.net/~bluesky
4 Alastair McKay, uncut.co.uk
5 *New York Times*, September 15 2007
6 Brown
7 Alastair McKay, uncut.co.uk
8 Peter Lewry, *Get Rhythm*, September 2001
9 Sylvie Simmons, *Mojo*, August 2000
10 Turner
11 Barney Hoskyns, *Mojo*, December 1996
12 Nick Tosches, *Journal Of Country Music*, 1995

Chapter 2

1 Harvey Kubernik, *Melody Maker*, August 16 1975
2 *NME*, March 5 1977
3 Philip Norman, *Sunday Times*, 1971

Chapter 3

1 Phil Sutcliffe, *Mojo*, October 2004
2 Turner

3 Turner
4 Cash (with Patrick Carr)
5 Larry Linderman, *Penthouse*, August 1975
6 Unpublished interview for *Q* by Steve Turner, 1988, available at *Rock's Backpages*, rocksbackpages.com
7 Turner
8 Mark Cooper, *Q*, May 1991
9 Jancee Dunn, *Rolling Stone*, June 1994

Chapter 4

1 Steve Pond, *Rolling Stone*, February 1993
2 Jancee Dunn, *Rolling Stone*, June 1994
3 Cash (with Patrick Carr)
4 Turner
5 Steve Pond, *Rolling Stone*, February 1993
6 Cash (with Patrick Carr)
7 Steve Pond, *Rolling Stone*, February 1993
8 Nathan Rabin, avclub.com
9 Steve Pond, *Rolling Stone*, February 1993
10 Barney Hoskyns, *Mojo*, December 1996
11 Steve Pond, *Rolling Stone*, February 1993

Chapter 5

1 Cash (with Patrick Carr)
2 Steve Pond, *Rolling Stone*, February 1993
3 Cash (with Patrick Carr)
4 Unpublished interview for *Q* by Steve Turner, 1988, available at *Rock's Backpages*, rocksbackpages.com
5 Mark Cooper, *Q*, May 1991
6 Opdyke
7 *Half A Mile A Day*, TV documentary (Hallway Group Productions 2000)

Chapter 6

1   *Guardian*, September 13 2003
2   Lisa White, gapersblock.com
3   Lisa White, gapersblock.com
4   U2
5   U2
6   Jancee Dunn, *Rolling Stone*, June 1994
7   U2
8   Steve Pond, *Rolling Stone*, February 1993
9   Unpublished interview for *Q* by Steve Turner, 1988, available at *Rock's Backpages*, rocksbackpages.com

Chapter 7

1   Steve Pond, *Rolling Stone*, February 1993
2   Turner
3   Liner notes to Johnny Cash *Unearthed*, by Sylvie Simmons
4   *Later With Jools Holland*, BBC2, June 25 1994
5   Harvey Kubernik, rocksbackpages.com
6   Alastair McKay, uncut.co.uk
7   Interview on 2003 CD reissue of Johnny Cash *Water From The Wells Of Home*

Chapter 8

1   David Kamp, *Vanity Fair*, February 2010
2   Brown
3   Cash (with Patrick Carr)
4   Turner
5   Mick Houghton, *Q*, April 1993
6   Jancee Dunn, *Rolling Stone*, June 1994
7   *The Word*, October 2006
8   *Chronicles Of Chaos*, September 30 2004
9   Jancee Dunn, *Rolling Stone*, June 1994

10 Cash (with Patrick Carr)
11 Streissguth
12 Brown
13 Brown
14 Russell Hall, gibson.com
15 Brown
16 Barney Hoskyns, *Mojo*, December 1996

Chapter 9

1   Nathan Rabin, avclub.com
2   Nathan Rabin, avclub.com
3   Cash (with Patrick Carr)
4   Adam D. Miller, beingtheremag.com
5   Jancee Dunn, *Rolling Stone*, June 1994

Chapter 10

1   Alastair McKay, uncut.co.uk
2   Steve Pond, *Rolling Stone*, February 1993
3   Brown

Chapter 11

1   Paul Gorman, *Music Week*, 1995
2   Interview by Chris Cornell on *MuchMusic* (TV channel), November 1996
3   David Kamp, *Vanity Fair*, February 2010
4   Sylvia Massey, mixonline.com
5   Paul Gorman, *Music Week*, 1995
6   Paul Gorman, *Music Week*, 1995
7   David Kamp, *Vanity Fair*, February 2010
8   Sylvia Massey, mixonline.com
9   Sylvie Simmons, *Mojo*, December 2002
10 *Guardian*, September 13 2003
11 Russell Hall, gibson.com

12 Russell Hall, gibson.com
13 Sylvie Simmons, *Mojo*, December 2002

Chapter 12

1   Cash (with Patrick Carr)
2   concertlivewire.com
3   Alastair McKay, uncut.co.uk
4   Lev Grossman, *Time*, September 22 2003
5   Lev Grossman, *Time*, September 22 2003
6   Russell Hall, gibson.com
7   concertlivewire.com
8   concertlivewire.com
9   Alastair McKay, uncut.co.uk
10 Alastair McKay, uncut.co.uk
11 concertlivewire.com
12 Alastair McKay, uncut.co.uk
13 David Kamp, *Vanity Fair*, February 2010
14 Alastair McKay, uncut.co.uk
15 David Kamp, *Vanity Fair*, February 2010
16 Lev Grossman, *Time*, September 22 2003
17 David Kamp, *Vanity Fair*, February 2010
18 Barney Hoskyns, *Mojo*, December 1996

Bibliography

Brown, Jake, *Rick Rubin In The Studio* (ECW 2009)
Campbell, Garth, *Johnny Cash: He Walked The Line* (John Blake 2003)
Cash, Johnny, *Man In Black: His Own Story In His Own Words* (Hodder & Stoughton 1975)
Cash, Johnny, *Man In White* (Westbow 2006)
Cash, Johnny with Patrick Carr, *Cash: The Autobiography* (Harper 1997)
Cash, Rosanne, *Composed: A Memoir* (Viking 2010)
Crouch, Kevin and Tanya, *Sun King: The Life and Times Of Sam Phillips, The Man Behind Sun Records* (Piatkus 2009)
D'Ambrosio, Antonino, *Heartbeat And A Guitar: Johnny Cash And The Making of 'Bitter Tears'* (Nation 2009)
Humphries, Patrick, *The Many Lives Of Tom Waits* (Omnibus 2007)
Irvin, Jim and Colin McLear (editors), *The MOJO Collection, Third Edition* (Canongate 2003)
Miller, Stephen, *Johnny Cash: The Life Of An American Icon* (Omnibus 2005)
Opdyke, Stephen, *Willie Nelson Sings America* (Eakin 1998)
Reineke, Hank, *Ramblin' Jack Elliott: The Never Ending Highway* (Scarecrow Press 2010)
Streissguth, Michael, *Johnny Cash At Folsom Prison: The Making Of A Masterpiece* (Da Capo 2004)
Turner, Steve, *The Man Called Cash* (Sceptre 2005)
Urbanski, Dave, *The Man Comes Around: The Spiritual Journey Of Johnny Cash* (Relevant 2003)
U2, *U2 By U2* (Harper Collins 2006)

Index

Words In Italics indicate
album titles unless otherwise
stated. 'Words In Quotes'
indicate song titles. Page
numbers in **bold** indicate
illustrations.

Acknowledgements

I would like to thank everyone who agreed to answer my questions for this book. They include: Dick Asher, Martyn Atkins, Earl Poole Ball, Rick Blackburn, Adam Clayton, 'Cowboy' Jack Clement, Anton Corbijn, Cathal Coughlan, Rodney Crowell, Andy Earl, Michael Eavis, David Ferguson, Gibby Haynes, Mick Houghton, Paul Kennerley, Jon Langford, Nick Lowe, Bruce Lundvall, Will Oldham, Steve Popovich, Marc Riley, Daniel Tucek, and Carey Womack. Particular thanks to Rosanne Cash and Chelsea Crowell.

Thanks also to everyone who helped facilitate the interviews, to my agent Stan at Jenny Brown Associates, and to my editor John Morrish.

As ever, the lion's share of love and appreciation is reserved for my family, particularly my wife and three children.

Picture Credits

Other books in this series:

MILLION DOLLAR
BASH: BOB DYLAN,
THE BAND, AND THE
BASEMENT TAPES
by Sid Griffin

ISBN 978-1-906002-05-3

HOT BURRITOS:
THH TRUE STORY OF
THE FLYING BURRITO
BROTHERS
by John Einarson with
Chris Hillman

ISBN 978-1-906002-16-9

BOWIE IN BERLIN:
A NEW CAREER IN A
NEW TOWN
by Thomas Jerome
Seabrook

ISBN 978-1-906002-08-4

BILL BRUFORD THE
AUTOBIOGRAPHY:
YES, KING CRIMSON,
EARTHWORKS, AND
MORE
by Bill Bruford

ISBN 978-1-906002-23-7

BEATLES FOR SALE:
HOW EVERYTHING
THEY TOUCHED
TURNED TO GOLD
by John Blaney

ISBN 978-1-906002-09-1

TO LIVE IS TO DIE:
THE LIFE AND DEATH
OF METALLICA'S CLIFF
BURTON
by Joel McIver

ISBN 978-1-906002-24-4

MILLION DOLLAR
LES PAUL: IN SEARCH
OF THE MOST
VALUABLE GUITAR IN
THE WORLD
by Tony Bacon

ISBN 978-1-906002-14-5

THE IMPOSSIBLE
DREAM: THE STORY
OF SCOTT WALKER
AND THE WALKER
BROTHERS
by Anthony Reynolds

ISBN 978-1-906002-25-1

JACK BRUCE:
COMPOSING
HIMSELF: THE
AUTHORISED
BIOGRAPHY
by Harry Shapiro

ISBN 978-1-906002-26-8

FOREVER CHANGES:
ARTHUR LEE AND THE
BOOK OF LOVE
by John Einarson

ISBN 978-1-906002-31-2

RETURN OF THE
KING: ELVIS PRESLEY'S
GREAT COMEBACK
by Gillian G. Gaar

ISBN 978-1-906002-28-2

A WIZARD, A TRUE
STAR: TODD
RUNDGREN IN THE
STUDIO
by Paul Myers

ISBN 978-1-906002-33-6

SHELTER FROM THE
STORM: BOB DYLAN'S
ROLLING THUNDER
YEARS
by Sid Griffin

ISBN 978-1-906002-27-5

SEASONS THEY
CHANGE: THE STORY
OF ACID AND
PSYCHEDELIC FOLK
by Jeanette Leech

ISBN 978-1-906002-32-9

WON'T GET FOOLED
AGAIN: THE WHO
FROM LIFEHOUSE TO
QUADROPHENIA
by Richie Unterberger

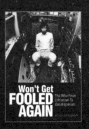

ISBN 978-1-906002-35-0

CRAZY TRAIN: THE
HIGH LIFE AND
TRAGIC DEATH OF
RANDY RHOADS
by Joel McIver

ISBN 978-1-906002-37-4